Helion & Company Limited
Unit 8 Amherst Business Centre
Budbrooke Road
Warwick
CV34 5WE
England
Tel. 01926 499 619
Email: info@helion.co.uk
Website: www.helion.co.uk
Twitter: @helionbooks
Visit our blog http://blog.helion.co.uk/

Text © Michal A. Piegzik 2023
Photographs © as individually credited
Colour artwork © Grzegorz Nowak and
    Jean-Marie Guillou 2023
Map drawn by Mark Thompson © Helion &
    Company 2023

Designed and typeset by Farr out
    Publications, Wokingham, Berkshire
Cover design by Paul Hewitt, Battlefield
    Design (www.battlefield-design.co.uk)

Every reasonable effort has been made to
trace copyright holders and to obtain their
permission for the use of copyright material.
The author and publisher apologise for any
errors or omissions in this work, and would
be grateful if notified of any corrections that
should be incorporated in future reprints or
editions of this book.

ISBN 978-1-804513-65-1

British Library Cataloguing-in-Publication
    Data
A catalogue record for this book is available
    from the British Library

We always welcome receiving book
proposals from prospective authors.

CONTENTS

Note: In order to simplify the use of this book, all names, locations and geographic designations are as provided in *The Times World Atlas*, or other traditionally accepted major sources of reference, as of the time of described events.

LIST OF ABBREVIATIONS AND SYMBOLS USED IN THE TEXT

#	seriously wounded in action		**Lt**	Lieutenant
(B)	*buntaichō* (division/group leader)		**LtCdr**	Lieutenant Commander
(C)	*chūtaichō* (flight leader)		**PO1c**	Petty Officer 1st Class
(F)	flagship		**PO2c**	Petty Officer 2nd Class
(H)	*hikōtaichō* (striking group leader)		**PO3c**	Petty Officer 3rd Class
(S)	*shōtaichō* (section leader)		**SLt**	Sub-Lieutenant
†	killed in action		**USAAF**	United States Army Air Force
CAP	Combat Air Patrol		**USS**	United States Ship
Cdr	Commander		**WO**	Warrant Officer
Ens	Ensign			

INTRODUCTION

まえがき
Maegaki

This two-volume book describes the Aleutian Islands campaign from June 1942 to March 1943. It was a part of the second phase of the Pacific War, when the Empire of Japan lost her initial strategic initiative and, despite launching a series of bold initiatives to regain it, was eventually forced to adopt a defensive strategy leading to the ultimate defeat in 1945. In historiography, the struggle for the Aleutians is often presented as a separate North Pacific theatre of war, which lost its significance after the American reconquest of Attu and Kiska.

Due to the specific nature of the Aleutian Islands campaign in 1942–1943, the book primarily focuses on naval and air warfare. The beginning of the struggle in the North Pacific was unquestionably marked by Operation AL and the capture of Attu and Kiska by the Japanese in early June 1942. The book ends on the battle of the Komandorski Islands at the end of March 1943, which led to the US Navy's domination in the North Pacific and allowed the Americans to start preparations to recapture Attu and Kiska. The monograph also presents some aspects of naval engagements after March 1943, mainly focused on the Japanese evacuation from Kiska, yet it does not detail the American landing on Attu (Operation Landcrab) and Kiska (Operation Cottage). The above-mentioned events deserve a more profound depiction in a separate work on land warfare. However, from the perspective of naval and air combat, a part of the campaign from early June 1942 to the end of March 1943 constituted the most critical stage of the Aleutian Islands campaign. As for me, it was also full of underestimated events that strongly influenced the course of the Pacific War in the other war theatres. It also enriched the belligerents' experiences, limited in many cases to the warfare in the hot and humid climate peculiar to South East Asia. Therefore, there is no doubt that the Japanese and Americans in the Aleutian Islands often found themselves lost in mist and freezing cold, sworn enemies of all soldiers, sailors, and aviators.

The main goal of *Into the Endless Mist* is to present the preparations, course, and effects of the naval and air campaign in the Aleutian Islands from June 1942 to March 1943. I also asked myself three questions to grasp the nature of the Japanese-American struggle in the North Pacific. Firstly, I wondered about the strategic significance of the Aleutian Islands campaign compared to the parallel fighting in the Pacific War. Secondly, I was curious whether the Japanese should have pursued its plan to seize Attu and Kiska after the disastrous defeat at the Battle of Midway. Finally, I wanted to assess if the Japanese effectively used their limited resources to secure the northern approach to the home islands and to prepare for the inevitable American invasion of Attu and Kiska in 1943. An analysis of military operations in the Aleutian Islands allowed me to comprehensively explain my findings on those questions as part of the last chapter.

Volume One comprises an introduction, nine chapters, three appendixes and a bibliography. Chapter One presents a brief geographical and historical outline of the Aleutian Islands. Chapter Two provides the Japanese plans to extend a defensive perimeter in the North Pacific. Chapter Three outlines the American plans to defend the Alaska and Aleutian Islands area from the enemy offensive. Chapters Four and Five detail the first and the second 2nd *Kidō Butai*'s air strikes on Dutch Harbor. Chapter Six presents the Japanese invasion of Attu and Kiska. Chapter Seven describes the first months of the aerial and naval struggle for the Aleutian Islands, focusing on American harassment of enemy positions on the captured islands. On the other hand, the summer of 1942 was also the period of active Japanese defence that resulted in some successes that limited the enemy's advance in the chain. Those events are outlined in Chapter Eight. The end of the narrative in Volume One is marked by the Japanese temporary evacuation from Attu and the American landing on Adak in September 1942. The rapid construction of a new airfield allowed for a more effective air war of attrition against Kiska and Attu.

Volume Two of the monograph covers the transitional period of autumn and winter of 1942 and 1943. During that period, the Japanese returned to Attu and tried to build up their garrisons in the Aleutians by sending numerous convoys. Parararell to those developments, the Americans seized Amchitka and continued harassing the enemy positions by regular air strikes and naval bombardment. Volume Two also presents the most crucial naval clash of the Aleutian Islands campaign – the battle of the Komandorski Islands (アッツ沖海戦; Attu oki kaisen) on 27 March 1943. Despite the Japanese tactical victory over Rear Admiral McMorris' task force, Vice Admiral Hosogaya abandoned the transport mission for Attu and withdrew from the area. Overwhelmed by the enemy's superiority in the air, the *Nippon Kaigun* gave up on the initial plan to send more convoys for Attu and Kiska in the following months. The book ends with a summary of the campaign in the North Pacific and the events leading to the Japanese evacuation from Kiska in June and July 1943. Since I raised three questions in the introduction, the ending also covers my answers and comments on the Aleutian Islands campaign.

The state of research on the struggle for the Aleutians in the United States is more complex and needs a brief explanation. American historians generally paid far less attention to the North Pacific combat than the Battle of Midway or the Guadalcanal campaign. Nevertheless, some published their research on the subject or a particular aspect of it. The list of authors in chronological order includes R. Bates' and the Naval War College analysis,[1] S.E. Morison and the monumental work on the history of the US Navy in World War Two,[2] B. Garfield and probably the most well-known monograph on the Aleutian Islands and Alaska,[3] J.A. Lorelli and the analysis of the battle of the Komandroski Islands,[4] J.H. Cloe and his detailed monographs on aerial warfare,[5] and the other notable mentions of R.L. Johnson's,[6] J. Dickrell's,[7] G.R. Perras',[8] B.L. Herder's publications.[9] The secondary American or English-language sources used in my research are listed in the bibliography.

Looking at the subject from the opposing side, the Aleutian Islands campaign has not been a prevalent research subject in Japan. Almost 80 years have passed since the struggle for the North Pacific finished, yet two volumes of the Official War History Series (戦史叢書; *Senshi Sōsho*) published in the late 1960s remain the primary source of information on the actions of the Japanese, namely the volumes covering the Army (*Nippon Rikugun*, vol. 21) and the Navy (*Nippon Kaigun*, vol. 29) operations.[10]

Due to significant English and Japanese-language research gaps on the Aleutian Islands campaign, the book is mainly based on Japanese and American archive documents. The Japanese sources belong to the Japan Center for Asian Historical Records (アジア歴史資料センター; *Ajia Rekishi Shiryō Sentaa*) being a part of the National Archives (国立公文書館; Kokuritsu Kōbunshokan) and the National Institute for Defense Studies (防衛研究所; Bōei Kenkyūsho). American sources were acquired from the National Archives and Records Administration and other local archives listed in the bibliography.

The natural consequence of choosing the Pacific War subject for research is the need to systematise Japanese terminology. As for spelling names, places, first names and surnames in Japanese, I have used the classic Hebon-Shiki Rōmaji – the traditional version of the Hepburn Transcription, representing kanji, hiragana and katakana in the Latin alphabet with diacritics characterising Japanese pronunciation. The exceptions are geographical names and terms that appear in English in a generally recognised form. For example, they include words such as Tokyo, Honshu, Hokkaido and the Kuril Islands. For practical and historical reasons, I kept the personal details of the Japanese persons in Japanese order, thus giving first a surname followed by a first name. Succumbing to the trends prevailing in the latest historiography, I also intended to use some Japanese words or passages next to the English ones to reflect the Japanese way of speaking or thinking and to promote further research on Japanese sources.

The campaign depicted in the book took place in a vast area near the International Date Line, which is why Japanese and American sources differ widely in describing the same events. In many cases, the time difference was 19 hours (between Honolulu and Tokyo time). For this reason, I used dates and times in local time (UTC-10:00 for the western Aleutians and UCT+10:00 for the Komandorski Islands), with minor exceptions explicitly noted in the text. As far as possible, I adopted the metric system except for distances specified in nautical miles (1 NM = 1,852 metres) and speed of vessels in knots.

The completion of this monograph would not be possible without the financial and institutional support of the Japanese Ministry of Education, Culture, Sports, Science and Technology (文部科学省, Mombukagakushō) and the Tokyo Metropolitan University (東京都立大学, Tōkyō Toritsu Daigaku), where I did my legal and historical research in 2016–2017 and 2020–2022. The book is the translated and significantly revised version of the monograph published in Poland in June 2022.[11]

Finally, I would like to thank my first reader (Polish version), Michał Kopacz, whose comments always let me look at the research problems differently. My friend and a passionate Pacific War researcher, Grzegorz Jeziorny, also has contributed significantly to my work, giving his helping hand and expert opinion on various matters that shaped the English version.

Acknowledgements must finally include my wife, Ola, who is not only a kind reviewer of my manuscripts but also the dearest person in my life who supports me and my scientific career. Thank you for your love and understanding.

Sagamihara-Edinburgh
2022–2023

1

ALEUTIAN ISLANDS: GEOGRAPHY AND HISTORY

アリューシャン列島とその地理および歴史
Ayūshan Rettō to sono Chiri oyobi Rekishi

The Aleutian Islands, commonly known as the Aleutians, are a chain of small islands in the northern part of the Pacific Ocean with an area of approximately 17,700km², stretching for 1,900km between the Kamchatka Peninsula and the Alaska Peninsula and bordering the Pacific Ocean from the south and the Bering Sea from the north. Most of the Aleutian Islands belong to the US state of Alaska, the westernmost part of American federal territory. From the geologic perspective, they are in the northern arc of the Pacific Ring of Fire, running along the Aleutian Trench, making them an area prone to frequent earthquakes and volcanic activity. The natural consequence of their location is that most of them are islands of volcanic origin.

The Aleutians comprise six smaller groups of islands: the Fox Islands, the Islands of Four Mountains, the Andreanof Islands, the Rat Islands, the Near Islands, and the Komandorski Islands. Five of the six groups of islands now belong to the United States, and the Komandorski Islands remained in the Russian Empire (the Russian Federation nowadays) when Alaska was sold to the American government in 1867. Undoubtedly, the most important and largest island of the Aleutians is Unalaska (part of the Fox Islands), with its main centre in the port town of the same name. In 2020, the Aleutian Islands were inhabited by only 5,230 people, including some belonging to the local Aleut group. Residents mostly make their living from fishing and benefit economically from the presence of US military bases. The harsh climate and the short growing season of around 135 days, from early May to late September, allow only the cultivation of potatoes and limited poultry farming.

The whole chain has a subpolar maritime climate, which derives from the collision of air masses from the

Lithograph of Grigory Shelekhov's settlement in Three Saints Bay. (Open source)

North Pacific and the Siberian Plain — frequent low atmospheric pressure results in long winters and short, cool, rainy summers. Gusty winds are recorded for most of the year, and the average annual temperature in Unalaska is only 3°C. This area is known primarily for the frequent dense fog, significantly reducing visibility and causing navigational troubles among seafarers.

The Aleutian Islands were first explored by the Danish cartographer, Captain Vitus J. Bering, and the navigator and skipper, Aleksey Chirikov, both in the service of the Russian Empire. In 1741, onboard *Saint Peter* and *Saint Paul*, they set out on the so-called Great Northern Expedition in the waters of the Pacific. A ferocious storm soon separated their ships, and Chirikov on *Saint Paul* sailed to the eastern part, while Bering on *Saint Peter* reached the western part of the Aleutians, soon deciding that both must return to home port. On the way back, the Danish captain crashed on the uninhabited Bering Island (part of the Komandorski Islands). Bering and 28 crew members, seriously ill with scurvy, did not survive the following winter. Georg W. Steller, a German botanist, saved the remaining 46 survivors by recommending the sailors diversify the diet composed of hunted seal meat with sea algae rich in essential vitamins.[1] After surviving the hardest of frosts and building a small boat from the wreck of *Saint Peter*, the crew reached Petropavlovsk in Kamchatka in August next year.

Along with stories of unknown islands, the survivors brought the tanned furs of the sea otters they encountered. Their softness, thickness and lightness were appreciated by Siberian traders, accelerating the Russian colonisation of Alaska. The increased demand for the new type of luxurious goods was a driving force for the British merchants, who also began searching for sea otter habitats. The price of one fur piece on the American market reached a dizzying value of $300 in 1772. Following that, in 1782, Russian hunters discovered the Pribilof Islands and the large population of otters. In just the first year more than 5,000 animals were hunted, and during the next 30 years of intensive exploitation powered by human greed, the entire otter species was brought to the edge of extinction.

Since the Bering and Chirikov expedition, the Aleutian Islands formally became part of the Russian Empire. In 1760, all Aleuts were officially granted Russian citizenship, and the first settlement with an Orthodox church was founded in Unalaska. In 1793, 10 missionaries arrived from the continent, and only one survived the next two severe winter seasons. His name was Herman, and soon after, he settled in a small village on Kodiak Island, becoming the defender of the natives against exploitation by Russian trading companies. Herman's devotion to protecting the weaker against all odds and despite apparent cultural differences made him a saint in the Orthodox Church.

In 1825, the Russian American Company brought several dozen Aleut families to Bering Island to secure the political interests of the empire and establish a waypoint on the trade route along the archipelago. The new inhabitants were mainly born on Atka and were soon joined by the first Russian merchants and officials, founding the permanent settlement of Nikolskoye. Five years later, the tsar's edict introduced the protection of sea otters to prevent the extinction of the entire species. The immediate effect of this decision was a decline in the profitability of the fur trade and less interest in exploring the region. In 1867, Alaska was sold to the United States, but the westernmost part of the Aleutians, the Komandorski Islands, remained within the Russian Empire's borders. Despite the Americans founding the first public school in Unalaska in 1883, until the beginning of the twentieth century, the Aleutian Islands remained a wholly forgotten and unknown place for most US citizens. It was not until 1924 that Congress granted American citizenship to the Aleuts, and following this event, the first hospital was opened in Unalaska in 1933.

When the Empire of Japan started actively looking for political changes in the North Pacific, the peaceful neighbourhood of Russians and Americans changed forever. Under the Treaty of Saint Petersburg of 1875, the Japanese took control of the Kuril Islands, stretching their sphere of influence south of the Kamchatka Peninsula.[2] One could predict that it was only an overture for a major reshuffle in the region as the unsettled status of Sakhalin and the frictions caused by the conflict of interests in Korea and Manchuria soon led to a war between the two empires, ending up in a disastrous defeat for the tsar's generals and admirals. The Portsmouth Peace Treaty of 1905 gave Japan control of Korea and South Manchuria, including Port Arthur and the railway that connected it with the rest of the region, along with the southern half of Sakhalin (Karafuto-chō).[3] For the

Hospital wards at Fort Mears, Dutch Harbor, around 1941. (NARA)

violent border clashes in the previous years.[6] An ambiguous peace with Stalin, resembling more a tactical truce than a genuine will to bury the hatchet for once and all was particularly beneficial to the Japanese Army which dreaded the opening of a new front by the Red Army in Inner Mongolia and Manchuria, and which would undermine any large-scale offensive in China. The non-aggression pact also secured the vital interests of the Japanese Navy, already fully committed to the preparations for war with the Allies, particularly the surprise carrier-borne strike on Pearl Harbor and the series of bold amphibious operations in South East Asia. The Empire of Japan, already struggling to bring China to its knees, decided to start another conflict to achieve undisputed supremacy in the Pacific. The Japanese determination to overcome the economic isolation and banishing the white man from East Asia also meant a time of upheaval for the remote and inaccessible Aleutian Islands.

first time in history, Tokyo permanently marked its presence in the North Pacific and expanded the Japanese territorial waters far north of Hokkaido. The October Revolution and the creation of the USSR created political turmoil in the region. Despite the relative balance of power, the imperial cabinet felt directly threatened by the expansion of communist ideology from the continent. In 1922, the United States and Japan reached an agreement wherein Japan promised not to construct defences in its newly acquired mandate of Micronesia, and the United States agreed not to fortify the Aleutians or any Pacific Islands west of Hawaii. However, after the Kwantung Army invaded Manchuria in 1931 and the beginning of a full-scale war with China six years later, uncontested control over the western part of the North Pacific area became one of the most critical principles of Japanese foreign policy. During the 1930s, the Japanese became increasingly interested in scientific investigations on the Aleutians, sending their fishing boats and biologists to Attu, Amchitka, Atka, Umnak, and Unalaska. The Americans suspected visitors of spying for the government in Tokyo, although there was no proof that they were collecting military data. Nevertheless, in early 1935 the Office of Naval Intelligence discovered Japanese spying on Unalaska before Navy Fleet Problem 16 Aleutian exercises planned for the summer of the same year.[4]

In 1938, the US Congress directed the US Navy to investigate the need for additional bases in the Pacific. The board, chaired by Rear Admiral A.J. Hepburn, recommended establishing seaplane and submarine bases at Dutch Harbor, Kodiak, Midway, and Wake and patrol plane bases at Sitka and Oahu. A year later, Congress approved the proposal. A civilian contractor, Siems Drake Puget Sound, began constructing the naval facilities at Dutch Harbor in July 1940, and the total cost was $44 million. The Naval Section Base was commissioned in January 1941, and the Naval Air Station on 1 September. The first Army troops arrived at Amaknak on 8 May 1941. On 10 September 1941, the army post was named Fort Mears in honour of Colonel Frederick J. Mears.[5]

Since the Soviet–Japanese Neutrality Pact, signed in April 1941, Tokyo and Moscow decided to maintain the *status quo* despite

Japanese Strategic Plans in the North Pacific
北太平洋における日本の戦略計画
Kitataiheiyō ni okeru Nihon no Senryaku Keikaku

Japanese strategic objectives in the North Pacific, including all internal *Nippon Kaigun* considerations leading to the genesis of Operation AL plan and its execution, are probably one of the biggest misconceptions in Western historiography in the last 80 years. For nearly six decades, American authors have convinced readers that the air raid on Dutch Harbor was merely a feint to distract the US Navy from the primary goals of the Combined Fleet in the Central Pacific. This view was for the first time widely presented by S.E. Morison in his monumental *History of United States Naval Operations in World War II* series, and successive generations of Western historians later repeated it.[7] Even though the "diversion theory" was refuted by J. Parshall and A. Tully in a ground-breaking monograph on the Battle of Midway published in 2005,[8] the most accurate and not misleading explanation of *Nippon Kaigun* intentions is still waiting to be revealed to the Pacific War researchers and enthusiasts. As the present-day reality shows, even Tully's and Parshall's most recent research has not eradicated old beliefs,[9] which proves the need for a more comprehensive clarification supported by Japanese sources.[10]

The meticulous analysis of Japanese operational plans and the post-war testimonies of *Nippon Kaigun* officers demonstrates that Combined Fleet and Navy General Staff had a keen interest in the North Pacific even before the outbreak of the conflict. On 5 November 1941, Commander-in-Chief of the Combined Fleet (*Rengō Kantai*), Admiral Yamamoto Isoroku, acting on Navy General Staff (*Gunreibu*) permission, issued the Combined Fleet Secret Operational Order No 1 (*Kimitsu Rengō Kantai Meirei Saku Dai 1-Gō*), in which he outlined strategic goals for the first and

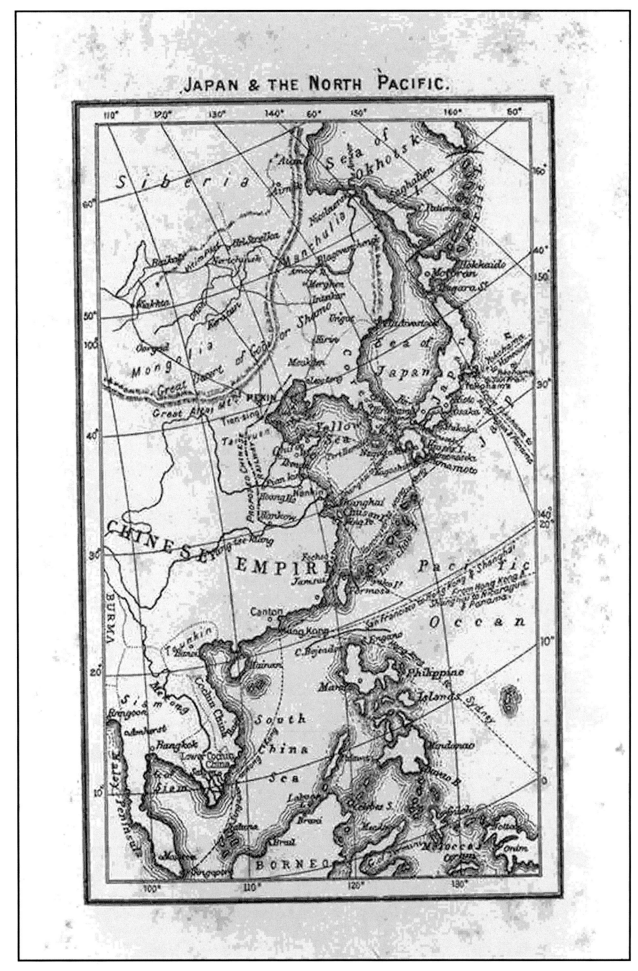

Manjirō Inagaki's map of Japan and the North Pacific. (NDL)

Commander-in-Chief Combined Fleet, Admiral Yamamoto Isoroku on board the battleship *Nagato* in 1940. (Open source)

Rear Admiral Fukudome Shigeru, Chief of the First Division (Strategic Planning), Navy General Staff. (NDL)

the second stage of the war. Among those objectives, Yamamoto mentioned "the necessity to either seize or destroy the crucial outer positions in the Aleutian Islands."[11] Two equally important reasons stood behind those plans. Firstly, the Combined Fleet intended to cut off the Americans from the northern approach to the Japanese islands. No matter how difficult it was for the enemy actually to reach them, from the Japanese perspective, the Aleutians seemed a natural bridge between the eastern and western parts of the Pacific Ocean. The biggest nightmare of the Navy was the carrier air raid on Tokyo, which constantly forced the Navy to maintain surface and air patrols in vast sectors. By expanding the defensive perimeter far to the northeast, *Nippon Kaigun* could rely on fewer warships and aircraft, using its limited resources in the other theatre of operations. Secondly, partly in connection with the belief to secure the mainland from the northern flank, Japanese military strategists also aimed to disrupt the US-Soviet communication lines in the North Pacific, making the transit of American planes to Siberia more arduous.[12] However, despite the clearly defined gains of advancing in the westernmost part of Alaska, the Combined Fleet did not decide to execute any offensive plans in the Aleutians unless carrying out detailed examinations.[13]

During that time, Combined Fleet and Navy General Staff submitted to Imperial General Headquarters (*Daihon'ei*) a detailed opinion on possible actions which could be taken in the Aleutians. It was advised to seize "*gaikaku yōchi*" – essential outer positions in the chain to establish a seaplane base on Kiska and maintain regular flying boat patrols to hamper any US Navy attempt to close to Japan from the North Pacific. Although the plan seemed reasonable, it was rejected due to the lack of free infantry and air forces and partly because the higher command did not want to provoke the Soviet

Union to take preventive measures against Japan. Nevertheless, the February 1942 war game simulating the progress of the offensive on Ceylon revealed the two most severe dangers that *Nippon Kaigun* had to face: the lack of strategy to halt American carriers from striking Japan's mainland and anticipation that the US Navy would establish military bases in Attu and the Semichi Islands and begin carrying out regular bombing missions against Tokyo with long-range strategic (Japanese described them as "*chō ōgata*" – super-heavy) bombers that, according to various sources, were at the advanced design stage. The first threat was not mere anxiety as American carriers hit the Japanese Navy garrisons in the Marshall and Gilbert Islands on 1 February, followed by the attempted strike on Rabaul in the second half of the month. With every single offensive operation of the US Navy carriers in the Pacific Ocean, which had become increasingly successful, *Nippon Kaigun* believed that the air raid on Tokyo was only a matter of time. Therefore, when the Operation MI initial plan was presented, along with the landing on Midway, the Navy General Staff also included seizing the western part of the Aleutians and establishing advanced reconnaissance outposts on two distant islands, covering 1,400 miles of patrol sectors in total, to minimise the chance of the enemy carrier strike on Japan. Eventually, the Navy General Staff entrusted the Combined Fleet with preparing and executing the plan of the envisaged operations in the Central and North Pacific. The Combined Fleet, having some surplus forces at disposal and, most importantly, suitable landing units, eagerly agreed to follow this strategy.[14] The US Navy intelligence could recognise the intentions of the Japanese Navy at the early stage since it intercepted the first dispatch containing a mention of strategic plans for the Aleutians on 9 March 1942.[15]

The importance of the offensive in the Aleutians concerning Yamamoto's grand strategy to crush US Navy carriers near Midway was underlined in a few official orders and some testimonies of the *Nippon Kaigun* officers. Although Combined Fleet and the Navy General Staff agreed to proceed with both operations, giving them equal priority, not every Japanese Navy officer was an enthusiast of the perilous expeditions to the Central and North Pacific, which were judged as putting all of their eggs into one basket, or from the other perspective, killing two birds with one stone. To grasp the significant diversity of opinions regarding the pivotal moments of the Pacific War, it is worth citing statements about the operation in the Aleutians.[16]

Rear Admiral Fukudome Shigeru, Chief of the First Division (Strategic Planning), Navy General Staff:

There is a high concern that even if we invade Midway, the US Navy, being in a disadvantageous position, won't counterattack. Therefore, since both islands are part of the United States, if we carry out the landing operation in the Aleutian Islands, there is a non-explicit conviction that it could serve as an additional measure to force the US fleet to sortie for Midway, so the implementation [of Operation AL] is desired.

Captain Tomioka Sadatoshi, Chef of the Operations Section, Navy General Staff

[Operation AL] could also become a strategic feint for Midway Operation.

Commander Miyo Kazunari, Operations Section Member, Navy General Staff:

I respect the idea of cutting the US-Soviet contacts and hampering the reinforcement of air bases in Siberia by American air forces, as well as denying the US bombers access to the western part of the Aleutians from where they could bomb our mainland.[18] However, as an air officer, I am opposed to advancing to Kiska and maintaining air patrols from there as it is assessed that it will be challenging for weather reasons and will bring high attrition of our aircraft.

As seen above, the Navy General Staff officers had a broad spectrum of views on Operation AL, from full approval to justified criticism. In addition, Captain Tomioka's notion became the binding interpretation of *Nippon Kaigun*'s plans in the Aleutians for the next few decades, even though the strategic feint to distract the US Navy from Midway was not the Japanese intention at any stage.

The issue of the strategic significance of the Aleutians became transparent to more staff officers at the end of February when the Combined Fleet organised a war game on board the battleship *Yamato* related to the planned operation against British forces on Ceylon. The Japanese predicted that during the offensive in the Indian Ocean, the Americans would like to test out their new "super-heavy" bombers in action and carry out air raids on Tokyo from the western part of the Aleutians, namely the new airfields on Attu or the Semichi Islands. The war game participants also deduced that at least one group of eight aircraft would get through poor air defence and drop bombs on the capital, causing minor damage

Captain Tomioka Sadatoshi, Chef of the Operations Section, Navy General Staff. The photo was taken in 1950s. (Open source)

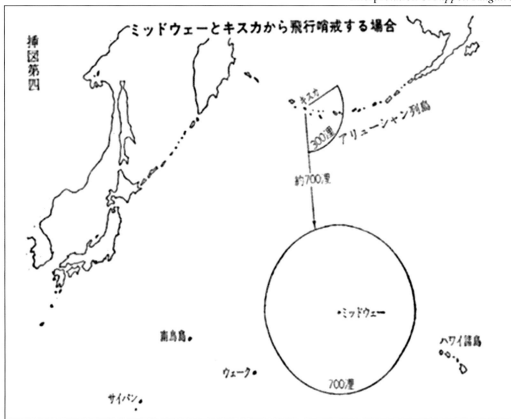

ミッドウェーとキスカから飛行哨戒する場合

挿図第四

キスカ
アリューシャン列島
300浬
約700浬

ミッドウェー

南鳥島
ハワイ諸島
ウェーク
700浬
サイパン

Planned reconaissance sectors from Kiska and Midway after seizing both islands and establishing air bases. Flying boats had to fly about 700 miles to cover the nothern part of the Pacific Ocean. (*SS vol. 43*)[17]

General Sugiyama Hajime, the Chief of Staff Army General Staff. (Open source)

to the city industrial complex but much more terror to the Japanese citizens.[19] In early March 1942, the American carriers proved their ability to penetrate the Japanese mainland's wide defence perimeter as they hit Minami Tori-shima (Marcus Island) and, a couple of days later, inflicted significant losses to Japanese forces in Lae and Salamaua on New Guinea, slowing their advance into the southern part of the island. In particular, the raid on Minami Tori-shima, distant less than 1,200 miles from Tokyo, was a painful lesson to *Nippon Kaigun*, which revealed that "the buffer zone" extending from the Kuriles to Guam, was only a theoretical concept and could not be protected by a group of second-rate warships.

The successful accomplishment of most strategic objectives from the first stage of the operations in mid-March freed some Japanese Navy resources, which could be used in the second stage of conflict. The Combined Fleet and the Navy General Staff were on the same page and advocated advancing into the North Pacific. Still, the staff in Tokyo, representing prudent and conservative views on using any precious *Nippon Kaigun* warships, was sceptical about Yamamoto's ultimate hand in Central Pacific. The failed attempt to question Operation MI almost led to Yamamoto's resignation, and the Navy General Staff planners wanted at least to secure part of their interests to have control over strategic initiatives. Using an original plot, they informed Captain Kuroshima Kameto, a Combined Fleet staff officer, that the Army General Staff gave a conditional agreement on executing Operation MI if Operation AL was also included in the Combined Fleet's schedule for June. On the other hand, General Sugiyama Hajime of Army General Staff denied that anyone from *Nippon Rikugun* demanded anything in return for allotting additional infantry battalions to secure Kiska. Although some back-stage negotiations between the Army and Navy could have happened in mid-March, in contrast to the statements of the Navy, Sugiyama's version is reflected in the report to the throne (*jōsō*).[20]

Nevertheless, the Combined Fleet and the Navy General Staff did not intend to crumple their copies for extraneous details, closing the discussion about the necessity to execute Operation AL to focus on more practical tasks. On 5 April, a Navy General Staff representative met with Army General Staff to informally assess if and what Army forces could participate in landing operations on Midway and Kiska. To convince the allied, but also often considered a rival branch of the armed forces within one state, he shared the Combined Fleet's plan

to strike American bases in Dutch Harbor and Adak, requesting to keep only an Army garrison on Kiska until the end of winter next year. In return, the Japanese Navy promised to remain in the Aleutian waters during that time and hold back the US Navy forces from the counterattack. The idea of securing the approach to Japan's mainland hit the jackpot, and the Planning Section of *Nippon Rikugun* right away ordered to prepare forces to carry out Operation AL. On 12 April, the Army and Navy representatives met in the broader group, and *Nippon Kaigun* officially presented its plan related to Midway and the Aleutians. Lieutenant General Tanaka Shin'ichi, the Chief of Operations in the Army General Staff, revealed genuine feelings of *Nippon Rikugun* towards those two initiatives:

> On 12 April, I heard from the Navy General Staff suddenly that the Combined Fleet had a strong desire to carry out Operations MI and AL, and this hit me like a bolt from the blue. Two Army battalions for Aleutians and the navy had eager hope for any participation of Army infantry during the amphibious operation on Midway. They also declared to proceed only with their [land] forces if we hesitated. The Army General Staff was primarily anxious about the hypothetical invasion of Hawaii, but when the Navy General Staff clarified that the plan of landing on Hawaii did not exist [yet], we could not say no. [21]

Tanaka's opinion was not unique, but the formal decision to use Army infantry forces was put on hold for unknown reasons to the other officers. Furthermore, despite stressing the importance of carrying out the operation in the North Pacific to protect Japan from air raids and US-Soviet cooperation, General Sugiyama reported to the emperor that he had not decided to deploy Army infantry forces to both MI and AL. Looking at the number of objectives in Operation AL (Dutch Harbor, Adak, Kiska, Attu), he assessed that it would be tough to detach enough infantry forces to accomplish all goals and suggested seizing only Kiska. Since the American garrison on the island was feeble, Sugiyama expressed his view that the Navy infantry forces (special landing forces) could solely conquer it. Moreover, he underlined that if *Nippon Kaigun* advocated capturing the Aleutians and Midway simultaneously, it should use [entirely] their independent land forces to proceed with the operation.[22]

By analysing various documents drafted by Sugiyama, present-day historians can only guess that he was not eager to commit his forces in the North Pacific due to the primary maritime character of the theatre of operations. The Army General Staff pointed out two main enemy air bases in Kodiak and Dutch Harbor and at least four smaller signal outposts on Adak, Kiska, Attu, and Kanaga. Although it was judged that the Americans possessed a relatively strong garrison just in Dutch Harbor, only planes and ships had open access to the vast chain of islands, considering weather limitations. Sugiyama was aware of the local climate and left a comment in which he emphasised that the year could be divided into three seasons: (1) from October to March – terrible weather; (2) from April to July – decent weather; (3) from August to September – fine weather. Given a few days with temperatures over 0 degrees and without snow or mist, the Army feared sending its troops to the remote islands and relying on unstable navy support, which also had to face the US Navy and USAAF with limited resources.[23]

Being unaware of the actual arrangements in the Army command but confident of obtaining necessary consent on staff-talks level, on 15 April, the Navy General Staff submitted to Emperor Hirohito the report entitled *Imperial Japanese Navy Operational Plans in the Second Stage of the Greater East Asia War* (*Daitōa Sensō Dai*

The Doolittle Raid significantly changed the Japanese Navy and Army's vision of the North Pacific campaign. (NARA)

Ni Dan Sakusen Teikoku Kaigun Sakusen Keikaku). At one point, the Japanese Navy stated that "the most important positions in the Aleutian Islands should be captured or destroyed as quickly as possible in a single operation, thus preventing any future US Navy action from the North Pacific."[24] The next day, the Navy General Staff issued Detailed Order No 85 (*Daikaishi Dai 85-Gō*), which modified the previously published Detailed Order No 1 from 5 November 1941, also known as the *Combined Fleet Secret Operational Order No 1. Nippon Kaigun* revealed its plans for the following months: (1) to strengthen defensive lines passing through the Andamans, Sumatra, Java, Lesser Sunda Islands, and the western part of New Guinea; (2) to protect its merchant fleet by destroying enemy ships attacking it; (3) to harass enemy shipping in the Indian Ocean and in Australian waters; (4) to seize Port Moresby, the Solomon Islands, Nauru, Ocean, Midway, and the western part of the Aleutians, which would form with existing Japanese positions on the Marshall and Gilbert Islands the greater defensive perimeter; and finally, (5) capture Fiji, New Caledonia and Samoa to cut off Australia from American support. In the last point, if circumstances permitted, the Japanese Navy planned to invade Hawaii at the end of the year.[25]

What was foreseen by *Nippon Kaigun* for long enough to get used to the idea of the enemy air strikes on the mainland happened at the least favourable time, right before the *Kidō Butai*'s return from the victorious Indian Ocean campaign. The surprise raid of *Enterprise* and *Hornet* on Tokyo on 18 April, better known as the Doolittle Raid, not only directly threatened the Japanese capital for the first time but also demonstrated the urgent need to take immediate measures to secure all approaches to the home islands from the enemy aircraft carrier task force. As T. Ishibashi proves,

the hitherto underestimated and sometimes even neglected area of the North Pacific suddenly gained crucial meaning in the eyes of the more sceptical Navy General Staff officers.[26] Although the distance from Pearl Harbor to Tokyo still precluded a large-scale offensive operation of aircraft carriers across the middle of the Pacific Ocean, the enemy could expand military bases along the Aleutian chain to try out hazardous but not entirely impossible hit and run tactics. In April 1942, the most advanced American outposts in the Aleutians were located on Attu Island, about 1,170km from the Kuriles and less than 3,200km from Tokyo, which the Japanese Navy could not ignore any longer.

Doolittle's raid reassured the Japanese command that the US Navy aircraft carriers were the deadliest American asset during the early stage of the war as they could seriously threaten the inner lines of communication within the defence perimeter at any moment. Another direct effect of the strike on Tokyo was a sudden shift in the views of the Japanese Army regarding the Navy's plans for seizing the Aleutians and Midway. Although the Army still could not promise to allot larger forces, on 21 April, it notified the General Navy Staff that the situation had changed, and several infantry units could be detached to support the Navy's amphibious operations in June.[27] At the same time, *Nippon Rikugun* intended to secure or destroy all airfields in China that American long-range bombers could use to harass the Japanese mainland. The land offensive would begin in mid-May from the Hangzhou area, followed by an advance from Nanchang at the end of the month, ending with two pincer forces meeting in early July.[28]

Since the Combined Fleet was responsible for carrying out Operations MI and AL, and the first one was the apple of

Vice Admiral Hosogaya Boshirō, the Commander of the Fifth Fleet. (Open source)

Vice Admiral Nakazawa Tasuku, the Chief of Staff, the Fifth Fleet. (Open source)

Yamamoto's eye which required his supervision, the latter had to be entrusted to another Navy unit. At the outbreak of the war in the Pacific, the *Nippon Kaigun* already had a force responsible for defending Japan's northern flank against the Soviet Union or the enemy air raids. The Fifth Fleet (*Dai 5 Kantai*) was reactivated in Yokosuka on 25 July 1941 after the personal intervention of the Chief of the Navy General Staff, Admiral Nagano Osami, to Emperor Hirohito.[29] Vice Admiral Hosogaya Boshirō was appointed its commander, and Vice Admiral Nakazawa Tasuku as the chief of staff.[30] Unlike many *Nippon Kaigun* officers, 54-year-old Hosogaya did not come from a notable family shaping the Japanese feudal upper class and was the fourth son of a farmer from the sleepy town of Minami Saku of the mountainous Nagano Prefecture. The Fifth Fleet initially comprised only the 21st Cruiser Squadron (light cruisers *Tama* (F) and *Kiso*) and torpedo boats *Sagi* and *Hato*.[31] On 1 October, it was reinforced with the 7th Base Force (10th Gunboat Division, 17th Minesweeper Division and 66th Subchaser Division). In November, its headquarters was relocated from Yokosuka to Ōminato. During the "Southern Operation" (*Nampō Sakusen*), Hosogaya patrolled the area around the Kuriles, Hokkaido, northern Honshū, and the Ogasawara Islands to protect the mainland Japan from the enemy air raid.[32]

The decision to advance into the Aleutians was in line with the views of the Fifth Fleet officers, who repeatedly tried to convince the Combined Fleet and the Navy General Staff to secure the northern

approach to Japan. The circumstances of drafting Operation AL remained unknown, but some believed their pressure on higher command was a fundamental factor in committing *Nippon Kaigun*'s effort to the North Pacific.[33]

Vice Admiral Nakazawa Tasuku, Chief of Staff, Fifth Fleet

In the Northern Forces [Fifth Fleet], the circumstances were not precise, but from the beginning, there was an expectation to seize the Aleutians; me and staff officers, during the talks with the Navy General Staff and the Combined Fleet, presented it repeatedly. However, I cannot recall any dispatch or documents with our recommendation.[34]

Imperial General Headquarters (Daihon'ei)
(Tokyo)

Navy General Staff (Gunreibu)
(Tokyo)
Admiral Nagano Osami

Army General Staff (Sambō Hombu)
(Tokyo)
General Sugiyama Hajime

Combined Fleet (Rengō Kantai)
(Truk)
Admiral Yamamoto Isoroku

Northern District Army (Hokubu Gun)
(Sapporo)
Lieutenant General Hamamoto Kisaburō

Fifth Fleet (Dai Go Kantai)
(Ōminato)
Vice Admiral Hosogaya Boshiro

Japanese chain of command during the Aleutian campaign, 1 June 1942. (Author)

Captain Ōno Takeji, the Commander of the Light Cruiser *Kiso*

I don't know where the initiative to seize Aleutians was born, but I think it was not the Fifth Fleet. As the Fifth Fleet, the morale was low since we were idle and did not have spectacular results. Everyone expects us to do the [job with the] Aleutians, and I often talked about that with the chief of staff. He told me he was negotiating [this matter] with the Combined Fleet.

Commander Matsugi Michiyo, a Member of the Fifth Fleet Staff

The studies related to the operation in the Aleutians area were carried out since the end of January, also by collecting the documents. I believe the initial idea was to move the patrol [defence] perimeter forward. It seems that even the Commander of the Combined Fleet himself considered it. I think the opinion of the Fifth Fleet appropriately reflected his and the Navy General Staff's views.

Drawing on the lessons learned during the first stage of the conflict, on 1 May, the Combined Fleet Staff organised the simulation of the possible course and the outcome of the second stage of operations. Played on the battleship *Yamato* "*zujō enshū*", a war game, was completed on the afternoon of 3 May and was followed by additional study and analysis sessions, which ended on the morning of 4 May. The rest of the day passed on discussions and advanced arrangements, but their content remained unknown due to a lack of detailed documents. Putting aside the considerations regarding the Battle of Midway, being out of the scope of this monograph, the simulation of Operation AL revealed that it might end with an undesirable result for the Combined Fleet. According to the war game, bad weather prevented the Japanese carrier task force from spotting the enemy fleet, and both sides accidentally ran into each other. The surprise encounter ended with the annihilation of Japanese forces, and the landing on Kiska was not covered in the following part of the simulation description. In response to this outcome, the Combined Fleet decided to increase the number of reconnaissance planes from the aircraft carriers and their fuel supply to increase the chance of spotting enemy warships.[35]

The cornerstone for Operations MI and AL was the Navy General Staff Order No. 18 issued on 5 May 1942.[36] Vice Admiral Nagano ordered Admiral Yamamoto to coordinate the cooperation of the Combined Fleet with the Japanese Army to invade Midway and the Aleutian Islands.[37]

Navy General Staff Order No. 18, 5 May 1942

1.   In cooperation with the Army, the Combined Fleet Commander will seize important positions of AF [Midway] and the western part of AO [the Aleutians].

2.   The Chief of Staff of the General Navy Staff will issue detailed instructions for the operations.

The same day, the Navy General Staff issued Detailed Order No. 94 specifying Operation AL objectives in 13 points.[38]

Navy General Staff Detailed Order No. 94, 5 May 1942

Following Navy General Staff Order No. 18, detailed instructions for cooperation between the navy and army commands in Operation "AF" will be provided in separate orders, and the cooperation between the navy and army commands in Operation "AO" will be based on [the following provisions]:

Cooperation of the army and navy commands related to the Aleutian Islands operation

- Objectives of operation
  To destroy and seize important positions in the western part of the Aleutians Islands to make the enemy's mobile [fleet] and air offensive operations difficult.
- Plan of operation
  The army and navy will seize Kiska and Attu [Islands] and destroy military facilities on Adak [Island].
- Outline of operation
  The army and navy will attack Adak first and thoroughly demolish local military facilities. Then, the Army will seize Attu and the Navy forces Kiska, holding both islands until the winter season.
  With its available forces, the Navy will escort the invasion forces, and prior to the amphibious operation, the carrier task force will hit and destroy the local enemy air force.
- Commanders and forces
  Navy
  Commander in Chief: Commander of the Combined Fleet
  Forces: Bigger part of the Combined Fleet
  Army
  Commander of North Seas Detachment, Major Hozumi Matsutoshi
  Forces: one infantry battalion, the core of one construction company
- Commencement of the operation
  This operation will begin with the Midway operation between the first and the second decade of June.
- Time and place of concentration
  Invasion forces will be gathered at Akkeshi Bay
  The date of concentration is set on [about] 23 May
- Command relation
  Since the concentration date in the indicated place, the Commander of Fifth Fleets takes control of the Army [detached] invasion forces.
  During the landing and ground operations, the Army forces will be led by the [Army] officer with the highest rank in all operational situations.
- Garrison duties
  The Navy will be mainly responsible for Kiska Island.
  Army [detached] forces will be mainly responsible for defending Attu Island.
- Communications
  Based on the army and navy command agreement, in [all] communications, "Midway Operation", "Aleutian Operation" and "Fiji Operation" will be used.
- Transport and supply
  To transport Army [detached] forces, the Navy will provide one transport ship during the operation.
  The Navy will be responsible for supplying the Army and evacuation of wounded soldiers.
  Maps and navigations maps [omitted]
- Time zone
  Central standard time [Tokyo time +9:00]
- Operation shortened nomenclature

This operation will be called "Aleutian Operation"

On 12 May, the Combined Fleet ordered a hasty concentration of forces at the Ōminato navy base, which was to last up to two weeks.[39] Eventually, the second stage of the *Nippon Kaigun* operations in the Pacific War was to comprise two phases: (1) capture of Port Moresby in early May and (2) Operations AL and MI in early June. Needless to say, the first phase was already in progress, and the Combined Fleet only awaited news from Fourth Fleet Commander, Vice Admiral Inoue Shigeyoshi, that MO *Kidō Butai* had crushed the American carrier task force in the Coral Sea and secured the successful landing on Port Moresby.

The final plan of Operation AL included the invasion of Attu and Kiska by the Army infantry detachment, preceded by the destruction of the American bases on Adak and Dutch Harbor.[40] Although the Japanese estimated that there were only a few military targets in the indicated area, protected by a naval force comprising a seaplane tender, two gunboats and a group of destroyers, the Navy General Staff recommended a carrier-borne strike to neutralise all enemy key positions, in particular airfields and air forces, to proceed with the successful amphibious operations.[41]

Table 1: List of identified US military targets and forces in the Aleutian Islands. [42]

Location	Targets and forces
Dutch Harbor (Amaknak/Unalaska)	harbour submarine base seaplane base seaplane tender and several warships a bigger Army garrison commanded by a General Major
Adak	signal post harbour for bigger warships
Kiska	signal post 200–300 man Navy garrison (unconfirmed) seaplane base
Attu	signal post smaller garrison (confirmed) seaplane base

Within days of issuing orders that set up the most important objectives of Operation AL, the US Navy and *Nippon Kaigun* clashed in the Coral Sea in the first carrier battle. Despite the sinking of *Lexington* and severely damaging *Yorktown*, the battle was a strategic loss for the Combined Fleet, which had to abandon plans to capture Port Moresby from the sea and cut off Australia from American support for a longer perspective. The first naval campaign in the South Pacific also had a colossal impact on Operation MI, leaving the 5th Carrier Squadron, composed of *Shōkaku* and *Zuikaku*, the *Nippon Kaigun*'s most modern aircraft carriers, in Japan due to necessary repairs and reconstruction of their air groups.[43]

The unfavourable outcome of the carrier confrontation at the Coral Sea did not affect the revision of the Japanese general plan to execute the decisive battle with the US Navy near Midway. However, on 8 May 1030 hours (Tokyo time), Rear Admiral Ugaki Matome, the Chief of Staff of the Combined Fleet, issued Combined Fleet Secret Dispatch No 29 – he modified the composition of forces in Operation MI and AL. Due to the loss of *Shōhō* on 7 May and significant damage to *Shōkaku* on 8 May, the Midway Invasion

Force was to be additionally covered by the 3rd Carrier Squadron (only *Zuihō*), as well as *Shōkaku* was removed from the *Kidō Butai*. Moreover, *Shōkaku* was battered so hard during the battle that Ugaki resigned from assigning her to the Fifth Fleet with some other vessels despite the initial thought to do so. The date of the air raid on Dutch Harbor was set three days before the landing on Midway (N-3), and part of the 1st Submarine Squadron received an order to proceed on reconnaissance patrols nearby Seattle to check the American defence readiness by N-5. By 20 May, the Combined Fleet eventually realised that the entire 5th Carrier Squadron was in poor combat condition and could not participate in any air operations at the beginning of June.[44] Based on Yamamoto's final instructions, on the same day, Hosogaya issued Northern Forces Secret Operational Order No 2, establishing the composition of the Fifth Fleet during the offensive in the Aleutians.

Taking advantage of the large-scale offensive in the Central Pacific, the Combined Fleet and the Naval General Staff believed in hassle-free execution of objectives in the Aleutians, namely speaking the air strike on Dutch Harbor and the capture of Attu and Kiska. The central role in Operation AL was attributed to the 2nd *Kidō Butai*, composed of the recently commissioned aircraft carrier *Jun'yō* and the light carrier *Ryūjō*, distinguished for active air support in China. Although the air groups of both carriers had a not very impressive striking potential (28 Zeros, 20 Kates and 18 Vals – counting by the number of available aircraft and crews), the American air forces in the North Pacific area were not considered a significant threat to the Fifth Fleet. Accompanied by three heavy cruisers, three light cruisers, 12 destroyers and other vessels, Hosogaya received an order to extend a defensive perimeter far to the northeast.

On 21 May, Hosogaya approved the plan for fuel consumption during Operation AL, previously reviewed by the Combined Fleet.[51] The next day, he also issued the final orders for Operation AL, slightly modifying the composition of forces (the 6th Destroyer Division replaced the 21st Destroyer Division) and explaining the objectives and the timetable:

- **Plan of operation**
  Crush enemy forces stationing in Dutch Harbor and Adak and destroy military facilities in both bases. Seize Kiska and Attu and be ready to defend them to prevent the enemy aircraft or mobile force from approaching [Japan] in the North Pacific. To achieve this, we:
- From the N-3 Day, using our mobile carrier force, we will strike Dutch Harbor to destroy local forces and military facilities and neutralise the entire base.
- Also, by the N-1 Day, we will strike Adak and Kiska and destroy local forces and military facilities.
- On the N Day, the Navy special landing troops will seize and secure Kiska. On the same day, the Army Northern Seas Detachment and Combined Fleet Special Landing Forces will carry out the raid on Adak and destroy the local military facilities.
- After neutralising Adak, the Army Northern Seas Detachment will move toward Attu and seize it.
- Submarine forces will be deployed close to Seattle.
- Flying boats will perform patrol duties towards Kiska.
- After landing on Adak, seaplane tenders' aircraft will carry out reconnaissance patrols in sectors north of the Aleutians.
- The mobile carrier force will search for the enemy fleet and destroy it as a second task.
  (…)
- **Outline of the 2nd Kidō Butai raid on Dutch Harbor**

Table 2: Technical characteristics of the Japanese aircraft carriers *Ryūjō* and *Jun'yō*.

	Ryūjō	*Jun'yō*
laid down	26 November 1929	20 March 1939
launched	2 April 1931	26 June 1941
commissioned	9 May 1933	3 May 1942
displacement	10,150 t	27,500 t
length and beam	180 x 20.3 metres	219.3 x 218 metres
draught	5.56 metres	8.15 metres
flight deck dimensions	154.5 x 23 metres 2 x elevators	210.3 x 27.3 metres 2 x elevators
propulsion	6 x Kampon water-tube boilers 65,000hp	6 x Kampon water-tube boilers 56,250hp
speed	29kts	25.5kts
range	10,000 miles/14kts	10,000 miles/19kts
anti-aircraft armament	4 x twin 127mm Type 89 guns 2 x twin 25mm Type 96 guns 6 x quadruple 25mm Type 96 guns	6 x twin 127mm Type 89 guns 8 x triple 25mm Type 96 guns
aircraft	14 Zeros (+2 spares) 20 Kates (no spares)[45]	14 Zeros (+? spares) 18 Vals (+? spares)[46]
aircraft tail code	D1-XXX	D11-XXX
complement	916	1,187
home port	Kure	Kure

Table 3: Organisation of Japanese Forces during Operation AL, 3-7 June 1942.[48]

Fifth Fleet (Northern Force), Commander-in-Chief, Vice Admiral Hosogaya Boshirō

Force	*Unit*	*Tasks*
Main Force, Vice Admiral Hosogaya Boshirō	heavy cruiser *Nachi* (F) 21st Destroyer Division (2nd Section) destroyers *Ikazuchi* and *Inazuma*	support during Operation AL

2nd *Kidō Butai*,
Rear Admiral Kakuta Kakuji
	4th Carrier Squadron
	    aircraft carrier *Jun'yō*
	    14 Zeros (+? spares)
	    18 Vals (+? spares)[49]
	    light carrier *Ryūjō*
	    14 Zeros (+2 spares)
	    20 Kates (no spares)[50]
	4th Cruiser Squadron (2nd Section)
	    heavy cruisers *Maya* and *Takao*
	7th Destroyer Division
	    destroyers *Ushio, Akebono, Sazanami*
	(tanker *Teiyō Maru*)
		air strike on Attu, Adak, Kiska;
		destroy the enemy task force

AQ [Attu] Invasion Force,
Rear Admiral Ōmori Sentarō
	1st Torpedo Squadron (less three destroyers)
	    light cruiser *Abukuma*
	    21st Destroyer Division
	    destroyers *Wakaba, Hatsuharu, Nenohi, Hatsushimo*
	(auxiliary minelayer/gunboat *Magane Maru*)
	Attu Landing Force
	    about 1,200 men of the Army Northern Seas Detachment
	    (Major Hozumi Matsutoshi)
	(transport ship *Kinugasa Maru* plus 10 seaplanes)
	(plus one transport ship)
		destroy the enemy positions on Adak; capture of Attu

Ryūjō (龍驤) was the first Japanese light aircraft carrier built from scratch to comply with the Washington Treaty limitations. The vessel was laid down on 26 November 1929 at the Yokohama Naval Shipyard. After launching, *Ryūjō* was towed to Yokosuka, where she was armed and entered service on 9 May 1933.

The operational history of the aircraft carrier began with the ill-fated manoeuvres of the Fourth Fleet in September 1935, during which a typhoon damaged her hull. After repairs and returning to service, in January 1937, she became the flagship of the 1st Carrier Squadron. Until then, *Ryūjō* served as a test vessel that enabled studying the offensive capabilities of carrier-based aircraft. In September 1937, she was sent to Shanghai, where she took part in bombing local ground targets and fought for air supremacy. By November, she operated in Chinese waters against targets such as Shanghai, Nanjing, and Guangzhou. After returning to Japan and the refit in March 1939, she again supported Army operations in southern China. In November 1940, *Ryūjō* became the flagship of the 3rd Carrier Squadron and, a year later, the flagship of the 4th Carrier Squadron. Parallel to *Kidō Butai*'s strike on Pearl Harbor, she took part in air operations in the Philippines. In early January 1942, the carrier supported the Twenty-Fifth Army in pursuing British forces on the Malay Peninsula. She participated in the Dutch East Indies campaign in February and March and then proceeded to Singapore to escort convoys to Burma. In early April, *Ryūjō* was assigned to

Vice Admiral Ozawa Jisaburo's Malay Force and played a major part in the offensive operation in the Bay of Bengal, contributing significantly to sinking many Allied cargo ships. On 18 April, her torpedo bombers were transferred to the Takao Navy Base in Taiwan, where additional training courses for crew members were conducted. On April 23, *Ryūjō* reached Kure, where she left her last aircraft ashore, which were soon incorporated into the *Saeki Kaigun Kōkūtai* as training planes. At that time, the Navy General Staff decided to fully modernise the air group of the aircraft carrier by replacing the older Claude fighters with the newest Zeros. Two days later, Captain Katō Tadao took command of the ship. On 28 April, *Ryūjō* went into drydock at Kure for planned maintenance and a refit. In late April, 16 Zeros were assigned to her air group. On 3 May, the newly commissioned aircraft carrier *Jun'yō* was attached to the 4th Carrier Squadron, becoming the *Nippon Kaigun*'s independent striking group. *Ryūjō* left drydock at Kure on 6 May and received an order to sail for Ōminato via Saeki and Tokuyama. On 22 May, after refuelling on the last leg of the route, the carrier finally headed north with *Jun'yō*, arriving at Ōminato three days later as part of the officially formed 2nd *Kidō Butai*. From then on, her air group was reorganised and comprised 14 Zeros (plus two spare aircraft) and 20 Kates (no spare aircraft).[47]

The full roster of *Ryūjō* during Operation AL is included in Appendix 1.

The light aircraft carrier *Ryūjō* seen in 1938. (Open source)

Table 3: Organisation of Japanese Forces during Operation AL, 3-7 June 1942 (*continued*)		

AOB [Kiska] Invasion Force, Captain Ōno Takeji	21st Cruiser Squadron
	    light cruisers *Tama* and *Kiso*
	6th Destroyer Division (1st Section)
	    destroyers *Hibiki*, *Akatsuki*
	destroyer *Hokaze* and auxiliary cruiser *Asaka Maru*
	13th Subchaser Division
	    subchasers *No. 25*, *No. 26*, *No. 27*
	Kiska Landing Force
	    about 550 men from 3rd "Maizuru" Special Naval Landing Force
	    (Lieutenant Commander Mukai Hifumi) with 8 guns and 4 machine
	    guns
	    about 700 workers with construction equipment
	(transport ships *Kumagawa Maru* and *Hakusan Maru*)
	escort ships *Hakuhō Maru*, *Kaihō Maru*, and *Shunkotsu Maru*
	(transport ship *Awata Maru*)
		capture of Kiska; patrolling Attu area

Table 3: Organisation of Japanese Forces during Operation AL, 3-7 June 1942 (continued)		

Submarine Unit, Rear Admiral Yamazaki Shigeaki	1st Submarine Squadron
	    submarine *I-9*
	2nd Submarine Division
	    submarines *I-15, I-17, I-19*
	4th Submarine Division
	    submarines *I-25* and *I-26*
		searching for the enemy

Seaplane Tender Unit, Commanding Officer of *Kimikawa Maru* (Captain Usuki Shuichi)	seaplane tender *Kimikawa Maru* 8 seaplanes (Jakes) destroyer *Shiokaze*	searching for the enemy
Navy Base Air Unit, Commanding Officer of *Tōkō Kaigun Kōkūtai* (Commander Itō ?)	*Tōkō Kaigun Kōkūtai* (part) 8 flying boats (Mavis) transport ship *Kamitsu Maru* gunboat *Dai Ni Hi no Maru* cargo ships *Dai Ni Hishi Maru* and *Dai Go Seitan Maru*	searching for the enemy, attacking the enemy
Attached Force, Fifth Fleet commander	tankers *Fujisan Maru, Nissan Maru, Teiyō Maru* transport ship *Awata Maru* and other one patrol boat 5th Weather Detachment	supply the other units

Time of launch: One hour after sunrise (N-4 Day, 2230 hours [Tokyo time]).

Position: 200 miles within Unalaska Island.

Composition of the striking group: 1st group – 15 dive bombers, 15 fighters, 9 torpedo bombers; 2nd group – 9 torpedo bombers, 3 fighters.

Movements: N-3 Day – raid on Dutch Harbor, N-2 Day – attack on Adak, Atka and Kanaga, N-1 Day – supply at 1500 hours near Kiska, N Day – reaching Point A at 1100 hours.

On 23 May, the Fifth Fleet's special meteorological detachment set sail from Akkeshi Bay and carried out a scrupulous weather reconnaissance east of the Kuriles. Two days later, having all the necessary and actual data, the Combined Fleet conducted the second war game and simulated the progress of Operation MI and Operation AL in a staff room on board the battleship *Yamato*. The outline and post-game conclusions were shared by Vice Admiral Nakazawa after the war, giving information on the positive outcome of landing operations on Attu and Kiska. The latter island was supposed to be supplied with construction materials by the seaplane tender *Chiyoda*, which was to depart Ōminato on 1 June. At the same time, the enemy base in Dutch Harbor was neutralised by the 2nd *Kidō Butai* strike and had limited capacities to conduct air operations. After the successful raid, the Japanese carriers were dispatched to proceed south and were replaced in the Aleutians' waters by the heavy cruiser *Nachi*.[52]

When the war game on *Yamato* was over, Hosogaya issued Northern Force Secret Operational Order No. 10. In fact, it was an address to the Fifth Fleet officers gathered on *Nachi* with an essential introduction of the Aleutian war theatre, their role during the upcoming operation and the importance of objectives.[53]

The Japanese carrier-borne torpedo bomber (*kankō*) Nakajima B5N2, better known as Kate. It was also used by the Nippon Kaigun as a reconnaissance aircraft. (Open source)

Table 4: Reconnaissance, anti-submarine, and CAP missions from *Ryūjō* and *Jun'yō*, 1 June 1942.[62]

Unit	No.	Pilot	Observer	Radio operator	Notes
1st *shōtai*/ Kates (*Ryūjō*) 80 degrees	1	Sea1c Futakuchi	SLt Satō (S)	PO2c Anzai	take-off: 0709 landing: 0918
	2	Sea1c Yamaguchi	PO2c Kobayashi	PO3c Izumi	
2nd *shōtai*/ Kates (*Ryūjō*) 60 degrees	1	PO2c Horiuchi	WO Uchimura (S)	PO3c Yamauchi	
	2	Sea1c Tanishiki	PO3c Nihei	Sea1c Toriyama	

Unit	No.	Pilot	Observer/navigator		Notes
? *shōtai*/ Vals (*Jun'yō*) Anti-Sub	1	(possibly Lt Abe)	Unknown		take-off: 1353 landing: ?
	2	Unknown	Unknown		
	3	Unknown	Unknown		
	4	Unknown	Unknown		

Unit	No.	Pilot	Notes
1st direct *shōtai*/ Zeros (*Jun'yō*) CAP	1	Unknown	take-off: 1452 landing: ?
	2	Unknown	
	3	Unknown	
2nd direct *shōtai*/ Zeros (*Jun'yō*) CAP	1	Unknown	take-off: 1624 landing: ?
	2	Unknown	
	3	Unknown	
? *shōtai*/ Zeros (*Ryūjō*) CAP	1	PO1c Kurihara (S)	take-off: 1600 landing: 1800
	2	Sea1c Tomoishi	
	3	PO3c Yoshihara	

A day later, at noon, the 2nd *Kidō Butai* secretly set off from Ōminato, heading for Unalaska.[54] After ascertaining that there were no American forces in the 500-mile arc, the Kiska Invasion Force left Sendai Harbor on 28 May at noon (except for the transport ship *Fujisan* Maru, which left Yokosuka and joined the rest of the group later). The bulk of the Attu Invasion Force departed Ōminato at 1100 hours the next day.[55] Hosogaya's Main Force departed Sendai Harbor on 29 May and proceeded to Kakumabetsu Bay, which he reached on 2 June, leaving it the next day after taking fuel from the oiler *Nachi Maru*.[56] The Combined Fleet intended to synchronise Operation MI and Operation AL to completely surprise the US Navy and prevent it from sending reinforcements to the North Pacific. However, due to unexpected delays in the movements of forces assigned to Operation MI, the air raid on Midway was rescheduled to the N-2 Day. Therefore, the air strike on Dutch Harbor must have been carried out one day faster than indicated in the plans of 22 May.[57]

Following the *Nippon Kaigun* doctrine, submarines and their scouting aircraft performed preliminary reconnaissance missions, which began the preparations for Operation AL. On 26 May, a seaplane from *I-9* circled over Kiska, Attu and Adak, confirming the absence of enemy aircraft, warships, and important military facilities. On 27 May, a seaplane from *I-25* proceeded as far as Kodiak and reported one Astoria-class cruiser, a destroyer, and two patrol ships in the local harbour. The crew also identified buildings described as barracks and warehouses and confirmed the existence of runways. On 29 May, a seaplane from *I-19* approached Dutch Harbor, reporting spotting two destroyers and several motorboats patrolling the harbour entrance. At the same time, on the return route, the aircraft came across two or three other destroyers of an unknown class. On 30 May, a seaplane from *I-26*, after completing a reconnaissance flight over Kodiak, found about 700 miles northwest

Rear Admiral Kakuta Kakuji, the Commander of the 2nd Kidō Butai. (Open source)

of Seattle two large cruisers (it was emphasised that one of them may have been a transport ship), which were probably on the route to the above-mentioned city.[58]

During the Japanese approach towards the Aleutians and before the strike on Dutch Harbor, air reconnaissance was provided by the 2nd *Kidō Butai*. On the early morning of 1 June, four Kates took off from *Ryūjō* (coordinates 43°44'N 173°51'E) and went in two pairs on reconnaissance missions in the 60–80 degrees sector for 120 miles distance. Bombers did not encounter the enemy and returned to the deck after two hours.[59] The afternoon reconnaissance conducted by four Vals from *Jun'yō* ended with the same result.[60] By the end of the day, Zero sections circled over the area in three consecutive patrols

Table 5: Reconnaissance, anti-submarine, and CAP missions from *Ryūjō* and *Jun'yō*, 2 June 1942.[65]					
Unit	No.	Pilot	Observer	Radio operator	Notes
1st *shōtai*/ Kates (*Ryūjō*) 130 degrees	1	Lt Samejima (S)	PO1c Yoshihara	PO2c Itō	take-off: 0645 landing: ?
	2	Sea1c Ōki	PO2c Kameda	PO3c Noda	
2nd *shōtai*/ Kates (*Ryūjō*) 100 degrees	1	SLt Morita (S)	PO1c Morishita	PO2c Urada	
	2	Sea1c Shitayoshi	PO2c Akiyama	Sea1c Takahashi I.	
3rd *shōtai*/ Kates (*Ryūjō*) 70 degrees	1	PO2c Kawahara	PO1c Kawaguchi (S)	PO3c Ōbata	
	2	Sea1c Mizoguchi	PO3c Shimada	Sea2c Nakajima	
Unit	No.	Pilot	Observer/navigator		Notes
? *shōtai*/ Vals (*Jun'yō*) Anti-Sub	1	Unknown	Unknown		take-off: 1453 landing: ?
	2	Unknown	Unknown		
	3	Unknown	Unknown		
	4	Unknown	Unknown		
Unit	No.	Pilot			Notes
? *shōtai*/ Zeros (*Jun'yō*) CAP	1	Unknown			take-off: 1059 landing: ?
	2	Unknown			
	3	Unknown			
	4	Unknown			
? *shōtai*/ Zeros (*Jun'yō*) CAP	1	Unknown			take-off: 1308 landing: ?
	2	Unknown			
	3	Unknown			
	4	Unknown			
? *shōtai*/ Zeros (*Jun'yō*) CAP	1	Unknown			take-off: 1453 landing: ?
	2	Unknown			
	3	Unknown			
	4	Unknown			
? *shōtai*/ Zeros (*Jun'yō*) CAP	1	Unknown			take-off: 1658 landing: ?
	2	Unknown			
	3	Unknown			
	4	Unknown			
1st direct *shōtai*/ Zeros (*Ryūjō*) CAP	1	PO1c Endō (S)			take-off: 0430 (first CAP) landing: 1110 (last CAP)
	2	PO1c Shikada			
2nd direct *shōtai*/ Zeros (*Ryūjō*) CAP	1	PO1c Koga (S)			
	2	PO2c Kitahata			
3rd direct *shōtai*/ Zeros (*Ryūjō*) CAP	1	PO1c Yoshizawa (S)			
	2	PO1c Miyauchi			
4th direct *shōtai*/ Zeros (*Ryūjō*) CAP	1	PO1c Sugiyama (S)			
	2	PO3c Morita			
5th direct *shōtai*/ Zeros (*Ryūjō*) CAP	1	PO1c Kurihara (S)			
	2	PO3c Yoshihara			
6th direct *shōtai*/ Zeros (*Ryūjō*) CAP	1	PO1c Tomoishi (S)			
	2	Sea1c Ishihara			

(two from *Jun'yō* and one from *Ryūjō*), providing the combat air patrol (CAP) for the entire team. Looking at the 2nd *Kidō Butai* ships' hulls from above, Lt Abe shared the sensation that the North Pacific was "*itsumade tsuzuku kiri*" – "an endless mist".[61]

On the morning of 2 June, the 2nd *Kidō Butai* resumed its search for the enemy, sending three pairs of Kates from *Ryūjō* (coordinates 44°21'N 174°43'E)

Table 6: Reconnaissance missions from *Ryūjō*, afternoon 2 June 1942.[67]					
Unit	No.	Pilot	Observer	Radio operator	Notes
1st *shōtai*/ Kates (*Ryūjō*) 76 degrees	1	Sea1c Futakuchi	SLt Satō (S)	PO2c Anzai	take-off: 1400 landing: 1756
	2	PO1c Ōshima	PO1c Yamano	PO2c Morita	
2nd *shōtai*/ Kates (*Ryūjō*) 58 degrees	1	Sea1c Takahashi	PO1c Nemoto (S)	PO2c Watanabe	
	2	PO2c Okuyama	PO1c Ōhashi	PO2c Ikehara	
3rd *shōtai*/ Kates (*Ryūjō*) 40 degrees	1	PO1c Oda	PO1c Miura (S)	PO2c Kurahashi	
	2	Sea1c Tamai	PO1c Motohashi	PO2c Fujiki	

in the 100–130 degrees sector for 120 miles distance and the 70 degrees sector for 60 miles distance. Due to heavy clouds and rain, the crews returned to the carrier after a few hours and did not encounter any suspicious aircraft or vessels. Rear Admiral Kakuta, reaching the area far enough from the Kuriles to receive reliable air support from Japanese bases, ordered an immediate reinforcement of the CAP to secure the approach to Aleutians. On that day, 10 sections of Zeros and four Vals vigilantly circled above the Japanese warships to hunt down enemy submarines if any were encountered on the route. Like Hosogaya, the 52-year-old 2nd *Kidō Butai* commander owed much in life to his career in the Navy since he was born in the paddy field village of Tsukida of Niigata Prefecture as the second son of the local family of farmers. However, Kakuta's long relationship with *Nippon Kaigun* did not necessarily mean he was the right person in the right place. According to Commander Fuchida, Kakuta was not the best choice for taking charge of naval air operations as he lacked the essential skills and traits of a carrier task force commander. Educated at gunnery school to follow conservative tactics but having a flaring personality pushing to attack the enemy at any opportunity, aptly described in the Japanese lexeme "*kenteki hissen*" (it is an inevitable battle if you spot the enemy), Fuchida was afraid he could eventually lead the 2nd *Kidō Butai* to a disastrous defeat.[63] Lieutenant Abe also picked out Kakuta's spirit of an ancient warrior rather than a typical aircraft carrier admiral and admitted that he

called him with his subordinates "*teppōya*" – "a gunman".[64] Despite those negative assessments, which could as well be attached to some of the US Navy's successful admirals, the first days of Operation AL passed without significant occurrences, and Kakuta carried out all reconnaissance missions in line with Navy procedures.

During the afternoon, the Ōminato garrison chief of staff sent the dispatch about the latest intelligence report of American forces in the Aleutians, indicating three to four warships, including one cruiser, in the Kodiak area and three to four warships, including one large, in the Dutch Harbor area. The more detailed search also revealed no enemy vessels near Sitka or proceeding northward to reinforce the local task force.[66]

On the evening of 2 June, just on the eve of Operation AL, Kakuta sent three pairs of Kates from *Ryūjō* (coordinates 46°8'N 174°W) for a final reconnaissance mission in the 40-, 58- and 76-degree sectors for 250 miles distance. The torpedo bombers were ordered to ascertain that US Navy had not set up an ambush for his forces. No enemy presence was notified on the radio by crew members, meaning the best possible scenario for the 2nd *Kidō Butai* and allowing the bold advance towards the Aleutians. Thrilled about what the next few hours might bring, staff officers anxiously awaited news from the Central Pacific, believing that a decisive victory over Americans near Midway would greatly facilitate the capture of Attu and Kiska.

2
AMERICAN DEFENCE PREPARATIONS

アメリカの防衛準備
Amerika no Bōei Jumbi

Notwithstanding positive news from the successive reconnaissance missions of the 2nd *Kidō Butai*, Japanese plans in the Aleutians had been well-known to the Americans since mid-May.[1] On 15 May, US Navy intelligence intercepted several enemy dispatches, and some of them indicated that one task force involved in the future offensive in the North Pacific area, namely the landing operation on Kiska, was coded as AOB Invasion Force.[2] On the night of 20 and 21 May, Admiral Chester Nimitz, Commander-in-Chief, US Pacific Fleet (CINCPAC), established Task Force 8 (TF-8; also known as the North Pacific Force; NORPACFOR) under Rear Admiral Robert Alfred Theobald, who was also given control of all Army and Navy forces, including Canadian troops in Alaska and the Aleutians.[3] On the same day, US Navy intelligence confirmed that the Japanese

had vigorously concentrated naval forces and supplies in Ōminato, delivered by transport ships directly from Tokyo. The Americans considered the last part of the dispatch as irrefutable evidence that the enemy was in the final stage of preparation for the offensive in the North Pacific.[4]

It is essential to mention that the US Navy did not accidentally pick up the intelligence data about the planned enemy advance in the Aleutians. On 29 April 1942, General George C. Marshall, Chief of Staff of the US Army, warned Lieutenant General John L. DeWitt of Western Defense Command that *Nippon Kaigun* command had just requested information and charts from Tokyo on the close-in waters along the Aleutians and as far eastward as Kodiak Island and to the north a little short of Nome. To Marshall, this kind of inquiry was the evidence of a contemplated threat against that region.[5] After receiving the more precise warning from the US Navy with

Rear Admiral Robert Alfred "Fuzzy" Theobald, the Commander of Task Force 8. (NARA)

Lieutenant General John L. DeWitt, Western Defense Command. (NARA)

the estimated date of the Japanese attack in the North Pacific on 1–3 June, on 18 May, DeWitt made arrangements for dispatching a squadron of P-40 fighters and four B-17 bombers to Alaska from the West Coast.[6]

In the crucial days of May, the US Navy's attention was focused on Midway and the Aleutians. The Americans were ready to commit to defending the North Pacific area regardless of the offensive actions taken by the enemy towards the Central Pacific. The Japanese loss in the battle of the Coral Sea and the aversion of the direct threat to Port Moresby allowed Nimitz to reinforce the Alaskan Forces with two heavy cruisers, three light cruisers, and a dozen destroyers. He also directly instructed Theobald to "oppose the advance of the enemy in the Aleutian-Alaskan area, taking advantage of every favourable opportunity to inflict strong attrition," and "be governed by the principle of the calculated risk", which meant that the TF-8 commander received permission to sacrifice part of his forces if he felt that there was any chance to weaken the *Nippon Kaigun* war potential significantly.[7]

American analysis of the scenario of an attack on Hawaiian and Alaskan bases from 26 May indicated the real possibility of the Japanese seizing advanced positions in the Aleutian Islands. Due to limited naval resources, the US Navy's initial goal was to consolidate its forces in the Kodiak and/or Cold Bay (Unimak) areas to act in response to the movements of the enemy. The Americans expected that *Nippon Kaigun* would deploy the aircraft carrier *Ryūjō* and another light carrier, three heavy cruisers (including *Nachi*), one older Tama-class light cruiser, 16 destroyers, and eight to 10 submarines. On the other side, Theobald was to gather off Kodiak by 5 June two heavy cruisers, three light cruisers, 12 destroyers, a seaplane tender, five minesweepers, 14 torpedo boats, 15 patrol boats, and six submarines, all supplied by three tankers.[8] TF-8 could also rely on air reconnaissance provided the part of the 4th Patrol Wing comprising 20 Catalina flying boats and nine seaplanes.[9]

On 27 May, US Navy intelligence confirmed the increased number of enemy surface vessels at Ōminato, intercepting detailed orders for carrier air groups relating to the new tasks in the North Pacific two days later. On 31 May, due to the expected commencement of Operation AL, the Japanese radio communication activity visibly decreased.[10]

The American forces assigned to the defence of Alaska and the Aleutians were too feeble to act independently in such a vast area. However, Nimitz's greatest concern was missing a fleet carrier in the North Pacific to counterbalance the two anticipated Japanese light carriers, even though their offensive potential was limited.[11] If defenders encountered enemy carrier-borne aircraft or any other type of plane, they were to rely on the support of the Eleventh Air Force (11 AF)[12] commanded by Brigadier General William O. Butler, who had four airfields to operate with his aircraft in the Aleutian theatre of war. In order from the westernmost to the easternmost, they were: (1) Cape Field/Fort Glenn at Otter Point on Umnak, (2) Fort Randall Army Airfield, Cold Bay, (3) Naval Air Station Kodiak, (4) Elmendorf Air Force Base in Anchorage.[13] According to the Control Division Office, the USAAF in Alaska comprised only 39 fighters, 20 bombers, and seven transport planes. Despite the gradually arriving aircraft from the West Coast, on 23 May, the Alaska command sent a cable to reinforce the local air wing with at least 54 torpedo bombers or dive bombers and a similar number of fighters.[14] After all, in the early hours of 3 June, the 11 AF had 95 fighters (49 P-40E, 20 P-38E, 15 P-36A, 11 P-39D), 45 bombers (21 B-26A, nine B-18A, seven A-29, nine B-17B/E, two LB-30), 12 transport planes, and four training aircraft.[15]

The Pacific War became a matter of fact in Alaska when the local radio program was suddenly interrupted at 0927 hours by an announcement that the Japanese were attacking Pearl Harbor. Major General Simon Bolivar Buckner Jr., the Alaska Defense Command (ADC) commander since July 1940,[16] immediately issued orders to recall all the troops away from the bases. During the following night, he also recommended the blackout of cities, causing huge discomfort to citizens uncertain of the near future. Local newspapers and strange reports of mysterious sightings of Japanese aircraft heated up the atmosphere of panic. All dependents of military and construction workers were evacuated south, and in line with the controversial US policy, Buckner took an order to remove all Japanese Americans from Alaska. On 7 April, the ADC proclaimed that 263 residents of Japanese ancestry would be relocated despite all odds. Their exodus ended by July, mainly with the last stop at Minidoka Internment Camp in Idaho.[17]

On the eve of the Japanese offensive in the North Pacific, the Alaskan garrison totalled about 45,000 men, deployed in

Brigadier General William O. Butler, Commander of the Eleventh Air Force. (The Pacific War Online)

Major General Simon Bolivar Buckner Jr., Alaska Defense Command. (NARA)

various bases, including tiny, remoted outposts in the Aleutians.[18] Responsibility for supplying the Army troops rested with Pearl Harbor and the major cities on the US west coast. Since arriving in Alaska, the ADC commander, a 56-year old Kentuckian from a distinguished Confederate family, soon turned out to be the energetic advocate of expanding military facilities and the air force in the North Pacific. Shortly after Pearl Harbor, he proposed to be given overall responsibility for all military forces in Alaska; however, his suggestion died in early January 1942 on the desks of Generals Marshall and DeWitt, who did not support any fundamental changes in the chain of command. Still, one could deny that Buckner's intelligence, sagacity, and insolence were beneficial in a place all Americans seemed to have forgotten existed. It was not until June 1940, after a series of disastrous articles predicting an imminent German-Soviet invasion of Alaska, Congress decided to invest $350 million in the local defence.[19]

As J.H. Cloe tries to convince the readers, before the Pacific War, many Alaskan politicians in the US Congress believed Alaska was

America's "Achilles Heel." The Alaska Territory Delegate, Anthony Dimond, in stressing the need to fortify the territory, pointed out that: "By bombing plane, one corner of this great territory is less than 15 minutes from the Soviet mainland, another corner is about three hours from a Japanese naval station, and a third corner is about three hours from Seattle."[20]

Besides politicians, the same anxiety was shared by the American armed forces, especially after the outbreak of the war with Japan. On 21 January 1942, General Marshall sent a memorandum to President Roosevelt and shared his concerns related to the Aleutians:

We have been anticipating at any moment a "destruction raid" on this region, especially at Dutch Harbor where our state of preparations is far from complete. Also there is the hazard of the destruction of barracks, storehouses, etc. at both Kodiak Island and Anchorage, which would involve a difficult situation in the winter period. As most of the construction is frame and of a temporary nature, it presents a serious fire hazard. General Buckner has been given the directions and has the funds, so far as they can be spent in that region in the winter, to prepare against such an eventuality. He is very resourceful and energetic, and with troop labor available, has undoubtedly decentralized his storage and otherwise improved the situation.

As a later development, I consider it probable that if Japanese successes in other areas release ships and troops, a positive effort toward actual occupation of our Alaskan bases will be undertaken.[21]

The American fear of the Aleutians' vulnerability was partly connected with the poor infrastructure of the entire region, particularly the insufficient number of airfields. In September 1940, Buckner surveyed Unalaska to identify possible army air base construction sites. Although any place near Dutch Harbor seemed the most natural selection, he discovered the local terrain at Unimak to be generally unsuitable. He also considered an alternative site close to Chernofski Harbor, but by April 1941, the Army Air Corps had agreed that an airfield on Unalaska was not advisable. Buckner did not give up and urged for building airfields at Otter Point on Umnak Island and Cold Bay and Port Heiden on the Alaska Peninsula. Leaving aside the discussion between the Navy and the Army about the rationales of locations pointed out by the ACD, authorisation for constructing the airfield on Umnak was issued on 9 December 1941. The 807th Engineer Battalion (Aviation) soon began to arrive at the place, hastily preparing the ground and laying down the Marston mat runway. On 1 April 1942, a Douglas C-53 Skytrooper made the first landing. Despite that, the engineers vigorously continued construction works at Umnak, and by June, the airfield was prepared for air operations against the Japanese.

The Cold Bay airfield construction started a little earlier than at Otter Point. By late April, a 1,520-metre paved runway had been laid, and it was classified as operational before the Japanese attack. The last air base at Port Heiden was not completed until July 1942.[22]

What could look like a great success on paper for American higher command looked more complicated from a more practical perspective. The conditions at both new fields, particularly at Otter Point, were primitive, especially for crews. While engineers had managed to build revetments for the aircraft, and there was sufficient gasoline, ammunition and bombs. Still, all other equipment, especially radio sets, was missing. Furthermore, Buckner's inspection revealed that engineers had not completed paving the runway at Cold Bay. The runway was neither perfect at Otter

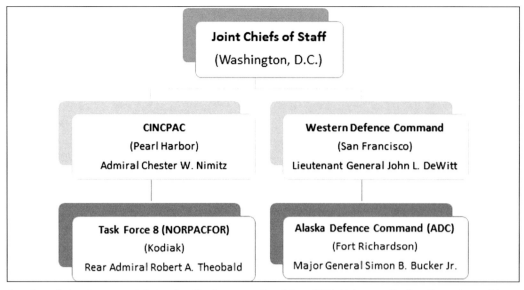

American chain of command during the Aleutian campaign, 1 June 1942. (Johnson, *Aleutian Campaign*, p. 7.)

Point, where the Marston mats were laid over the hastily prepared surface. The pilots who landed there had to fight for control over their aircraft and felt like landing on a trampoline, while during the take-offs, mats tended to ripple up in front of the wheels. General Butler also signalled another issue – the lack of space. Pilots who landed at Otter Point "were forced to land one after another like carrier planes, as on a carrier's deck, and then taxi back, so their wheels were just on the edge of the runway to make way for other ships." The planes were packed so close that Butler feared that dive bombers could destroy them in a single approach.[23]

Time for preparations had relentlessly passed, and besides the technical issues, the Americans faced another nuisance. When on 27 May Theobald arrived in Kodiak, he immediately entered a bitter personal conflict with Buckner. The ADC commander could not accept that he would have to submit to a person with no practical experience in serving in severe weather conditions of the northern seas. Nor did he respect preservative US Navy officers, constantly spreading his spiteful opinion that they had "an instinctive dread of Aleutian waters, feeling that they were inhabited by a ferocious monster that was always breathing fogs and coughing up williwaws that would blow the unfortunate mariner onto uncharted rocks and forever destroy his chances of becoming an admiral." However, B. Herder states that Buckner coped well with the agreeable, competent Captain Ralph C. Parker, a US Navy officer appointed in October 1940 as Alaska sector commander of Seattle's Northern Coastal Frontier, better known as the 13th Naval District.[24]

Fifty-eight-year-old "Fuzzy" Theobald, a quick-mind Californian, repaid Buckner's fervent comments and, frequently enough to upset the ADC commander for good, undermined the Army's authority, emphasising the prominent role of the US Navy in the upcoming struggle for the Aleutian Islands.[25] The verbal skirmishes between the two Americans and their senseless stubbornness went down in the United States armed forces history as the embodiment of the distrust between the Army and Navy. Even Admiral Nimitz, doing his utmost to reconcile both parties and avoid any incidents before the decisive clash with the Japanese, only fuelled the conflict by insisting on creating a space for "mutual cooperation"[26] instead of firmly supporting Theobald's leadership and putting pressure on the US Army staff to temper Buckner's ambitions. B. Garfield shared his valuable insight that stable and voluntary collaboration of strong personalities in the higher command was more difficult than fighting the common enemy.[27]

Theobald and Buckner may not have liked each other, but they shared the same problem: poor hydrographic and topographical knowledge of Alaska and the Aleutians. Some American staff maps were still based on Russian sketches and documents from 1864, which made utterly alien Africa a better-known area than its state territory in the North Pacific. More importantly, Alaska and the Aleutians have a longer coastline than the rest of the continental part of the United States, making strategic planning with limited naval and air forces a herculean task. However, it should be mentioned that Buckner spent most of his first months after arrival in July 1940, travelling throughout the state to become familiar with the territory. He also joined Major Davis in making survey flights, including a flight over the Bering Sea islands of Little Diomede and the Russian-owned Big Diomede three miles to the west across the International Date Line.[28]

Ironically, Buckner implicitly trusted the US Navy intelligence reports and believed that the Japanese would strike directly at Dutch Harbor. In his opinion, it was necessary to gather the bulk of the American forces in this area and only await the enemy's attack. In an ideal scenario, the ADC commander would like to see a joint Army-Navy action towards Japan from Alaskan and Siberian bases, though this idea was rejected due to primarily defensive goals in the region and a lack of Soviet response to involving airfields in Siberia.[29]

Theobald did not support any straightforward strategy as he feared that Combined Fleet could ignore military bases at Unalaska and land closer to Alaska, thus outmanoeuvring the US Navy in a single move.[30] The Japanese seemed capable of doing it; after all, the western part of the Aleutians was much closer to Tokyo than the bases on the west coast. The length of the supply lines also could not strictly determine the course of the future campaign. After the surprise attack on Pearl Harbor, few Japanese initiatives could astonish the US Navy. Buckner and DeWitt agreed with the Navy that the Navy was responsible for defending the Aleutians and other offshore islands while the Army would take care of the rest of Alaska. They also agreed with their Navy counterparts that the defence of the mainland was dependent on securing the eastern Aleutians, for the loss of Dutch Harbor would isolate western and northern Alaska.[31]

The TF-8 commander also disagreed with Nimitz's prediction that the western Aleutians, particularly Attu and Kiska, were the likely targets for *Nippon Kaigun*. On 29 May, Theobald stated in his memorandum that Japanese radio transmissions could be bait for the US Navy to abandon strategic positions off Kodiak.[32] To avoid falling into an ambush, he proposed using all operational flying boats and submarines to patrol the Aleutians regularly. The concept was aligned with official arrangements that surveillance along the chain was a Navy function,[33] but the plan had two major flaws. First, even if Theobald intended to track enemy movements only around the most important islands, he had too few PBY Catalina patrol aircraft to organise reconnaissance missions for over 2,000 miles daily. Secondly, the unstable weather conditions of the North

An SCR-268 Radar. The example shown was set up on Baker Island, Central Pacific. (Pacific Eagles.)

A B-17E of the USAAF. (Open source)

Pacific soon became his worst nightmare, especially the thick fog typical of the coastal subpolar zone, which reduced visibility to a minimum. All vessels had to be careful not to collide with each other at the anchorage accidentally, and the aircraft crews had to be careful not to crash into the steep slopes of the local mountains.

Given such a hurdle, seeing anything on the water surface from above seemed pure fiction. Still, Catalinas were equipped with ASV radar and did not have to rely entirely on visual identification, remaining Theobald's most reliable scouting aircraft. Eventually, the TF-8 commander abandoned his plan of conducting regular long-

Table 7: Order of Battle of the American forces in the Aleutians under Operational Plan 1-42, 3 June 1942.[38]

Task Force 8: Rear Admiral Robert A. Theobald

Task Group 8.6 (Main Force), Captain Thomas T. Raven
- heavy cruisers *Indianapolis, Louisville*
- light cruisers *Nashville* (F), *Honolulu, St. Louis*
- destroyers *McCall, Gridley, Humphreys, Gilmer*

Task Group 8.4 (Destroyer Group), Commander Wyatt Craig
- destroyers *Case* (F), *Reid, Sands, King, Kane, Brooks, Dent, Waters, Talbot*

Task Group 8.2 (Search Group), Captain Ralph C. Parker
- navy air bases at Dutch Harbor, Kodiak, Sitka
- gunboat *Charleston*
- minesweeper *Oriole*
- coast guard cutters: *Haida, Onondaga, Cyane, Aurora, Bonham*
- 15 motor torpedo boats (Lieutenant Commander Charles E. Anderson)

Task Group 8.9 (Tanker Group), Captain Houston L. Maples
- tankers *Sabine, Brazos, Comet*

Task Group 8.5 (Submarine Group), Lieutenant Commander Burton G. Lakes
submarines *S-18, S-23, S-27, S-28, S-34, S-35*

Task Group 8.1 (Scouting Group), Captain Leslie E. Gehres
Patrol Squadrons at hand in the Aleutians (28 May 1942):
- VP-41: 10 x PBY-5A, Captain Paul Foley (Dutch Harbor/Umnak)
- VP-42: 10 x PBY-5A, Captain James Russell (Cold Bay)

a)   Seaplane Tender Unit
Casco at Cold Bay servicing 4 x PBY
Gillis at Dutch Harbor servicing 12 x PBY
Williamson at Sand Point servicing 4 x PBY

b)   Kodiak airfield
2 x LB-30 (B-24A), 1 x B-17E
(all aircraft were radar-equipped)

Task Group 8.3 (11 AF), General Brigadier William O. Butler
a)   Fort Randall – Cold Bay (Unimak)
21 x P-40E
12 x B-26A
2 x B-18A

b)   Fort Glenn – Otter Point (Umnak)
12 x P-40E
6 x B-26A
1 x B-17B

c)   Kodiak
17 x P-40E
5 x P-36A
3 x P-39D
3 x B-18A
6 x Boeing B-17E heavy bombers (from 3 June)
Elmendorf Field (Anchorage)
3 x P-36A
2 x P-40E
28 x P-38E
5 x P-39D
11 x B-26A
9 x B-18A

distance reconnaissance flights but did not give up ad hoc patrols with radar-equipped PBYs, which could help to trace the enemy approach towards the Aleutians. The flying boats' usefulness was confirmed on 29 May when one of them, taking off from Dutch Harbor, tracked down a Japanese submarine on the sea's surface.[34]

The threat of the imminent offensive of the enemy made the commander of TF-8 finally decide to leave nine destroyers in Makushin Bay (Unalaska) under Lieutenant Commander Wyatt Craig. At first glance, these forces may seem quite large, but most of the vessels could remember the times of the First World War. Craig had only one task: to prevent the Japanese from landing on Unalaska. Meanwhile, Theobald, with five cruisers and four destroyers, planned to take up safer positions about 300 miles south of Kodiak and watch the following developments. Buckner criticised this idea since the core of the US Navy surface forces in the North Pacific was to avoid action and stay passive in vain almost 500 miles from Dutch Harbor.

It should be noted, however, that Theobald did not intend to avoid checking the enemy's advance but was afraid to come within range of the Japanese carriers, which could send his ships to the bottom, leaving the rest of Alaska at their mercy. Therefore, the US Navy strongly relied on the USAAF support, particularly B-26A and B-18A bombers, the only aircraft that could be equipped with torpedoes and menace the 2nd *Kidō Butai*. At last, Theobald ordered six submarines to set sail for war patrols and motor torpedo boats to proceed far west of Dutch Harbor to avoid the Japanese striking group.

Speaking of Dutch Harbor, the American base had been preparing for the potential Japanese strike since 24

Fort Randall Army Airfield in 1942. (USAAF)

March 1942, when Lieutenant Captain William N. Updegraff, Commanding Officer of Naval Air Station, sent there his deputy, Lieutenant Commander Thomas C. Thomas. The arrangements included rigorous training programs (chemical warfare, rifle instruction and aircraft identification practice), digging trenches, erecting concrete pill boxes, and establishing observation posts on high points. The naval personnel were moved out of the barracks and dispersed among the other establishments, along with supplies and food. Yet, Dutch Harbor was unfit to take any severe blow, and Commander Foster assessed in his report from 15 May that the base was "still in its infancy and was far from being an air station or a submarine base." He pointed out the lack of an air defence system, including a deficiency of anti-aircraft artillery practice and a shortage of ammunition. The SCR-271, scheduled for installation near Dutch Harbor, was still in its packing crate. The three short-ranged SCR-268 anti-aircraft searchlight radars that provided the only ground-based coverage were masked by nearby mountains. Although observation posts had been established, there was no command system to process and forward the information. Control of aircraft operations and communications between Dutch Harbor and Otter Point were inadequate, described as "in a kindergarten stage of development". Foster repeated his opinion that the Otter Point airfield construction was a mistake. Airstrips on Umnak were too far remoted – a 140-mile round trip limited the time the fighters could spend defending Dutch Harbor.[35]

Recognising the seriousness of the situation in the Aleutians, at the last moment, the USAAF command decided to reinforce the 11 AF with six new B-17E, which were already in transit according to the 26 May plan. On 3 June, the long-awaited Flying Fortresses equipped with SCR-521 radars arrived and were sent to Kodiak. They were immediately put to work flying combat patrols.[36] In

the meantime, Theobald onboard *Nashville* was already with Task Group 8.6 at sea some 350 miles to the southeast and directed all ships in his formation not to use TBS except in an emergency. Crews were also informed about the possibility of meeting friendly Russian merchantmen on a trade route or American submarine *S-27* crossing ahead of track of the formation during the dark hours of 2–3 June.[37]

On 1 June, the entire US west coast, from Nome to Seattle, was put on 24-hour combat alert. All aircraft on reconnaissance missions were to fly to the limits of their range, and additional fighters from various states began their transfer route to the west.[39]

A day later, the electrifying news reached the Americans, which had been waiting for the opening moves for almost two weeks. Based on observations of radio transmissions, US Navy intelligence indicated that the enemy aircraft carrier was operating approximately 400 miles south of Kiska. The Japanese striking force was to consist of an aircraft carrier, three heavy cruisers, and four destroyers south of the Aleutian Islands. In addition, two heavy cruisers, two converted cruisers, and six destroyers would approach main American positions from the west along the northern side of the chain. A force of auxiliaries with transports and cargos protected by two light cruisers was believed to be heading for the Bering Sea, ready to descend upon the islands selected for landings when the opportune time arose. Based on available intelligence and meteorological reports, which showed the frontal weather and a band of rain and mist approaching the Aleutian chain, it was estimated that an attack would materialise between the morning of 3 June and the morning of 4 June.[40] In reaction to the imminent threat, the 11 AF command deployed most of its operational bombers to the outermost airfields at Cold Bay and Otter Point. Nothing more could be done at that moment; the next day was to reveal if the Americans were right to expect a Japanese attack.

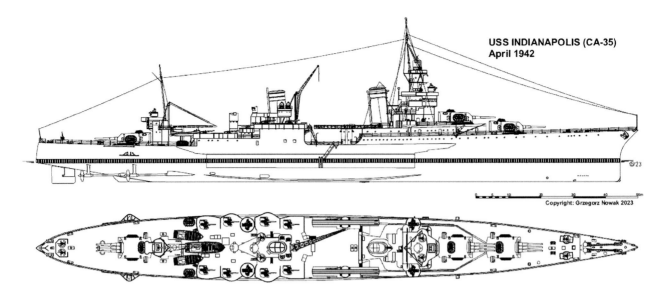

USS INDIANAPOLIS (CA-35)
April 1942

Copyright: Grzegorz Nowak 2023

USS *Indianapolis* (CL/CA-35) was a Portland-class heavy cruiser (the third class of "treaty cruisers") launched in 1931 and commissioned in 1932. Like her sister, she was designed as a fleet flagship to accommodate the flag officer and his staff. The cruiser could carry as many as four seaplanes and had two aircraft catapults amidships. Her main armament comprised nine 8-inch (203 mm) guns and eight 5-inch (127 mm) anti-aircraft guns. During the outbreak of the Pacific war, she was at sea near Johnston Atoll and returned to Pearl Harbor on 13 December. As a part of Task Force 11, Indianapolis escorted *Lexington* and participated in the action off Bougainville on 20 February 1942. The following month, she supported *Yorktown* during the successful raid against Lae and Salamaua. She was then briefly refitted in the Mare Island Naval Shipyard, and after escorting a convoy to Australia, she was dispatched to the North Pacific, where she became a crucial part of Rear Admiral Robert Alfred Theobald's Task Force 8. (Drawing by Grzegorz Nowak)

3

3 JUNE 1942, THE FIRST RAID ON DUTCH HARBOR

ダッチハーバー第一次空襲、6月3日
Dacchi Haabaa Dai Ichiji Kūshū, Rokugatsu Mikka

Well before the dawn of 3 June, Kakuta found himself less than 200 miles south of Unimak and ordered *Ryūjō* and *Jun'yō* to launch the first striking group comprising 14 Kates, 15 Vals and 16 Zeros led by Lieutenant Shiga Yoshio as its *hikōtaichō*.[1] Ten torpedo bombers were armed with two 250kg land bombs and four aircraft with one 250kg land bomb and in total fifteen 60kg general-purpose bombs.[2] The group had to proceed northeast, and their primary objective was to strike the US Navy base at Dutch Harbor.[3]

Just 30 minutes after take-off (*Ryūjō*'s coordinates: 51°53'N 168°43'W), a *shōtai* of Zeros led by Lieutenant Kobayashi unexpectedly flew into the storm clouds and soon had to turn back on the carrier. The 2nd *Kidō Butai* command did not want to leave the torpedo bombers without proper fighter support, at 0410 hours, a *shōtai* led by PO1c Endō scrambled from *Ryūjō* and soon caught up with the formation of Kates.[4] A quarter later, at 0427 hours, the striking group from *Jun'yō* detected one enemy flying boat returning to Dutch Harbor. Warrant Officer Kitahata's *shōtai* was ordered to intercept the lonely aircraft. A short pursuit ended with no credible claims as the Catalina, described as "smoking badly", managed to disappear into clouds. Zeros joined the formation of planes from *Ryūjō*, continuing the approach to the American base. In the meantime, the rest of the *Jun'yō* striking group was facing a severe problem. Val crews reported terrible weather conditions, particularly thick fog and low clouds, when they were close to Unimak. Lieutenant Abe, fighting with his thoughts – a sense of duty or safety of his subordinates and meaningless loss of the planes – at 0505 hours, made a painful decision to return to the carrier with all dive bombers and was joined by Shiga's 11 fighters.[5] Despite the fear

that Kakuta might be unsatisfied, he supported Abe's judgement, soothing him that the attack would be renewed the next day.[6] The planes from *Ryūjō* had much more luck as they avoided clouds and gusty wind by flying at higher altitudes.

At about 0540 hours, the seaplane tender *Gillis'* radar picked up a dozen unidentified aircraft in a 25 miles distance,[8] approaching Dutch Harbor at 3,000 metres. Operators instantly passed the warning to Captain Updegraff, who did not doubt that the incoming group of boogies was the long-awaited Japanese carrier-borne strike. Alarm sirens sounded all over Dutch Harbor, and in less than five minutes, the crew members and soldiers had taken up their battle stations, the ships' boilers were fired, and Catalinas were vigorously prepared for emergency take-off. In the meantime, P-40E scrambled from the neighbouring Cold Bay airfield and dashed towards Dutch Harbor to close the 180 miles gap between the two bases. Kodiak and Anchorage also received a warning about the enemy air raid, and even Theobald at sea was among the recipients of this dispatch. However, due to a failure of the communication system, the message about the approaching Japanese striking group was not sent to the nearest Fort Glenn army airfield, where its personnel were unaware of the danger and did not raise the alarm. As a result of this mistake, the P-40E fighter pilots of the 11th Fighter Squadron, ready to intercept the enemy group, entirely missed the morning engagement over Dutch Harbor.[9]

At 0545 hours, the Americans spotted the first enemy planes approaching the base. They were six Kates led by Lieutenant Samejima Hiroichi escorted by three Zeros. The Japanese immediately noticed one Catalina taxiing in the water, visibly trying to get out of the base before the enemy arrived. In the one-sided skirmish, the flying boat piloted by Lieutenant (jg.) Jack Litsey of

Table 8: The composition of the 2nd *Kidō Butai* first striking group during the attack on Dutch Harbor, 3 June 1942.[7]

Unit	No.	Pilot	Observer	Radio operator	Notes	Expended ammunition/ bombs
4th *shōtai* Kates/*Ryūjō*	1	Lt Samejima (S)	PO1c Yoshihara	PO2c Itō	take-off: 0340 landing: 0750	1 x 250kg land bomb (each)
	2	Sea1c Ōki	PO2c Kameda	PO3c Noda		15 x general-purpose 60kg bomb (in total)
6th *shōtai* Kates/*Ryūjō*	1	PO2c Kawahara	PO1c Yamaguchi (S)	PO3c Ōbata	take-off: 0340 landing: 0750	
	2	Sea1c Mizoguchi	PO3c Shimada	Sea2c Nakajima		
5th *shōtai* Kates/*Ryūjō*	1	SLt Shibata (S)	PO1c Itō	PO2c Kikuta	take-off: 0340 landing: 0750	2 x 250kg land bomb (each)
	2	PO1c Oda	PO1c Miura	PO2c Kurahashi		
	3	Sea1c Shitayoshi	PO2c Akiyama	PO2c Takahashi I.		

Unit	No.	Pilot			Notes	Expended ammunition/ bombs
1st *shōtai* Zeros/*Ryūjō*	1	Lt Kobayashi (S)			take-off: 0340 landing: 0430 (replaced by Kobayashi *shōtai*)	None
	2	PO1c Kurihara				
	3	PO1c Tomoishi				
2nd *shōtai* Zeros/*Ryūjō*	1	PO1c Endō (S) #			take-off: 0410 landing: 0745	840 x 7.7mm 238 x 20mm (in total)
	2	PO1c Koga				
	3	PO1c Shikada				

Unit	No.	Pilot	Observer	Radio operator	Notes	Expended ammunition/ Bombs
1st *shōtai* Kates/*Ryūjō*	1	PO1c Nishimura	Lt Yamagami (B)	PO2c Endō	take-off: 0430 landing: 0745	2 x 250kg land bomb (each)
	2	Sea1c Shimada	PO2c Satō	PO2c Hoshino		
3rd *shōtai* Kates/*Ryūjō*	1	PO2c Horiuchi #	WO Uchimura (S) #	PO3c Yamauchi #	take-off: 0430 landing: 0745	70 x 7.7mm (in total expended)
	2	PO1c Tanishiki #	PO3c Nihei #	Sea1c Toriyama #		
2nd *shōtai* Kates/*Ryūjō*	1	Sea1c Futakuchi #	SLt Satō (S) #	PO2c Anzai #	take-off: 0430 landing: 0745	2 x 250kg land bomb (each)
	2	PO1c Takahashi	PO1c Nemoto	PO2c Watanabe		
	3	PO1c Yamaguchi	PO2c Kobayashi	PO3c Izumi		

Unit	No.	Pilot			Notes	Expended ammunition / bombs
1st *chūtai* 11th *shōtai* Zeros/*Jun'yō*	1	Lt Shiga (H)			take-off: 0325 landing: 0545	none
	2	PO1c Yamamoto				
1st *chūtai* 12th *shōtai* Zeros/*Jun'yō*	1	WO Kitahata (S)			take-off: 0325 landing: 0835	?
	2	PO2c Sasakibara				
1st *chūtai* 13th *shōtai* Zeros/*Jun'yō*	1	PO1c Kubota (S)			take-off: 0325 landing: 0545	none
	2	PO2c Hasegawa				
2nd *chūtai* 14th *shōtai* Zeros/*Jun'yō*	1	Lt Miyano (C)			take-off: 0325 landing: 0545	
	2	PO1c Ōzeki				
	3	Sea1c Yoshida				
2nd *chūtai* 15th *shōtai* Zeros/*Jun'yō*	1	PO1c Okamoto (S)			take-off: 0325 landing: 0545	
	2	PO3c Tanaka				
2nd *chūtai* 16th *shōtai* Zeros/*Jun'yō*	1	PO1c Kamihira (S)			take-off: 0325 landing: 0545	
	2	PO2c Yotsumoto				

VP-41 was shot down by PO1c Endō's *shōtai*, killing RM3c Martin H. Zeller and AM2c Rolland Geller. A third crew member was wounded and jumped out of the rear blister window of the PBY and drowned trying to reach the shore. Litsey managed to beach the damaged plane, which did not explode or burn and was salvaged.[10]

According to the Patrol Wing 4 report, the remaining Catalinas were either returning from night patrols or dispersed in coves near Dutch Harbor at the time of the attack. Still, several flying boats had brief contact with enemy planes, but they all avoided being shot down. Lieutenant (jg.) Kirmse of VP-41 reached cloud cover, and Ensign

Table 8: The composition of the 2nd Kidō Butai first striking group during the attack on Dutch Harbor, 3 June 1942.[7] (*continued*)

Unit	No.	Pilot	Observer/navigator	Notes	Expended ammunition/ bombs
1st *chūtai* 21st *shōtai* Vals/*Jun'yō*	1	Lt Abe (B)	WO Ishii	take-off: 0325 landing: 0545	none
	2	PO3c Takei	PO1c Harada		
	3	PO3c Nakatsuka	PO2c Kimura		
1st *chūtai* 22nd *shōtai* Vals/*Jun'yō*	1	PO1c Ōishi	WO Yamamoto (S)	take-off: 0325 landing: 0545	
	2	PO3c Okada	PO2c Sugie		
	3	PO2c Ikeda	PO2c Miyazaki		
1st *chūtai* 23rd *shōtai* Vals/*Jun'yō*	1	PO1c Numata (S)	PO2c Takano	take-off: 0325 landing: 0545	
	2	Sea1c Nagashima	PO2c Nakao		
2nd *chūtai* 24th *shōtai* Vals/*Jun'yō*	1	PO1c Kawabata	Lt Miura (C)	take-off: 0325 landing: 0545	
	2	PO3c Yamakawa	PO2c Nishiyama		
	3	Sea2c Murakami	PO2c Kataoka		
2nd *chūtai* 25th *shōtai* Vals/*Jun'yō*	1	WO Harano (S)	PO1c Nakajima	take-off: 0325 landing: 0545	
	2	PO3c Kosemoto	Sea1c Nakata		
2nd *chūtai* 26th *shōtai* Vals/*Jun'yō*	1	PO2c Miyatake	WO Tajima (S)	take-off: 0325 landing: 0545	
	2	PO2c Gotō	PO2c Yamano		

Seaplane tender USS *Gillis* (AVD-12) on 14 February 1941. (Open source)

William R. Doerr of the same squadron encountered fighters and bombers without suffering any damage. Ensign James T. Hildebrand of VP-41 was less fortunate as Endō's *shōtai* attacked him off the southern coast of Unalaska but fought back with his machine guns. The American crew reported sending one fighter down in flames, but neither *Ryūjō*'s nor *Jun'yō*'s reports confirmed this claim.[11]

During the initial hunt for American flying boats, the other two Zeros from *Jun'yō* focused on strafing military facilities with machine

guns and 20mm cannons. At 0550 hours, the first formation of four Kates led by Samejima attacked Fort Mears from 2,750 metres, dropping 60kg general-purpose bombs throughout the complex, destroying three warehouses, two navy barracks buildings, and three Quonset prefabricated barracks and killing 25 and wounding 25 men. Additionally, Japanese torpedo bombers inflicted minor damage to three barracks, two officers' quarters, an officers' mess, and two cold storages. The only serious loss was a SCR-271 fixed,

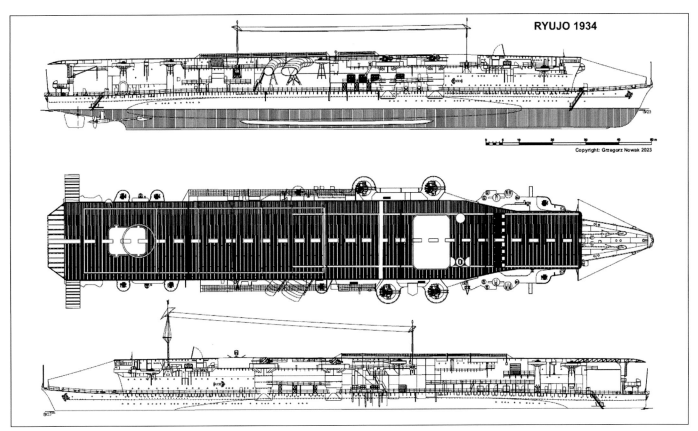

Ryūjō (龍驤) was the first Japanese light aircraft carrier built from scratch to comply with the Washington Treaty limitations. The vessel was laid down in November 1929 and entered service in May 1933. Her operational history covered ill-fated manoeuvres of the Fourth Fleet in September 1935 and operations in Chinese waters against Shanghai, Nanjing, and Guangzhou during the Second Sino-Chinese War. Parallel to *Kidō Butai*'s strike on Pearl Harbor, she took part in air operations in the Philippines. In early January 1942, the carrier supported the Twenty-Fifth Army in pursuing British forces on the Malay Peninsula. She participated in the Dutch East Indies campaign and headed to Singapore to escort convoys to Burma. In early April, *Ryūjō* was assigned to Vice Admiral Ozawa Jisaburo's Malay Force and played a major part in the offensive operation in the Bay of Bengal, contributing significantly to sinking many Allied cargo ships. In April, the Navy General Staff decided to fully upgrade her air group by replacing the older Claude fighters with the newest Zeros. *Ryūjō* went into drydock at Kure for planned maintenance and a refit and left it on 6 May. Soon after, she formed the 2nd Kidō Butai with *Jun'yō* to support Operation AL. (Drawing by Grzegorz Nowak)

long-range aircraft warning radar set intended for Cape Winslow on the north side of Unalaska. After a while, three more Kates, led by Sub Lieutenant Shibata, appeared over Mount Ballyhoo, flying southerly and then circled to the left to the 55 degrees course. They dropped six 250kg "land" bombs, yet all of them glided too far from Fort Mears, falling right into the nearby soft ground and a trench, where they killed one soldier taking cover but did no material damage. The third group of torpedo bombers, coming from the opposite direction, destroyed the radio transmitter and the adjacent Quonset hut, killing a civilian employee of Siems Drake Puget Sound. Bombs narrowly missed Dutch Harbor's radio shack, spraying it with shrapnel and prompting the American yeoman to transmit, "That one knocked me off my chair!".[12] The fourth and the last group of three Kates, led by Sub Lieutenant Satō, approached from the east and targeted Power House Hill, over-shooting the wooden oil tanks. One bomb struck the hard ground near a Navy fire-watchers pillbox, killed one enlisted man outside, and severely wounded one man inside. Another struck on the edge of a road, demolishing an Army truck, and killing the driver. A third struck in soft ground near a trench and killed one Marine private. The other three bombs exploded harmlessly on soft ground. After the attack, all planes disappeared northward. They were again sighted at about 0800 hours by M.V. Point Reyes, flying northeast over Beaver Inlet and then southwest to sea over Udagak Strait.[13]

The first raid of the 2nd *Kidō Butai* on Dutch Harbor lasted less than 30 minutes. All American ships stationed in the base participated in the defence. In addition to the seaplane tender

Gillis, the support fire was provided by flush-deck destroyers *King* and *Talbot*, the US Coast Guard cutter *Onondaga*, the transports *President Fillmore* and *Morlen*, and the submarine *S-27*. Japanese aircraft were also deterred by anti-aircraft artillery consisting of twelve 3-inch (76.2mm) M1918 guns, fourteen 37mm AA guns and twenty-four 0.5-inch (12.7mm) M2 Browning heavy machine guns. The Americans also had four 155mm M1 coastal guns from the 250th Coast Artillery Regiment, but they were useless against planes attacking Dutch Harbor. The great struggle and dedication to fight off the Japanese plane can be seen through in *President Filmore*'s action report:[14]

[points 1 and 2 omitted]

3. At 0557 General Quarters were sounded. All men including the Naval personnel attached to the ship, Naval personnel in transit, officers and men of Battery G, 260th CA (AA), and officers and men of the Merchant Marine crew rushed to battle stations without confusion, just as if they were veterans. At 0600 all guns reported manned and ready. I directed fire of all guns from the flying bridge by means of the telephone system.

4. Enemy planes were sighted. Visibility was excellent, inasmuch as at the hour in the Land of the Midnight Sun we were favored with a clear Arctic Sky. "Tojo" came over in formations of three and four planes, totalling nineteen bombers and fighters, and generally followed the same tactics that he used at Pearl Harbor; i.e., squadrons approaching from the south and west

simultaneously, flying straight and level, crossing, turning and coming back from the north and east.

5. At 0602 the order was given to commence fire. All guns which could bear on target opened fire. The ship's battery consisted of: two 3" 50 cal. AA guns, two .50 cal. Browning machine guns, and two .30 cal. Lewis machine guns. One 3" was located forward and one aft. The .30 cal. were on the flying bridge. The .50's were located on the boat deck just abaft the stack. Battery G'S armament consisted of: Eight 37 Millimeter cannons and four .50 cal. Browning machine guns. Two of the .50's were on the forecastle and other two on the poop deck. Four of the 37's were located on A deck forward; the other four on A deck aft. The field of fire of G Batter's eight 37's and four .50's was limited by the boom cables and superstructure. The 3" batteries opened fire with fuse 6 settings. No. 1 3" gun had a hangfire on the first salvo and the gun was out of action for the remainder of the raid. Since the ship was loaded with detonators, torpedoes, and all types of high explosives, I thought it was best to wait at least fifteen minutes before giving the order to unload. The gun was finally unloaded and the shell was examined and thrown overboard. You could see where the firing pin struck home. I came to the conclusion that it contained a faulty primer.

6. The planes flew at an altitude ranging between 14,000 and 18,000 feet, with frequent attempts to "peel off" for low altitude bombing. The bombers made one trial run before dropping their cargo. After the bombing started, they kept it up until their mission was completed.

7. One shell from the after 3" gun exploded just ahead of the second formation of bombers, causing the starboard plane to shake and fall out of formation, as evidenced by enclosures (B) and (F). Apparently we damaged the plane, but she later rejoined the formation.

8. One plane in the last formation of bombers was hit by a shell from the after 3" gun, as evidenced by enclosures (B) and (F) and was last seen smoking and in flames falling in the mountains behind Unalaska.

9. A Japanese fighter plane broke through the barrage of fire and commenced to machine gun a destroyer in the harbor. My .30 cal. machine guns opened fire. Some of the .25 cal. bullets used by the fighter plane landed on the deck, almost cutting in half ropes and cables suspended from the booms.

10. The ship, a survivor of five sustained attacks at Suez, is apparently "charmed," for a "dud" landed on the dock about 15 feet from the ship near the stern. The "dud" broke in half and was kicked into the water by a sailor.

11. At 0614 the order was given to cease fire. A few minutes later we were ordered to leave the dock. The ship maneuvered and stood out of the harbor, and commenced to circle clockwise just five miles northwest of Priest Rock. At 1708 the ship reentered the harbor and moored starboard side to the Dutch Harbor dock. There were four alerts that day, but only one attack.

P-40Es that took off from Cold Bay arrived too late to intercept the striking group. Ironically, the Americans could not find the intruders, but in return, four Warhawks were spotted by several Kates off western Unalaska. The Japanese torpedo bombers were already on their return course and avoided engaging the enemy, visibly dashing towards Dutch Harbor.[15]

The general landscape after the battle did not give the Americans much cause for optimism. Dutch Harbor was enveloped in thick acrid black smoke, and the scattered bodies of the dead at Fort Mears and the screams of the wounded spoke for themselves. After putting out the fires and helping people in urgent need, it was possible to summarise the Japanese strike. Even though the enemy's air domination was unquestionable, due to a horizontal bombing by 14 torpedo bombers, only the Fort Mears barracks were damaged, and half burned down. The signal facility on which one bomb was dropped did not report significant damage. The most critical equipment for the Americans – the radio station and antenna – remained operational, and none of the radio operators was killed. After hastily refuelling, three of the four flying boats returned safely to base and went on reconnaissance missions to the southwest.[16]

The Americans reported shooting down at least two enemy fighters and three bombers, but the first striking group returned all hands on-deck. Despite three torpedo bombers and one fighter being damaged by anti-aircraft shell splinters, they remained fully operational after quick repairs.[17] During the short talk with the commanders of air groups, Kakuta realised that the raid could not neutralise the enemy base.[18] On the eve of the attack on Dutch

Fort Mears afire after the Japanese attack on 3 June 1942. (Naval History and Heritage Command)

Tank farm afire after Japanese attack on 3 June 1942. Radio station in foreground. (Naval History and Heritage Command)

Navy machine gun crew watches intently as Japanese aircraft depart scene after the attack on 3 June 1942. (Naval History and Heritage Command)

Apart from offensive moves, Kakuta also remained vigilant in the event of an American counterattack. On his order, at 0510 hours, four Kates scrambled from *Ryūjō* and went on a routine scouting patrol in 70, 90, 265, and 270 degrees for 60 miles distance. Less than two and a half hours later, all torpedo bombers landed on the carrier, reporting no threat to the entire team.

Reading the news from the 2nd *Kidō Butai* raid on Dutch Harbor, Theobald knew that the Japanese had insufficient knowledge of the important positions in the Aleutians. In a 3 June report, he indicated that if the correct location of his forces had been known, instead of Dutch Harbor, airfields on Umnak or in Cold Bay should have been attacked first. Taking advantage of the enemy's ignorance, the TF-8 commander intended to move most of the bombers to Umnak and wait for an opportunity to counterattack. Circumstances indicated that such a moment would come during the attempted landing of Unalaska, which Theobald believed was the most likely objective of Operation AL.[21]

Besides Patrol Wing 4, which search capacity was limited due to the number of PBYs, the 11 AF also joined in looking for the enemy carriers. Captain Owen "Jack" Meals, the commander of the 77th Bombardment Squadron, scrambled with six B-26s from Otter Point and went southwest, where he expected to find the 2nd *Kidō Butai*. Nonetheless, his mission ended without any sightings, and on landing,

Harbor, *Nippon Kaigun* had no current photographs of military facilities in Unalaska, and the air strike was more or less improvised. The crews of each bomber chose targets at their discretion, guided by intuition and current assessment of the battlefield. Although no enemy fighters were encountered, the mission was hampered by bad weather, as it also prevented the whole formation of dive bombers from reaching Dutch Harbor. Even several Vals, which certainly had higher chances to hit ground targets than torpedo bombers, could be a priceless asset during the opening hit of Operation AL.

around 1400 hours, one of the wheels of his bomber slid off the wet steel runway matting into the mud. The landing gear collapsed, and a torpedo slung under the Marauder broke free and skidded down the runway but luckily did not explode. Meals and his crew climbed unharmed from the bomber.[22]

Before the first striking group returned to the decks, Kakuta learned about the spotting of five enemy destroyers in Makushin Bay and soon decided they would become his next target. Carrier maintenance personnel eagerly awaited bombers and fighters to appear on the horizon, which had to loosen their formation in

Table 9: The 2nd *Kidō Butai* claims after the first strike on Dutch Harbor, 3 June 1942.[19]

Unit	Claimed results
Zeros from *Ryūjō*	set three Catalinas afire strafed fuel tanks site
Zeros from *Jun'yō*	one Catalina shot down
Kates from *Ryūjō* (Lt Samejima 7 x torpedo bombers)	three direct hits with 250kg bombs and 15 hits with 60kg bombs on group of barracks and set them on fire, one direct hit and three near misses with 250kg bombs on communications facility
Kates from *Ryūjō* (Lt Yamagami 7 x torpedo bombers)	direct hit and medium damage to military warehouse direct hits and set fire to two fuel tanks sites, direct hit on the AA post

case any American flying boats snooped them to track the entire task force. Another reason for the dispersal was the deteriorating weather, making it impossible to go along the shortest route. As the 2nd *Kidō Butai* maintained radio silence, navigators on Kates had to find their carriers by dead reckoning. Yet, overcoming all difficulties, the Japanese aircraft found their ships and landed by 0835 hours without further complications.

Preparations for sending the second striking group lasted over an hour, during which the planes were refuelled and rearmed. Starting at 1045 hours, 17 Kates, 15 Vals and 15 Zeros, led by Lieutenant Shiga, scrambled from *Ryūjō* and *Jun'yō*. The dive bombers and

their escorts from *Jun'yō* took off first, followed by the first batch of torpedo bombers and fighters from *Ryūjō* a quarter of an hour later. In less than an hour, the remaining group of Kates and Zeros also lifted into the air.

More than an hour after the departure, planes from *Jun'yō* went into gusty winds, thick fog, and a rain squall, making it challenging to find the enemy destroyers. On that day, the weather did not favour air operations. However, in less than 15 minutes, Zeros accidentally encountered one Catalina lurking around the area. During the short pursuit, the flying boat was machine-gunned, and the Japanese pilots saw the black smoke coming out of her tail while she escaped into the thick clouds at the last moment. They were uncertain about the outcome of the chasing run and did not report a victory.

Still, circling above Unalaska helplessly to find any targets was too dangerous. At 1215 hours, Shiga ordered the entire group to return, including the *Ryūjō* torpedo bombers that had just scrambled. The Zeros did not meet any enemy fighters coming to intercept their bombers. Instead, the six-plane formation stumbled upon the second PBY and, like a quarter earlier, machine-gunned her and saw only the trail of smoke, claiming a possible victory.[24]

To increase the potential damage to the enemy, Kakuta also ordered to prepare four Dave reconnaissance floatplanes, each armed with two 60kg bombs, to attack the American destroyers. They were catapulted from the heavy cruisers *Takao* and *Maya* and were supposed to go to the location indicated in the dispatch. On the route, in the vicinity of Umnak, though, two Daves encountered a large group of American fighters. Six P-40Es of the 11th Fighter Squadron hurriedly took off from Otter Point for the signal of observers, who spotted the intruders flying over the base. The Japanese crews were utterly taken aback and did not know how quickly the enemy got behind their backs. According to the description of the flight officer on *Takao*, Lieutenant Obata, one of the seaplanes cornered by two P-40Es, piloted by First Lieutenants John B. Murphy and Jacob Dixon, intentionally rammed the enemy fighter and disintegrated in mid-air. The 11th Fighter Squadron history claims only that Murphy fired just two shots and the enemy crashed at the end of the runway into the bay.[26] The other Dave was much luckier and, despite being full of bullet holes, ditched, and her crew left the sinking aircraft in time.[27] Seeing no other option, two seaplanes from *Maya* escaped into the dense clouds and set off on a return course.[28] Although the American pilots dominated the enemy, they could speak of great luck because the Japanese did not notice that

Table 10: Reconnaissance missions from *Ryūjō*, morning 3 June 1942.[20]

Unit	No.	Pilot	Observer	Radio operator	Notes
x *shōtai* Kates/*Ryūjō*	1	PO1c Ōshima	PO1c Yamano	PO2c Morita	take-off: 0510 landing: 0736
	2	PO2c Okuyama	PO1c Ōhashi	PO2c Ikehara	
	3	PO2c Fujii	PO1c Morishita	PO2c Itasaka	
	4	Sea1c Tamai	PO1c Motohashi	PO2c Fujiki	

Fort Glenn Army Air Base at Otter Point, built on Umnak Island in 1942. (Open source)

Table 11: The composition of the 2nd *Kidō Butai* striking group during the second (unsuccessful) attack on Dutch Harbor, 3 June 1942.[23]

Unit	No.	Pilot			Notes
1st *shōtai* Zeros/*Ryūjō*	1	Lt Kobayashi (B)			take-off: 1100 landing: 1340
	2	PO1c Kurihara			
	3	PO1c Tomoishi			
2nd *shōtai* Zeros/*Ryūjō*	1	PO1c Yoshizawa (S)			
	2	PO1c Miyauchi			
	3	PO1c Ishihara			
? *shōtai* Zeros/*Ryūjō*	1	WO Uemura (S)			take-off: 1150* landing: 1315
	2	PO1c Sugiyama			
	3	PO2c Kitashino			

Unit	No.	Pilot	Observer	Radio operator	Notes
4th *shōtai* Kates/*Ryūjō*	1	Lt Samejima (S)	PO1c Yoshihara	PO2c Itō	take-off: 1100 landing: 1340
	2	PO1c Oda	PO1c Miura	PO2c Kurahashi	
	3	Sea1c Ōki	PO2c Kameda	PO3c Noda	
5th *shōtai* Kates/*Ryūjō*	1	PO2c Kawahara	PO1c Yamaguchi (S)	PO3c Ōbata	
	2	Sea1c Tamai	PO1c Motohashi	PO2c Mogi	
	3	Sea1c Mizoguchi	PO3c Shimada	Sea2c Nakajima	
1st *shōtai* Kates/*Ryūjō*	1	PO1c Nishimura	Lt Yamagami (B)	PO2c Endō	take-off: 1150* landing: 1315
	2	PO1c Ōshima	PO1c Yamano	PO2c Morita	
	3	Sea1c Shimada	PO2c Satō	PO2c Hoshino	
3rd *shōtai* Kates/*Ryūjō*	1	PO2c Horiuchi	WO Uchimura (S)	PO3c Yamauchi	
	2	PO1c Tanishiki	PO3c Nihei	Sea1c Toriyama	
4th *shōtai* Kates/*Ryūjō*	1	Sea1c Futakuchi	SLt Satō (S)	PO2c Anzai	
	2	Sea1c Takahashi	PO1c Nemoto	PO2c Watanabe	
	3	Sea1c Yamaguchi	PO2c Kobayashi	PO3c Izumi	
5th *shōtai* Kates/*Ryūjō*	1	SLt Shibata (S)	PO1c Itō	PO2c Kikuta	
	2	PO2c Fujii	PO1c Morishita	PO2c Itasaka	
	3	Sea1c Shitayoshi	PO2c Akiyama	Sea1c Takahashi I.	

Unit	No.	Pilot			Notes
11th *shōtai* Zeros/*Jun'yō*	1	Lt Shiga (H)			take-off: 1045 landing: 1335
	2	PO1c Kubota			
	3	PO1c Yamamoto			
12th *shōtai* Zeros/*Jun'yō*	1	Lt Miyano (C)			
	2	PO1c Okamoto			
	3	PO1c Kamihira			

the Otter Point airfield was below them. The defenders, however, expected that it was only a matter of time before the 2nd *Kidō Butai* command deduced the location of the hitherto unknown air base by analysing various reports about encountering American fighters in the same area.[29]

The second striking group landed on the decks of the aircraft carriers by 1340 hours. Due to the upcoming evening and dark, Kakuta did not intend to retry the attack on Dutch Harbor and limited himself to sending eight Zeros from *Ryūjō* for CAP duties. His warrior soul was temporarily sedated, and he focused on protecting the 2nd *Kidō Butai* from the counterattack of the enemy. Despite the bad weather, his fears were not unfounded since, in the morning hours, one of the American reconnaissance planes managed to find

the Japanese task force, and its crew sent a warning "affirmative large carrier large bombing plane on deck". This message of great value, which could initiate the 11 AF response to Operation AL, was lost on the air and never reached Dutch Harbor nor any other base in the area.[30]

The Catalina piloted by Lieutenant (jg.) Lucius Campbell of VP-42 had another chance to locate the enemy's carrier task force. Around 1700 hours, the flying boat spotted the Japanese fleet at 52°45'N 167°54'W and alerted the base of her discovery.[32] Again, the warning did not reach the land signal station, and Campbell had to save himself from chasing Zeros, which had to destroy the intruder at all costs before he could transmit the message to the end. Machine gun fire wounded one of the deck gunners in the thigh,

Table 11: The composition of the 2nd *Kidō Butai* striking group during the second (unsuccessful) attack on Dutch Harbor, 3 June 1942.[23] (*continued*)

Unit	No.	Pilot	Observer/navigator	Notes
1st *chūtai* 21st *shōtai* Vals/*Jun'yō*	1	Lt Abe (B)	WO Ishii	take-off: 1045 landing: 1335
	2	PO3c Takei	PO1c Harada	
	3	PO3c Nakatsuka	PO2c Kimura	
1st *chūtai* 22nd *shōtai* Vals/*Jun'yō*	1	PO1c Ōishi	WO Yamamoto (S)	
	2	PO3c Okada	PO2c Sugie	
	3	PO2c Ikeda	PO2c Miyazaki	
1st *chūtai* 23rd *shōtai* Vals/*Jun'yō*	1	PO1c Numata (S)	PO2c Takano	
	2	Sea1c Nagashima	PO2c Nakao	
2nd *chūtai* 24th *shōtai* Vals/*Jun'yō*	1	PO1c Kawabata	Lt Miura (C)	
	2	PO3c Yamakawa	PO2c Nishiyama	
	3	Sea2c Murakami	PO2c Kataoka	
2nd *chūtai* 25th *shōtai* Vals/*Jun'yō*	1	WO Harano (S)	PO1c Nakajima	
	2	PO3c Kosemoto	Sea1c Nakata	
2nd *chūtai* 26th *shōtai* Vals/*Jun'yō*	1	PO2c Miyatake	WO Tajima (S)	
	2	PO2c Gotō	PO2c Yamano	

Table 12: *Jun'yō* fighter group claims during the second (unsuccessful) strike on Dutch Harbor, 3 June 1942.[25]

Unit	No.	Pilot	Claims
11th *shōtai* Zeros/*Jun'yō*	1	Lt Shiga (H)	two Catalinas damaged
	2	PO1c Kubota	
	3	PO1c Yamamoto	
12th *shōtai* Zeros/*Jun'yō*	1	Lt Miyano (C)	
	2	PO1c Okamoto	
	3	PO1c Kamihira	

Lieutenant Yoshio Shiga, the *hikōchaichō* of the *Jun'yō*'s air group. (NDL)

tore off the starboard wing's forward fin, damaged the control lines, and punctured a fuel tank, igniting a fire inside the aircraft. The Catalina was salvaged by rapidly lowering the ceiling and escaping into dense clouds. With the fighters finally lost, Campbell set course for Akutan. Unfortunately for him, the Japanese damaged the right tank, which was not self-sealing, unlike the left one. He increased the power of the engines to the maximum to regain altitude and thus extend the range of the mauled flying boat. This decision had its negative effect as at about 40 miles from Akutan, he ran out of fuel. The plane started to descend gradually from 2,000 metres, and eventually, Campbell had to ditch at sea. The crew left the aircraft and tried to plug the bullet holes to secure the Catalina from sinking.

The survivors were soon spotted by an Allied flying boat, which informed the nearest Coast Guard cutter *Nemaha*. Her skipper also received the SOS signal from the crew and rushed to pull them out of the freezing water. The damaged Catalina was taken in tow, but in the meantime, she took too much water and sank. Campbell later blamed himself for making a mistake during the emergency landing and further damaging the flying boat. However, an essential thing in his desperate struggle was that he saved all his comrades, for which he was awarded the Distinguished Flying Cross.[33]

In the summary of the first day of air operations over the Aleutians, the 2nd *Kidō Butai* claimed to destroy and set

Table 13: The 2nd *Kidō Butai* CAP missions from *Ryūjō*, afternoon 3 June 1942.[31]

Unit	No.	Pilot	Claims	Notes
1st direct *shōtai* Zeros/*Ryūjō*	1	Lt Kobayashi (S)	None	take-off: 1715 (first *shōtai*) landing: 0320 (last *shōtai*)
	2	PO1c Kurihara		
2nd direct *shōtai* Zeros/*Ryūjō*	1	PO1c Sugiyama (S)		
	2	PO3c Morishita		
3rd direct *shōtai* Zeros/*Ryūjō*	1	PO1c Yoshizawa (S)		
	2	Sea1c Ishihara		
4th direct *shōtai* Zeros/*Ryūjō*	1	PO2c Miyauchi (S)		
	2	PO3c Yoshihara		

The heavy cruiser *Takao* seen in 1939. (Open source)

fire to several military facilities in Dutch Harbor, shooting down three aircraft (with two more probable victories), and demolishing seven reconnaissance aircraft on the ground. The Japanese losses were limited to two of *Takao*'s seaplanes. As a reason for the poor performance during the air strike, Kakuta blamed terrible weather, which hindered all crews from the very morning. According to his report, the landing on Kiska and Attu was impossible at the time and depended on weather improvement in the following days.[34] The invaders still knew nothing about the American airfields on Umnak

and the position of other American warships. Throughout 3 June, Theobald remained with his cruisers and destroyers at a safe distance from Kodiak, avoiding coming within range of Japanese carriers.[35]

Regardless of the decisions made by both sides, the first day of Operation AL could not bring a decisive result. Kakuta moved southwest to carry out an air strike on Adak the next day. Above all, the 2nd *Kidō Butai* command awaited a message from the Combined Fleet informing of the annihilation of the US Navy in the Central Pacific and the seizure of Midway.

4
4 JUNE 1942, SECOND RAID ON DUTCH HARBOR

ダッチハーバー第二次空襲、6月4日
Dacchi Haabaa Dai Niji Kūshū, Rokugatsu Yokka

The late hours of 3 June and no more Japanese planes over Dutch Harbor did not mean a moment of respite for the defenders since they were aware that the main enemy attack in the Aleutians would come in the following days. By sending Catalinas and Army bombers on night patrols, the Americans intended to find the Japanese carriers before air operations resumed on the morning of 4 June. As the crews later recalled, that night over Alaska and the Aleutians, the brutal weather made it hard to find anything other than the tip of their aircraft. Moreover, during the reconnaissance missions on 3 June, Patrol Wing 4 lost one more Catalina. The PBY piloted by Lieutenant (jg.) Jean Cusick of VP-41 did not return from the mission, and all crew members were presumed dead.[1]

The fate and the story of Cusick and his crew came out after the war. They took off from Otter Point at 0300 hours on 3 June on patrol over the North Pacific. Their Catalina, passing through the heavy overcast, squalls and light rain near the 2nd *Kidō Butai*, was the one which *Jun'yō*'s Zeros from the first striking group found at 0427. The Japanese caught the PBY crew by surprise. After the first salvo from machine guns and cannons, the Catalina's right engine was damaged for good, the wing caught fire, and the radio was destroyed. A bullet

pierced through Cusick's arm. The crippled flying float was forced to ditch in the rough sea while Zeros made successive passes to deliver her a *coup de grâce*. Cusick and AP1c Clark W. Morrison somehow managed to bring the Catalina down onto the water about 200 miles, bearing 210 degrees from Umnak. Yet, the crew did not have time to secure the bow and tunnel hatches under the heavy fire. The PBY immediately began taking water and sinking. After the war, Lieutenant (jg.) Wylie M. Hunt, then Ensign, described the rest of this dramatic story from a more personal perspective:

> The plane captain and the remainder of the crew got out the large seven man life raft and attempted to launch this raft. I stopped and picked up the small two man life raft and launched it. I then assisted the first pilot away from the burning plane and into the raft. After we were aboard the raft, we saw that the crew were having trouble getting the large raft launched. In the small raft, besides Lieut. (jg) Cusick and myself, were Brown S1c, third mechanic of the plane and Creamer AOM3c, gunner. The large raft had bullet holes in it and would not float so two more men swam over and hung on to the side of the two man raft. These men were the plane captain, Siler, and the enlisted pilot, Morrison. Siler stayed with our raft for a few minutes and then,

seeing the large raft still afloat, swam back to it and tried once again to make it seaworthy. He was unable to do so and as we were drifting quite rapidly with the high wind, he was unable to reach us again. Morrison remained holding to the side of the raft for approximately one hour before he died of exposure. Lieut. (jg) Cusick died from his wound and the cold about one hour after Morrison.[2]

Three survivors from the Catalina were adrift for about five hours. Finally, they were rescued by *Takao*, which appeared around noon and took them aboard, giving a hot bath, hot food and drink (milk and sake), and Japanese, but still dry clothing. After a medical examination and an hour of rest, three Japanese officers interrogated Hunt. They asked about the number of ships, their classes, and how many planes were in the Dutch Harbor area with disposition on American forces. Hunt constantly pretended that he knew nothing, and the Japanese gave up and allowed him to go to sleep. However, it was not the end of his troubles, as they repeated the same three questions for the next three days, also threatening to push him overboard with a weight tied around his waist. Hunt believed it was his final moments, but the Japanese felt convinced he told the truth and decided to keep him alive. On 25 June, he arrived in Ōminato and, with his comrades, were put on a train and sent to the Ōfuna interrogation camp. Moving from place to place around Japan, their captivity lasted until the end of the war.[3]

Patrol Wing 4's fatal streak was broken on 4 June by a PBY piloted by Ensign Marshall C. Freerks of VP-42. At 0650 hours, he was already eight hours in the air and came out of the storm without any damage to his plane. On the way back, approximately 160 miles southwest of Umnak, his ASV's radar picked up an unidentified object on the water's surface. Freerks knew it could not be an island or an American ship, so he decided to lower the ceiling and check the area. To his surprise, he ran straight into the 2nd *Kidō Butai* and was not detected by the Japanese observers on the ships.

The Catalina hurriedly sent a message to the base, warning about one aircraft carrier and two destroyers at coordinates 50°07'N 171°14'W, on course 150 degrees. After making sure the cable was received, the flying boat was to maintain visual contact with the Japanese task force. Less than an hour later, Patrol Wing 4 command instructed Freerks to return. Despite this order, he wanted to try his luck and drop bombs on one of the Japanese ships before moving away. His attack was unsuccessful, and he lost one of his engines to anti-aircraft fire but eventually landed at base safely.[4]

To keep track of the 2nd *Kidō Butai*'s moves, Freerks was to be replaced with the next flying floats. The first one, piloted by Lieutenant (jg.) Eugene W. Stockstill of VP-42 took off from Cold Bay and arrived at the place an hour later. The Japanese fighters noticed the intruder this time and took advantage of the decent visibility. With several Zeros on his tail, Stockstill had to escape, but he was too slow to avoid machine gun fire, which seriously damaged the PBY. He did not reach the base with his aircraft aflame, and the eight-man crew was lost.

The next on stage was Lieutenant Commander Charles E. Perkins of VP-42, who took off from Dutch Harbor. His Catalina was armed with one torpedo and two 227kg bombs in case she could, at any rate, get closer to the enemy. Around 1100 hours, Perkins found the Japanese task force and reported to the base that he had spotted one aircraft carrier and two heavy cruisers on 360 degrees course, bearing 215 degrees, 165 miles from Dutch Harbor. He soon received orders to follow the 2nd *Kidō Butai* until the 11 AF bombers arrived. However, due to delays in the transmission of radiograms, 12 B-26As from Cold Bay and Umnak took off with over an hour delay.

Like Freerks, Perkins wanted to test his fortune and turned his Catalina straight against *Jun'yō*. The Japanese carrier did not seem surprised and opened an anti-aircraft fire, which destroyed the flying boat's right engine and knocked her stability off. Perkins had the choice of either continuing the suicidal approach or making a

Catalinas were crucial aircraft for the American reconnaissance in the Aleutian Islands campaign. This photograph shows four PBY-5s in flight over a glacier in the Alaskan coast, 22 August 1942. (Open source)

U-turn to withdraw. Not eager to risk the lives of his entire crew, he jettisoned the torpedo and two bombs into the water and disappeared in a squall cloud, leaving three Zeros from *Jun'yō* chasing his back. When he was sure his Catalina was out of danger, he half-emptied the tanks to reach the base with only one working engine.[5]

Before Perkins attacked the enemy, Ensign Hildebrand of VP-41 appeared on the scene. Not many details are known about his mission since the Catalina was never seen again. This was the fifth and still not the last flying boat lost by Patrol Wing 4 on 3–4 June since another one was shot down during the second strike on Dutch Harbor. According to the unit's war diary, four complete crews were presumed lost, and despite some of the men being found later or surviving in captivity, the death toll was terrifying.[6]

The 11 AF personnel felt deep down inside that the sacrifice of PBYs could not go to waste. Led by Meals, five B-26As scrambled from Otter Point. Yet, despite all efforts to join the action,

Table 14: Patrol Wing 4 losses on 3 and 4 June 1942				
PBY	Unit	Fate	KIA and MIA	POW
Litsey	VP-41	shot down during the first strike on Dutch Harbor on 3 June	RM3c Martin H. Zeller, AMM2c Rolland Geller AP1c Merlyn B. Dawson	None
Cusick	VP-41	shot down during the reconnaissance mission on 3 June	Lt Jean C. Cusick, RM3c John F. Collins, AMM2c Alton J. Davis, AMM2c Burdette B. Siler, ARM2c Louis E. Yurec, AP1c Clark W. Morrison	Lt Wylie M. Hunt, AOM3c Carl Creamer, S1c Joseph R. Brown
Campbell	VP-42	damaged during the reconnaissance mission and ditched at sea on 3 June	None	None
Stockstill	VP-42	shot down during the reconnaissance mission on 4 June	Lt Eugene W. Stockstill, AP1c Henry M. Mitchell, AM1c Cyril A. Day, ARM3c Glen E. Ray, ARM3c Oscar J. Alford, S1c David D. Secord, S1c Frank E. Birks, AP1c Merlyn B. Dawson	None
Hildebrand	VP-41	shot down during the reconnaissance mission on 4 June	Ens. James T. Hildebrand, Ens. Leonard J. Hurley, AP1c William B. Laing, AP1c Frank D. Geiger, AMM1c Lester W. Dietrich, AMM3c Willis H. Sweeney, AMM3c Anthony H. Duesing, RM3c William J. Glover	None
Mitchell	VP-42	shot down during the second strike on Dutch Harbor on 4 June	Ens. Albert E. Mitchell Ens. Joseph M. Tuttle, AMM1c Wheeler H. Rawls, AMM1c Frank G. Schadl, ARM3c Burton J. Strom, ARM3c Neal R. Sparks S1c James D. Pollit	None

they could not track the Japanese carriers based on the received data. None of the bombers was equipped with radar, and Perkins' Catalina was already on its return way. Once again, changeable weather marked its presence. A rain squall and thick fog made air reconnaissance with traditional optical equipment impossible. The B-26As had to cruise at higher altitudes to avoid violent turbulence, and they could only dream of detecting any ship under the thick layer of clouds. Precious time and fuel started to run out, and Meals had no choice but to retreat to Otter Point.

In the meantime, the bombers that took off from Cold Bay experienced a more dramatic course of action. Sick of waiting for the recon results, at 1220 hours, Colonel William O. Eareckson led five B-26As, armed with torpedoes, according to the instructions of the Navy personnel. After take-off, the group headed for the area indicated in Perkins' dispatch, but they eventually flew into a thick and dark fog. The American planes lost visual contact with each other and had to increase altitude to regain it. Although the climb lasted only a few minutes, the bombers piloted by Captains George W. Thornbrough and Henry S. Taylor lost track. As the only two aircraft in the formation, they decided not to abort the mission

and continued the search for Japanese carriers. Fate rewarded their persistence, as they soon managed to locate the 2nd *Kidō Butai*.

With only one torpedo at their disposal, Thornbrough and Taylor knew this was a unique opportunity to alter the course of Operation AL in American favour. Taylor, who had become separated from Thornbrough, got out of the squall and nearly collided with *Jun'yō* as his B-26 was below a 100-foot ceiling. Since the enemy task force was in front of his eyes, he headed for one of the Japanese ships. One could deny that the 2nd *Kidō Butai* was also puzzled but ships immediately opened an anti-aircraft fire. Shortly afterwards, a small calibre round hit the bomber's nose and wounded the bombardier, Lieutenant Vern Peterson. Taylor escaped into the clouds while the co-pilot pulled Peterson from the position at the aircraft's nose. Still, Taylor was doggedly determined to throw a proper jab at the Japanese and made another torpedo approach, receiving the next hit with an AA shell. Temporarily increasing the distance from the enemy, he tried to make the third attempt, but this time the B-26 was swarmed by fighters from CAP. Taylor did not want to risk the confrontation with deadly Zeros, especially with the damaged aircraft, and flew into the clouds, jettisoning his torpedo and heading for Otter Point.

A Martin B-26 Marauder bomber. (The Aviation History Online Museum)

A Boeing B-17E Fortress. This example is seen over Panama in 1942. (Open source)

Nearly simultaneously, Thornbrough made two torpedo runs. Yet, he lacked the space and time to carry out a textbook attack, so he turned his plane down sharply against the narrow frontal target and acted like a dive bomber. Thornbrough hoped that during the approach, he would be able to arm the torpedo and use it as a bomb. He picked not the biggest but the closest aircraft carrier as the target, and Ryūjō's crew quickly noticed the deadly threat falling from the sky. Anti-aircraft guns roared, though it was too late to redirect Zeros from CAP to intercept the enemy aircraft. Thornbrough made a turn and found himself directly opposite on one of the carrier's sides. In her long service, Ryūjō had never been so helpless and could only hope the anti-aircraft guns would knock down the B-26A or at least distract the pilot. Despite all odds, the bomber continued the risky approach and released the torpedo at the decisive moment, which glided towards the carrier's deck. The closer it got to the target, the

more its trajectory changed, and finally, it fell just over 60 metres behind the ship, raising a huge water column behind her.

The Japanese were relieved and could continue Operation AL without hindrance. Conversely, Thornbrough was furious that he had missed his only opportunity to sink an aircraft carrier. But he was not going to give up so quickly and turned back to base to refuel, arm the bomber, and set off again. Due to thick clouds, he had to land in Cold Bay instead of Otter Point. Once there, he shared a detailed account of his attack and learned that the other five bombers of his formation had safely returned to base.[7] Without waiting for the orders, he jumped into the bomber with all the crew members and went to look for the Japanese task force in the fog. This was the last time Thornbrough and his companions were seen alive. Before midnight, a signal was received from his plane, informing about an attempt to break through the clouds to the base from about

3,000 metres. The radio operator on the seaplane tender *Casco* tried to figure out how to guide the bomber in complete darkness, yet the B-26A eventually crashed during the approach for landing. A month later, a half-burned wreck with bodies tangled in seat belts was found on the beach at Unimak, approximately 40 miles from Cold Bay.[8] The Americans named the runaways in Cold Bay the Thornbrough Airport in honour of the heroic service and sacrifice.

That afternoon, the 11 AF sent several reconnaissance missions to find the Japanese carriers. At 1535 hours, led by Captain Donald Dunlop, five B-17Es and one LB-30 of the 36th Bombardment Squadron, transferred from Kodiak to Cold Bay after the first strike on Dutch Harbor, went looking for the 2nd *Kidō Butai*. Their search was fruitless, and they all returned to Cold Bay by 1945 hours. However, other American planes had more luck as mechanical problems of one of them delayed their start. Lieutenant Thomas F. Mansfield's B-17E was still at Cold Bay when Thornbrough landed after the unsuccessful torpedo attack. The remaining Flying Fortress scrambled in the late afternoon and went to the location indicated by the Marauder's crew.

While proceeding southwest to find the enemy, he was joined by a B-17B, piloted by Captain Jack Marks, who took off from Otter Point for a scouting mission. Using the ASV radar, the two B-17s found Kakuta's task force and decided to make a bold approach. Marks descended to only 300 metres and dropped five bombs on a group of ships, missing all. At the same time, Mansfield chose the heavy cruiser *Takao* as a target. However, he went too low in his greed and was directly hit by one of the anti-aircraft rounds. The Flying Fortress burst into flames and crashed near the attacked vessel. Most of crew members did not leave the aircraft in time since it rapidly took on water and sank. *Takao* rescued the only survivor.[9] Marks could not help his comrades and returned to Otter Point, where he reported the failed attack.

Kakuta feared an enemy counterattack, though he did not expect to be harassed by small groups of bombers for most of the afternoon. It was much easier for the Japanese to avoid separate attacks than the coordinated strike of the entire air wing based in the Aleutians and Alaska, one of the few positive factors for the Japanese that day. As initially planned, on the morning of 4 June, the 2nd *Kidō Butai* was to hit the enemy positions on Adak. However, the terrible weather over the island throughout the night and most of the morning convinced Kakuta that it would be more reasonable to repeat the raid on Dutch Harbor since the weather over Unimak had significantly improved.[10]

As a precaution, at 1154 hours, Kakuta sent a pair of Kates from *Ryūjō* in the 46 degrees sector for over 144 miles to gather the latest data on weather conditions over Dutch Harbor. The Japanese torpedo bombers encountered one enemy plane on the way but did not engage it. At 1315 hours, they finally arrived at the American base and sent a message recommending an air strike. Kakuta was still unsure if the weather would not get worse and refrained from making hasty decisions. At 1444 hours, he sent a second pair of Kates to scout the 49 degrees sector for over 150 miles to check the avenue of the second raid on Dutch Harbor. More than an hour later, at 1555 hours, the bombers give the green light to

carry out the air offensive operations. At the same time, both crews informed the 2nd *Kidō Butai* of spotting one enemy destroyer south of Unalaska.[11]

Preparations for the launch of the striking group lasted about 35 minutes. By this time, the 2nd *Kidō Butai* had come within 100 miles of Dutch Harbor. Starting at 1630 hours, nine Kates, 11 Vals and 12 Zeros, led by Lieutenant Shiga, scrambled from both carriers (*Ryūjō*'s coordinates 52°12'N 169°7'W). All torpedo bombers were armed with two 250kg "ordinary" bombs, except for three equipped with two more 60kg "ordinary" bombs. The dive bombers took off with one 250kg high-explosive bomb under their bellies. Less than 20 miles after the departure, one of *Jun'yō*'s fighters reported engine failure and turned back.[13] Because the pilot expressed by his hand gestures the concern that he might not reach the carrier, he was accompanied by one of the dive bombers in case he was forced to an emergency landing on water. Despite these initial setbacks, both planes landed safely on *Jun'yō*'s deck by 1705 hours.[14]

When Kakuta believed things were finally going according to the plan, the Fifth Fleet received with some delays Operational Dispatch No. 155, sent at 1420 hours by the Commander-in-Chief of the Combined Fleet. Admiral Yamamoto ordered all forces in the area to attack the American carrier task force north of Midway. The 2nd *Kidō Butai* was to immediately break off its operations in the Aleutians and link up with the 1st *Kidō Butai*. Operational

Lieutenant Zenji Abe, the *buntaichō* of the *Jun'yō* dive bombers. (NDL)

Table 15: The 2nd *Kidō Butai* weather reconnaissance flights over Dutch Harbor (*Ryūjō*), 4 June 1942.[12]

Unit	No.	Pilot	Observer	Radio operator	Notes
X *shōtai* Kates/*Ryūjō* 46 degrees	1	Sea1c Futakuchi	SLt Satō (S)	PO2c Anzai	take-off: 1154 landing: 1450 (spotted one damaged flying boat and one destroyer)
	2	Sea1c Yamaguchi	PO2c Kobayashi	PO3c Izumi	
X *shōtai* Kates/*Ryūjō* 49 degrees	1	Lt Samejima (S)	PO1c Yoshihara	PO2c Itō	take-off: 1444 landing: 1850 (spotted one destroyer)
	2	Sea1c Ōki	PO2c Kameda	PO3c Noda	

Dispatch No. 156, sent at 1510 hours and arrived at the Fifth Fleet slightly later, specified that only the invasion of the Aleutians and Midway was temporarily postponed.[16] Hosogaya could not read the intentions of the Combined Fleet, especially since he was not yet aware of Nagumo's ominous defeat at Midway. Nevertheless, he asked Yamamoto to reconsider his decision and take steps towards continuing Operation AL to fulfil at least some of its objectives.[17]

Based on the memoirs of the Chief of Staff of the Fifth Fleet, Vice Admiral Nakazawa, one can reconstruct a broad spectrum of opinions among the Japanese officers participating in Operation AL. *Nippon Kaigun* zealously believed that if Nagumo succeeded in seizing Midway, the Aleutian Islands would fall into Japanese hands without much hassle. Yamamoto's dispatches were generally misinterpreted and not read as a veiled disclosure of the greatest defeat in the history of the Imperial Navy. The faith and confusion intervolved even more when at 1930 hours, Yamamoto acceded to the request of the Fifth Fleet and, in Operational Dispatch No. 157, ordered to carry on an invasion on Attu and Kiska, as well as the return of the 1st Torpedo Squadron and 1st Submarine Squadron to the main forces.[18]

Notwithstanding the decisions in the Combined Fleet command, Kakuta did not call off the striking group that set out for Dutch Harbor. On its last stretch of the journey towards the enemy base, the leading *Ryūjō*'s *shōtai* ran into the Catalina piloted by Ensign

Table 16: The composition of the 2nd *Kidō Butai* striking group during the second attack on Dutch Harbor, 4 June 1942.[15]

Unit	No.	Pilot			Notes
1st *shōtai* Zeros/*Ryūjō*	1	WO Uemura (S)			take-off: 1630 return: 1840
	2	PO1c Sugiyama			
	3	PO2c Kitashino			
2nd *shōtai* Zeros/*Ryūjō*	1	PO1c Endō (S) #			
	2	PO1c Koga†			
	3	PO1c Shikada #			

Unit	No.	Pilot	Observer	Radio operator	Notes
1st *shōtai* Kates/*Ryūjō*	1	PO1c Nishimura	Lt Yamagami (B)	PO2c Endō	take-off: 1640 return: 2015
	2	PO1c Ōshima	PO1c Yamano	PO2c Morita	
	3	Sea1c Shimada	PO2c Satō	PO2c Hoshino	
2nd *shōtai* Kates/*Ryūjō*	1	PO2c Horiuchi	WO Uchimura (S)	PO3c Yamauchi	
	2	PO2c Okuyama	PO1c Ōhashi	PO2c Ikehara	
	3	PO1c Yashiki	PO2c Nihei	Sea1c Toriyama	
3rd *shōtai* Kates/*Ryūjō*	1	PO2c Kawahara	PO1c Yamaguchi (S)	PO3c Ōhata	
	2	Sea1c Tamai	PO1c Motohashi	PO2c Mogi	
	3	Sea1c Mizoguchi	PO3c Shimada	Sea2c Nakajima	

Unit	No.	Pilot	Observer/navigator	Notes
1st *chūtai* 21st *shōtai* Vals/*Jun'yō*	1	Lt Abe (B) #	WO Ishii (S) #	take-off: 1650 return: 2026
	2	PO3c Takei #	PO1c Harada #	
1st *chūtai* 22nd *shōtai* Vals/*Jun'yō*	1	PO1c Ōishi†	WO Yamamoto (S) †	
	2	PO3c Okada†	PO2c Sugie†	
1st *chūtai* 23rd *shōtai* Vals/*Jun'yō*	1	PO1c Numata (S) †	PO2c Takano†	
	2	Sea1c Nagashima #	PO2c Nakao #	
2nd *chūtai* 24th *shōtai* Vals/*Jun'yō*	1	PO1c Kawabata #	Lt Miura (C) #	
	2	PO3c Yamakawa #	PO2c Nishiyama #	
2nd *chūtai* 25th *shōtai* Vals/*Jun'yō*	1	WO Harano (S) †	PO1c Nakajima†	
	2	PO3c Kosemoto	Sea1c Nakata	
2nd *chūtai* 26th *shōtai* Vals/*Jun'yō*	1	PO1c Miyatake	WO Tajima (S)	returned with Zero (1705)

Unit	No.	Pilot		Notes
11th *shōtai* Zeros/*Jun'yō*	1	Lt Shiga (H)		take-off: 1650 return: 2015
	2	PO1 Yamamoto		
12th *shōtai* Zeros/*Jun'yō*	1	Lt Miyano (S)		
	2	PO1c Ōzeki #		
14th *shōtai* Zeros/*Jun'yō*	1	WO Kitahata (S) #		
	2	due to an engine failure, the pilot turned back shortly after take-off (1705)		

Albert E. Mitchell of VP-42. Since the Japanese had the advantage in altitude and numbers, he had no chance to avoid the faster and more agile enemy aircraft while trying to get out from Dutch Harbor.[19] The burning flying boat crashed into a nearby bay, and the crew members evacuating from the cockpit were killed by machine gun fire.[20]

This loss, painful as it may be, did not go in vain as at 1737 hours, Fisherman's Point Army observation post reported a Catalina shot down in flames near Egg Island, and three minutes later, it sighted three flights of bombers headed for Dutch Harbor. Almost simultaneously, Unalaskan radar picked up several unidentified aircraft closing the distance, and they could not be presumed as allied. The radio personnel alerted all the surrounding airfields to wait in full combat readiness for further orders. At 1745 hours, the Army observation posts at Priest's Rock and Eider Point reported seeing many planes. At 1752 hours, the Mount Ballyhoo observation post noticed enemy aircraft circling the mountain and warned to watch for three flights of bombers. Shortly afterwards, seven fighters and 11 bombers were seen flying south close to the west slope of Mount Ballyhoo. All continued south until lost from sight for a while. Yet, the Japanese fighters suddenly marked their presence and made a fast low-flying strafing attack from the south, and at 1800 hours, the fire was opened with anti-aircraft guns. The second raid on Dutch Harbor had begun.[21]

This time, the Japanese had photographs of the military installations which were taken the previous day. Their route towards Dutch Harbor after reaching Unalaska was well planned and coordinated. The first to arrive directly over the base were dive bombers escorted by fighters. As they did not encounter the American fighters, the Zeros strafed US Navy military facilities in the harbour. In the meantime, two *shōtai* of Vals dropped bombs from about 300–400 metres on four new steel oil tanks, filled a few days earlier with 22,000 barrels of fuel. Even though the Americans lost all this stock, they could still speak of great luck. As a result of the explosion, the largest diesel fuel tank also burned down, but the flames did not spread to the area where the main fuel depot was located.[22] The third *shōtai* of dive bombers headed straight for the anchorage, where they spotted three vessels. Two of them, the seaplane tender *Gillis* and the transport ship *President Filmore*, opened an anti-aircraft fire that damaged two enemy Vals and discouraged the entire formation from attacking. In retaliation, the invaders targeted a third vessel, a converted transport ship *Northwestern*, serving as a civilian hotel for Army and Navy personnel. Due to her size, the Japanese believed that they had caught a lonely warship. In anticipation of the next enemy carrier-borne strike, the Americans removed most of the ships from the port, leaving only those of no strategic importance. One well-aimed bomb hit *Northwestern* and set her on fire. The last Vals dropped bombs on the local warehouse, workshop, and abandoned aircraft hangar. A more detailed summary of the damage caused by the Japanese dive bombers was covered in Updegraff's report:

- Indian Affairs Hospital at Unalaska – hit and one wing demolished.
- Four new steel (6,666-barrel), fuel oil tanks commissioned on May 31, 1942, and filled by the U.S.S. BRAZOS on June 1, were hit and totally destroyed with their contents of 22,000 barrels of fuel oil. The adjacent steel diesel oil tank (15,102 barrel capacity) was punctured and its contents destroyed by fire. The wisdom of having installed these tanks in bunkers was proved

when the resulting fire was contained in two bunkers and all other tanks and their contents in the tank farm were saved.
- The Northwestern, barracks ship for Siems-Drake Puget Sound and which supplied steam and electrical power to the Air Station, was hit forward on the port side and set on fire. Fire was spread to the adjacent issue warehouse by an unfavorable wind; this warehouse and its contents were destroyed. The Northwestern burned for three days. The third day her boilers were found undamaged, were lit off and are now supplying steam to the station.
- An Army 37mm gun emplacement on the Air Station was hit, demolishing the gun and burying the crew. Two members of the crew were killed and two men were seriously injured. The other crew members were dug out; their injuries were slight.
- The Naval Air Station pier was struck near the sea side of the southeast corner shearing off piles and splintering the deck. This damage has now been repaired. The bomb that made this hit was the only dud noted. Two bombs dropped into the water near the pier.
- The incompleted hangar was struck in the center of the roof by one bomb. The bomb pierced the roof and detonated before reaching the floor. A hole fifty feet in diameter was blown in the roof. Debris showered the Catalina damaged in the previous raid, tore the fabric of the tail and wings, and pierced the hull in several places.
- Three bombs exploded harmlessly in soft earth.[23]

The attack by dive bombers was also described in less official language by PO3 Yamakawa:

The enemy anti-aircraft guns opened fire. We carefully looked at the barrage trying to be safe from it. Our plane was swung by the blast of the explosions. However, our attack formation remained intact and gave it a shot to charge.
Yamakawa *Heisō*,[24] there is one destroyer next to the cliff wall, but no ship looking like a submarine in the harbour?
PO2c Nishiyama sitting in the back seat told it to me.
There was a base supplying submarines, but unfortunately, no single enemy ship. I headed for the destroyer and the place with the depot near the cliff wall, which became the target for our leading planes in the formation. In the southern part of the main port there was a seaplane base but no seaplanes in it. Looking at the first dive bomber in our formation I said:
Nishiyama *Heisō*, I ask for permission to attack the target
Nishiyama leaned forward and confirmed the target.
Striking group made a circle over the valley of clouds. *Buntaichō*'s plane made a light "bang", passing soon the signal to take an assault formation.
All planes, charge!
Buntaichō gave an order and his plane attacked as the first, followed by the next ones which also went into the dive. The first planes aimed for the destroyer and the warehouse. We were left with only with fuel tanks as the target.
Nishiyama *Heisō*, I go for a dive!
I said that to the observer and went for a diving run with my beloved aircraft.
Okay, altitude: 5,000 metres!
I got the confirmation from the back seat.
Target: the cliff wall tanks!
Putting the plane's cockpit to 65 degrees, I contacted the back seat. Slowly, but maintaining the speed, the pointer was moving.

Damaged Bureau of Indian Affairs Hospital after Japanese air raid. (Naval History and Heritage Command)

Three bombers dropped five bombs into the harbour between the sand spit and the Naval Air Station dock. These planes flew high over the broken clouds and smoke from the tank farm fire. They turned to the west over the harbour and disappeared over Mount Ballyhoo, hitting with one bomb the south summit of Mount Ballyhoo. In less than five minutes, five Kates dropped 10 more bombs south of Mount Ballyhoo along the magazine road with a range pattern of 1,500 feet. The first nine exploded harmlessly, and the tenth struck near a Navy 20mm gun emplacement, killing the battery officer and three of the gun's crew. Since this attack was highly ineffective, Updegraff pointed out in his report that "the heavy anti-aircraft fire and the cloud conditions prevented the horizontal bombers from making successful attacks. Of the sixteen bombs observed to have been dropped by horizontal bombers, only one was effective".[26]

At 1915 hours, the Japanese planes were sighted behind Mount Ballyhoo and, nine minutes later, were reported over Hog Island. After several sightings by various army outposts, they eventually disappeared in the south by 2010 hours. The afternoon raid was succinctly described by *President Filmore*'s skipper, Gus S. Stravos, in his report dated 14 June:

14. One Thursday afternoon, June 4, the alert sounded. The ship followed its usual procedure of heading for the straits to drift around. A half-hour later the "all-clear" was sounded. At 1640 the second alarm sounded and all men rushed to their battle stations. Twenty-three Jap planes in formations of three, four and five appeared at 1750, coming from the south and west. They circled the mountains and attacked Dutch Harbor. The Japs used dive-bombing tactics against what seemed to be pre-determined targets.

15. They split up as if they knew exactly where they were going, picking such targets as the oil tanks, the 3" guns, the dock and "hotel ship," the Northwestern. They bombed Dutch Harbor for about an hour.

16. First the Jap fighters would appear and attract the attention of the AA batteries, then the dive bombers would zoom in and bomb their objectives and sneak off before anyone realized what was happening. In the midst of all this the bombers would drop their loads from above.

17. About two of the oil tanks were hit. One hit was registered on the dock, and one bomb from the stick hit the Northwestern, which the Japs apparently had mistaken for the President Fillmore.

18. In the midst of all this, three Jap fighters dived on and strafed the ship; the attacks coming during an interval of fifteen minutes. They came in at a range of about 250 yards and a height of 200 feet, with a speed of close to 250 knots. The planes resembled the

Altitude: 4,000 metres!

Second by second, I was informed about the altitude. The enemy opened fierce anti-aircraft fire. From that moment, I was stuck to the sighting device.

Altitude: 3,000 metres!

Without any doubt, the target became bigger.

Altitude: 2000 metres!

Despite the enemy barrage, our sighting device was already set. I opened fire from the machine guns. When I thought the target was closer and closer, the plane in front of us dropped its bomb. What's that?

The plane before us targeted the same fuel tanks we planned to attack. There was no need to hit it with two 250-kilogram bombs, so we had to change the target. We were already at 1,000 metres. I decided to go for the tanks with red supports in front of me. The fuel tank exploded, raising possibly the 300-metre pillar of fire. Our beloved plane was at a 70-degree angle. We went for another target, so I had to increase the angle even more, almost to the vertical position.

Altitude: 600 metres! Be ready ...

The bomb was released. I pulled the flight stick with all my strength. The plane was still falling, and after the dive ended, it started to climb with great speed. I lost consciousness for a while. Subliminally I came back to the position in front of the stick. My eyes recovered from the dark vision. Before me, there was a pillar of fire.

A direct hit with a bomb!

I was informed by Nishiyama. When I recall, I can remember the buildings near target ablaze and covered in black smoke, erupting like a volcano.[25]

Less than 10 minutes later, the formation of nine Kates also appeared over Dutch Harbor and carried out a horizontal attack.

Nakajima "97's". They were instantly fired upon by the .30 and .50 cal. machine guns and 37 milimeter cannons.

19. Two of the three fighters were riddled with machine gun bullets and when last seen were smoking and afire, and with props dead fell out of sight. The destroyer U.S.S. Gillis, which was about four miles away from the Fillmore, saw the planes crash as evidenced by enclosure (E). Several of the men aboard saw the planes fall, as evidenced by enclosures (C) and (D).

20. After the bombers had emptied their loads on Dutch Harbor they joined in flights of five. One formation of bombers flew over the ship but did not drop any bombs. The 3" AA immediately opened fire.

21. 1955--Ceased fire. The "all clear" sounded at 2048, and ship returned to dock. There were several more alerts during the day. Up until the ship left Dutch Harbor, there were at least two alerts daily.[27]

Unlike the previous strike, on 4 June, the Japanese could no longer feel utterly prevailing over Dutch Harbor. Enraged anti-aircraft gun crews made their lives as difficult as possible, particularly for dive bombers and fighters who dared to come too close. Two Vals and one Zero were severely damaged and had to withdraw from the area. The other planes also did not intend to stay over the enemy base too long – immediately after dropping the bomb, they took a return course. To expend all ammunition and inflict more damage, some fighters also strafed Fort Glenn. However, by 1830 hours, the central part of the Japanese raid was over. Now, the defenders had a chance to get back at the enemy.

By a strange twist of fate, the Japanese aircraft were to meet up after the strike on Dutch Harbor near the western tip of Unalaska.[28] Around 1830 hours, on their way to the rendezvous point, six Zeros encountered the seaplane tender *Williamson* and machine-gunned her. No significant damage was done to the ship, but more importantly, the Zero pilots accidentally discovered an outline

The Siems Drake warehouse afire just after the Japanese strike, with firefighting parties at work and the burning SS *Northwestern* . (Naval History and Heritage Command)

SS *Northwestern* burning after being hit by a bomb. (Naval History and Heritage Command)

of runways and tents on the neighbouring island. They suddenly realised that the Americans had a fully operational airfield with an observation post at Umnak. It was not only used to warn and support Dutch Harbor during air operations but also served as a perfect place from where the enemy could chase the striking group and locate the 2nd *Kidō Butai*.[29]

The Otter Point crew knew that the enemy was in the area from the B-17B crew that had stopped at Umnak to refuel. When it got into the air, it yelled back on the radio that a whole formation of Japanese planes was at its tail. The men on the ground saw the hostile aircraft moving on either side of the island, hugging the water. Four P-40Es immediately took off and joined the other few Warhawks already in the air on patrol. The 11th Fighter Squadron pilots had been waiting for this moment for a long time and positioned themselves in the rear of three dive bombers flying in a tight formation. During the first approach, Second Lieutenants Lester M. Chancellor, James A. Dale, and Herbert C. White were each accredited with one Val, while the fourth dive bomber found in the front was crippled but escaped at the last moment. Other Vals also noticed P-40E, and Abe recalled later the moment of this surprising encounter and dogfight:

My God, so far, I thought that all planes could safely return to the carrier and then suddenly, I got this strange hunch.

Enemy fighters!

It wasn't mere words, and I felt a lump in my throat.

- An ambush!

I stiffened up from the tension. One, two, three… nine planes! P-40 fighters. Or maybe they are friendly planes?

I looked back, and we had only three aircraft. Three against nine was a nightmare, especially for a two-seat dive bomber. To my right and left, there was an island hidden in clouds. They had an anti-aircraft gun on the ground. But I didn't lose my nerves. To return to our carrier, nothing was left but to push through the strait by all means. How to pass through? It was a move that I had to decide on as a commander.

Formation? Single line? I was confused for a while, but there was a 300-metre cloud under us, yet it could not be a pleasant flight. I made up my mind, and without changing the formation, we cut across it.

We appeared at 200 metres altitude. Enemy fighters divided into two groups and started to close from the right and left like scissors. I was patient but keeping on the same track was suicide for us. Suddenly we broke our formation, and I stuck to one P-40's tail. We dragged into the vertical circling between the clouds and the sea's surface. The other P-40 started to follow me. My first half-turn was tight. By making another turn away from the chased plane, my tactic was to separate the enemy fighters from each other. Then, I was pinned down by 13 mm bullets from attacking P-40.

Going for 60 degrees dive, I made an abrupt turn. By 60 degrees, I mean it was like taking a position in which wings are directly pointed towards the ground. Harano's plane went after the P-40, which targeted me. Enemy, allied, three enemy aircraft, we chased each other to get at its back. At that moment, I finally made a turn looking like an elliptic circle.

The enemy plane was tenaciously facing me. Machine guns roared. The dogfight show of three versus three planes, and I didn't have a chance to consider that there was no time or fuel for that. Losing myself in shooting, I only made a turn after the turn. The other six P-40s were cruising nearby. We didn't have any option to continue the turns against each other. However, if we did like that, we could scatter the enemy planes and escape.

With the crosshair of my fixed machine gun, I set aim at one enemy plane and shot him up frantically. He swung upwards like crazy, and then I confirmed that he was falling. This and another plane set ablaze were swallowed by the sea. I noticed that Harano's and Numata's aircraft were missing when our formation

was scattered. Feeling that my backs were soaking wet with sweat, I knew they flew into the cloud. Even though we shot down three enemy planes, we also lost two of our shōtaichō, and that devastated me. I was so disappointed that I went directly into the cloud and headed south. Just alone…

One hour to the carrier

I heard the upset voice of Ishii.

Our fuel tank has been shot; we have about 30 minutes.

I down know which plane reported it, but we received the message. Then, I noticed a big hole in my wing, about one metre in diameter.

Taichō, it was Yamamoto with that fuel tank. (…)[30]

Although Abe's testimony gave a detailed picture of the dogfight from the Japanese dive bombers' perspective, it was not entirely precise regarding American losses since Vals could not be credited for any victory against P-40E. Neither could he see the clash between fighters when Second Lieutenant John J. Cape Jr. shot down one Zero, claiming the first victory in his career. He did not have time to celebrate the success as another Japanese fighter took advantage of his tunnel vision and showed up at the back. Using his plane's better position, speed and agility, the Japanese pilot did not miss the opportunity and dealt a killing blow from his machine guns. Ammunition exploded in the P-40E, turning the fighter into a torch. Cape did not leave the cockpit in time, and his plane crashed into the bay.

After the first jab from the Warhawks, the Zeros shook out of the slump and visibly took the initiative in the dogfight over Umnak. The P-40E of Second Lieutenant Winfield E. McIntyre had trouble getting rid of the Japanese fighter on his back. Eventually, a quick salvo of 20mm cannons set his engine on fire. Through the plunge towards the ground, he tried extinguishing the flames but soon realised he could not start the damaged engine. McIntyre miraculously crash-landed on a nearby beach on another part of the island. He signalled a Navy patrol boat by using his parachute and was rescued. He returned to camp by 1800 hours with only a nasty gash on his forehead.[31]

Two victories over P-40Es were sufficient for the Japanese to let the dive bomber formation take cover in a dense cloud and escape further clashes. Neither Zeros had the craving to continue the dogfight. Two Vals were crippled, and one fighter reported a hole in the fuel tank and a leakage. The pilot, PO1c Koga Tadayoshi from *Ryūjō*, reduced the speed to extend the engine operation to the maximum range. This plan did not bring the expected result because the plane began to descend. Koga did not have many options and decided to stay over Akutan, where he had a chance to make an emergency landing. He sent a radio message about his situation, counting the Japanese submarines circling the Aleutians could take him back. *Ryūjō*'s pilot was accompanied by both wingmen to the very end, who observed the terrain conditions and tried to advise him in this difficult moment.

About 1,500 metres from the coastline, the Japanese found a packed grassy plain suitable for an emergency landing. Koga pulled out the landing gear and was about to land, but at the last moment, his wingmen realised that the grassy plain was a swampy terrain, and it was essential to put the aircraft on its "belly", same as for ditching at sea. However, Koga did not have time to retract the landing gear. His Zero stuck into the marshy ground like a needle in a soft pillow and rolled over its back. Koga broke his neck, probably dying immediately. Ironically, his fighter was not damaged, and this fact was visible even from above.

P-40Es of the 11th Fighter Squadron stationing at Otter Point. (NARA)

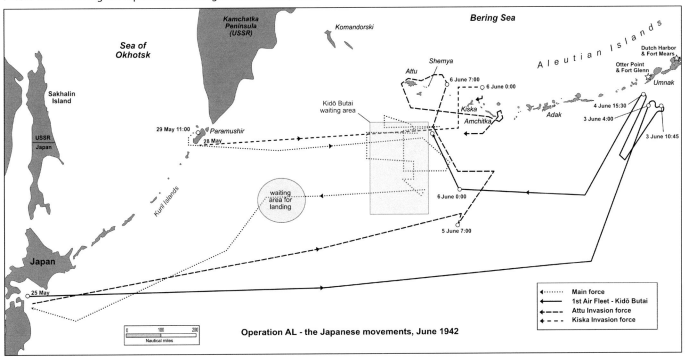

Japanese movements during Operation AL in June 1942. (Map by Mark Thompson).

Nippon Kaigun procedures instructed Japanese crews to destroy any Zeros that landed behind enemy lines. Koga's wingmen should have machine-gunned and set fire to his fighter, but they were not sure if he had survived the crash landing. Strafing the plane would be a death sentence. After a brief consideration, they moved away from Akutan, hoping that Koga would get out of the cockpit and be rescued by one of the submarines. Despite noble intentions, this decision later turned out to be a grave mistake, which became another factor that wallowed the Japanese Navy in a longer perspective.

The striking group returned on decks by 2026 hours. The last to land on *Jun'yō* were the dive bombers that suffered the most during the raid on Dutch Harbor and the dogfight with the American fighters. Three Vals were certainly lost over Umnak, and one crashed into the water before reaching the 2nd *Kidō Butai*. The Japanese sent one destroyer to rescue the crew, yet it had not been found.[32] Five of the remaining six aircraft were damaged, but fortunately, without additional casualties among the crews. Lieutenant Abe reported 10 big bullet holes in his dive bomber, while Lieutenant Miura, the next most crippled plane, had only five. *Jun'yō*'s air group action report mentions that only two out of 11 Vals that scrambled against Dutch Harbor were fully operational. Out of five Zeros, two were hit by lone bullets.[33] Casualties on *Ryūjō* were limited to one lost and two damaged Zeros (which remained operational) and four slightly damaged Kates. Although Koga's death was recorded in the action report, the accounts of both wingmen made the Japanese uncertain whether he had died during the emergency landing.[34]

The Japanese carrier-borne dive bomber, Aichi D3A, known by the Allied codename "Val". (NDL)

Fire and smoke from Navy oil tanks burning after the bombing of Dutch Harbor, 4 June 1942. (Naval History and Heritage Command)

In the summary of the second raid on Dutch Harbor, the Japanese reported blowing up and setting fire to the docks, hangar for large flying boats, two sites with fuel tanks, command post, and a communications facility. They also claimed shooting down three flying boats, one large bomber and 10 fighters. In addition to aircraft

claims, pilots reported destroying a large transport ship. The more detailed account can be again reconstructed based on available Japanese documents:

Table 17: The 2nd *Kidō Butai* claims after the second strike on Dutch Harbor, 4 June 1942.[35]	
Buntai (Unit)	**Kōka (Claimed results)**
Zeros from *Ryūjō*	one Catalina shot down
Zeros from *Jun'yō*	six P-40s shot shown, strafed one submarine with no visible results
Vals from *Jun'yō*	four P-40s shot down, direct hit and setting fire to one transport ship, setting fire to two sites with fuel tanks, one direct hit to flying boat's hangar but without setting it on fire, three direct hits to the command post
Kates from *Ryūjō*	setting fire to hangar for large flying boats

In addition to the above-mentioned Japanese claims, the American report also indicated the destruction of part of the military hospital. However, in the case of aircraft, the Japanese reports were exaggerated. In two days of struggle over the Aleutians, the 11 AF and Patrol Wing 4 lost two P-40Es, one B-17E, one B-26A and six PBYs. Also, one LB-30 washed out of Kodiak while returning from Elmendorf field, and one B-26A was badly shot up and out of commission.[36] Due to two carrier-borne raids on Dutch Harbor, personnel casualties accounted for 33 Army, eight Navy, one Marine Corps, and one civilian killed, plus about 50 wounded. The only severe material casualties were the loss of four 6,666-barrel fuel oil tanks, 22,000 barrels of fuel, 625,000 gallons of diesel oil, the burning of the *Northwestern*'s upperworks and interior, and the

Table 18: The 2nd *Kidō Butai* CAP, 4 June 1942.[39]

Unit	No.	Pilot	Claims	Notes
1st direct *shōtai* Zeros/*Ryūjō*	1	Lt Kobayashi (S)	none	take-off: 1130 (the first *shōtai*) landing: 2100 (the last *shōtai*)
	2	PO1c Kurihara		
2nd direct *shōtai* Zeros/*Ryūjō*	1	PO1c Tomoishi (S)	two Martin B-26s bombers damaged	
	2	Sea1c Ishihara		
3rd direct *shōtai* Zeros/*Ryūjō*	1	PO1c Kurihara (S)	none	
	2	PO3c Yoshihara		
4th direct *shōtai* Zeros/*Ryūjō*	1	PO1c Yoshizawa (S)	one Martin B-26 bomber damaged	
	2	PO1c Miyauchi		
? *shōtai* Zeros/*Jun'yō*	1	PO1c Numata (S)	two flying boats shot down	take-off: 1133 landing: 2040
	2	PO1c Okamoto		
	3	PO1c Kamihira		

burning of the warehouse. Efficient firefighting supervised by Major G. P. Groves of the Marine Corps and Fire Chief Harold Joe Davis prevented the spreading of fire from the warehouse to the wooden oil tanks.[37]

While defenders at Dutch Harbor were dealing with the damage inflicted by the enemy, the 2nd *Kidō Butai* was preparing to cease air operations before night falling. However peculiar it may seem; it was not the end of active combat on 4 June. The news about the successive groups of bombers encountering the Japanese carrier task force, and then, the second raid on Dutch Harbor reached Umnak, where Captain Meals decided to give his crews another opportunity after a futile search in the morning. He recalled: "We rolled our planes back into their protective revetments as fast as we could get them there while our fighters took off after the Japs."[38] Five B-26As were armed with torpedoes and started to roll out of Otter Point at 2030 hours while it was still bright. One Marauder with a flat tire never took off; the next reported engine trouble and had to turn back. Meals had to continue his mission with only three bombers, yet before 2100 hours, he found the Japanese carriers. His attack was described in the following words:

… all of sudden in front of me I saw the outline of a large vessel. We came onto it so unexpectedly that the Japs must have been as surprised as we were. Poor visibility and the dull light prevented me from identifying the ship's type. And there wasn't much time

for that anyway. I flashed the news over the radio to the other two planes piloted by Capt Kenneth W. Northamer and Lieut Brady Golden. I could just make out one of my 26s in the far distance. The other was completely out of sight. We squared away to make our torpedo run. I swept in low and my co-pilot, Lieutenant Patch, released the torpedo. We climbed into the overcast fast to get out of range of the Jap AA fire. But before the ship was gone from our view, my rear gunner saw the torpedo strike the port bow, about a third of the way back in the ship and saw a large explosion as flame and water shot high into the air. The gunners said they also spotted some bursts of AA fire but none of them were very close. By this time Captain Northamer had rushed back after picking up my radio call. It was his plane that I had discerned in the distance. He went in for his torpedo attack and was close enough before pulling away to identify the ship as a Jap cruiser. His torpedo was believed to have exploded in the stern. We returned our own separate ways to Umnak. When we got there we learned that Lieutenant Golden had never located the cruiser.

Indeed, despite claiming to hit one cruiser, none of the enemy ships suffered from the torpedo attack. The Americans had a unique opportunity to deliver the hit at the least expected moment, but conditions were difficult. Surprisingly, Meals did not mention encountering any Japanese fighters. During this attack, the 2nd *Kidō Butai* had already been preparing to call back pilots from the CAP missions, but the last remaining in the air PO1c Yoshizawa's *shōtai* from *Ryūjō* noticed the intruders. Two Zeros machine-gunned one bomber and, looking at its unsuccessful approach, gave up from chasing the formation of B-26s in the dusk.

5
6-7 JUNE 1942, INVASION OF ATTU AND KISKA

アッツ島・キスカ島の占領、6月6−7日
Attsu-tō, Kisuka-tō no Senryō, Rokugatsu Muika/Nanoka

In normal circumstances, on the late evening of 4 June, the Fifth Fleet command would have discussed the effects of two strikes on Dutch Harbor and one on Adak, analysing reasons for the meagre tactical successes and losses in the carriers' air groups. This time, however, the Japanese had much more severe troubles to worry about since the strategic situation in the Central Pacific was more than uncertain. Even though Hosogaya convinced the Combined

Fleet to continue Operation AL, it could not be carried out as initially planned. At 2015 hours, the Fifth Fleet commander issued Operational Order No. 89, advising that all groups apart from the 2nd *Kidō Butai* should proceed with their tasks without any changes to the schedule.[1]

Table 19: Japanese aircraft losses during Operation AL, 3-4 June 1942		
Aircraft	Date	Crew
Dave/*Takao*	shot down by P-40Es on 3 June	lost
Dave/*Takao*	damaged by P-40Es and ditched on 3 June	survived
Zero/*Ryūjō*	shot down by P-40Es on 4 June	lost
Val/*Jun'yō*	shot down by P-40Es on 4 June	lost
Val/*Jun'yō*	shot down by P-40Es on 4 June	lost
Val/*Jun'yō*	shot down by P-40E on 4 June	lost
Val/*Jun'yō*	damaged by P-40Es and ditched on 4 June	lost

Immediately after retrieving the striking group, Kakuta's task force hastily headed southeast to be prepared to link up with the 1st *Kidō Butai* in case of further developments. He awaited further orders from the Combined Fleet for the rest of the evening and night of 4/5 June. Once at 0455 hours, Yamamoto was sure that Nagumo had lost all four carriers, so he ordered Operation MI to be aborted immediately. The Fifth Fleet commander was also informed about the tragic defeat. Hosogaya issued new interim instructions for all units at 0815 hours to avoid panic among his subordinates.

Fifth Fleet Secret Operation Dispatch No. 803[2]

5 June, 0815 hours

1. The destruction [of enemy positions] during Operational AL is postponed.

2. All invasion forces will immediately head west and await the orders.

3. Submarine force will take the "G" scouting line to find the enemy.

4. Main force will merge with AQ [Attu] Invasion Force and act together.

The Fifth Fleet decided to give up the raid on the American positions on Adak and withdraw with transport ships westwards yet be ready to proceed with the landing operations. Its command tried to remain clear-headed, but Vice Admiral Nakazawa's memories revealed true Japanese beliefs. As he describes, many Fifth Fleet officers were convinced that the beating in the Battle of Midway squandered the entire plan for the North Pacific. Even if the western part of the Aleutians could be seized, they felt that establishing reconnaissance outposts in the North Pacific was of no strategic importance, especially since four Japanese carriers had been lost. Therefore, the 2nd *Kidō Butai* could not be in danger of being detected by the Americans or Soviets near the Aleutians anymore. The Fifth Fleet presented its opinion to the Combined Fleet; however, Captain Kuroshima and Flight Officer Captain Sasaki Hanku did not support it. They emphasised that the primary goal of Operation AL was to cut off the US Navy from the North Pacific to carry out air raids on Japan's mainland. After the long debate, Hosogaya had no alternative but to prepare his fleet for landing operations.[3] At 1730 hours, he issued additional orders and postponed seizing Attu and Kiska to the N+1 Day.[4] To deceive the enemy, all units were to act like they never knew about any changes in the schedule.[5] After all, discussions over the rationale of the invasion of both islands were cut off by the Navy General Staff at 1930 hours when it sent a cable ordering the Combined Fleet and the Fifth Fleet to proceed with

landing operations if circumstances allow for them. The Fifth Fleet copied the message to all its units three hours later.[6]

The confusion in the Japanese highest command was so great that it also influenced the situation on the battlefield. Throughout 5 June, the 2nd *Kidō Butai* was in unspecified retreat, and Kakuta did not even issue the orders to provide routine reconnaissance or CAP missions.[7] On the other hand, the Americans continued the search for the enemy during the night and early morning, particularly in the area south of Unalaska. None of the aircraft found the Japanese vessels, and all returned to base. During the landing at Kodiak, the LB-30 piloted by Lieutenant Frederick C. Andrews slid off the runway and crashed into nearby Chiniak Bay. No one got hurt, but the aircraft was out of commission.[8]

The second day in a row, Theobald remained with his task force about 400 miles south of Kodiak, avoiding detection by the Japanese. He considered it necessary to maintain numerous reconnaissance missions along the Aleutians to find where the 2nd *Kidō Butai* could have gone during the night of 4/5 June. At the same time, he was aware that Patrol Wing 4 was left with 14 PBYs, and their crews were exhausted after 48 hours of continuous air operations in awful weather.[9] The need to keep radio silence prevented Theobald from discussing his next steps with the other units' commanders, so in the morning, he decided to go to Kodiak with *Nashville* at 27 knots. Captain Edward W. Hanson, on the heavy cruiser *Indianapolis*, took command of the rest of the team in his absence.[10]

Apart from Theobald, the meeting in Kodiak was attended by Commander Air Search Group, Commander Alaskan Sector, and Commander Air Striking Group. They all agreed that the Air Striking Group should concentrate all aircraft for immediate attack when the enemy objective has been located. Additionally, the Task Force and Task Force Commander were to be informed of the progress of operations by sending all available cables without delays.[11] The most likely scenario seemed to be the Japanese landing on Unalaska, so it was intended to wait for the right moment to counterattack. The Americans believed it could be during the enemy amphibious operation on Dutch Harbor when all troops and equipment would be gathered in one place and anchored transport ships would become easy targets for bombers.

For more than 12 hours, the 2nd *Kidō Butai* had been in retreat, but the Americans still believed that the enemy was planning a third approach towards Dutch Harbor. The defenders' predictions were partly confirmed by subsequent reports, which indicated at least one carrier, one heavy cruiser and two destroyers bearing 330 degrees and distant 25 miles from Otter Point.[12] This meant that the Japanese could have sneakily entered the Bering Sea from where they intended to proceed with the landing on Umnak or Unalaska. To track the position of the enemy, the 11 AF hastily sent six B-17E bombers equipped with ASV radars, which could help find the carriers in deteriorating weather. At some point, the formation of American planes informed the base of a successful attack on a group of Japanese ships. However, as it turned out late, no vessels were there, and bombs were dropped on the uninhabited part of the Pribilof Islands.[13] The other report of Patrol Wing 4 also informed TF-8 of spotting one carrier and one cruiser with supporting units 90 miles southwest of Otter Point in the early morning, which brought even more confusion.[14]

Patrol Wing 4 eventually found the enemy task force on the morning of 6 June when a PBY piloted by Lieutenant (jg.) John T. Bowers Jr. was returning from overnight patrol in sector 6. The flying boat made a radar contact and later reported "a large number of ships". The Catalina could not investigate the situation closely as

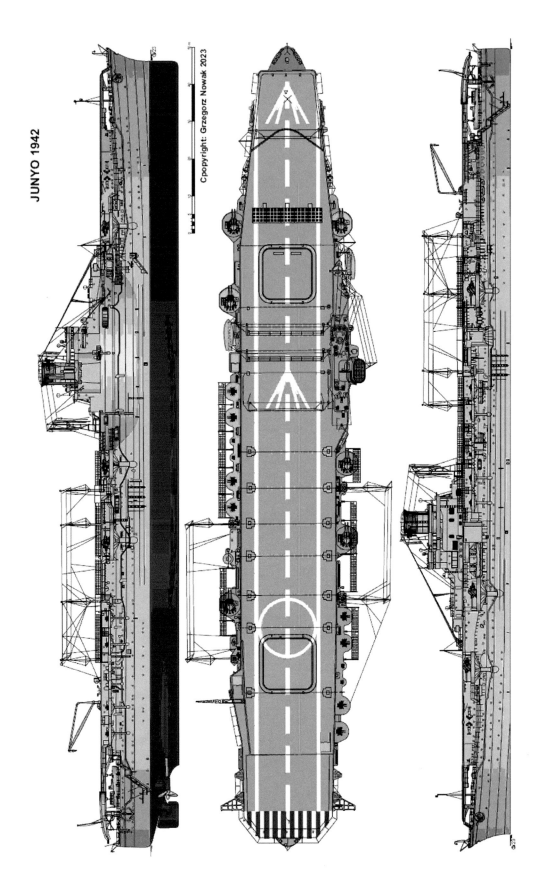

JUNYO 1942

Cpopyright: Grzegorz Nowak 2023

Jun'yō (隼鷹) – one of the two Hiyō-class aircraft carriers, which were initially designed as a *Nippon Yūsen* transoceanic passenger ship (with possible conversion into an aircraft carrier) in connection with the planned organisation of the Olympic Games in Tokyo in 1940. In mid-1940, the Navy General Staff decided to convert those passenger ships into fleet aircraft carriers and thus, the future *Jun'yō* was launched at the Mitsubishi shipyard in Nagasaki in June 1941. After completion of the armament, the aircraft carrier entered service on 3 May 1942. Compared to the latest standard set by the Shōkaku-class, *Jun'yō* was slower by more than 8 knots (25.5 vs 34 kts). She was also inferior to the older *Sōryū* and *Hiryū* to a similar extent, lacking other advantages, such as an armoured flight deck, the merits of which were noticed during the battles of the Coral Sea and Midway. However, according to naval planners, the *Jun'yō* and *Hiyō* air groups were to have 48 operational aircraft each (plus five spares), which made their offensive potential similar to *Sōryū* and *Hiryū*. Together with *Ryūjō*, she formed the 2nd *Kidō Butai* to support Operation AL. (Artwork by Grzegorz Nowak)

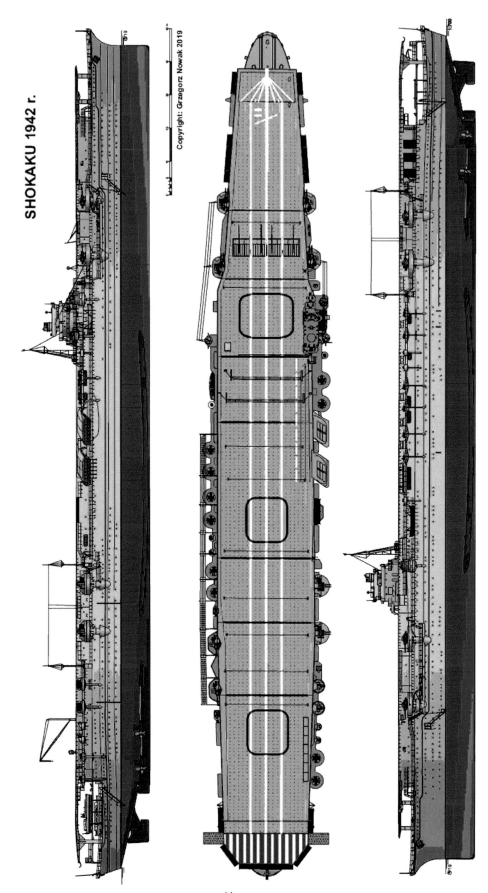

SHOKAKU 1942 r.

Copyright: Grzegorz Nowak 2019

Shōkaku (翔鶴) – The first 'Crane' of the newest aircraft carrier class (鶴, *tsuru* = crane), which was the second generation of Japanese aircraft carriers, becoming a critical reinforcement for the Imperial Japanese Navy before the outbreak of the Pacific War. *Shōkaku* was the flagship of the 5th Carrier Division, which formed in August 1941. At the time of the attack on Pear Harbor, the ship was incorporated into *Kidō Butai*, and in January 1942, took part in the landing on Rabaul. She participated in the Indian Ocean operation in early April and in the battle of the Coral Sea in early May, where she was badly damaged. Due to the necessary repairs in Japan, the carrier would not see action during the battle of Midway, yet in the second week of June 1942, the Combined Fleet planned to send her to the North Pacific to oppose the possible American counteroffensive. Finally, only her sister, *Zuikaku*, was ordered to link up with the 4th Carrier Squadron (*Ryūjō* and *Jun'yō*). Finally, the Americans decided to adopt a war of attrition against Kiska and Attu and all the Japanese carriers were withdrawn from the area. After the enemy landing on Guadalcanal, the Aleutian Islands campaign became a secondary theatre of operations for the Combined Fleet. (Artwork by Grzegorz Nowak)

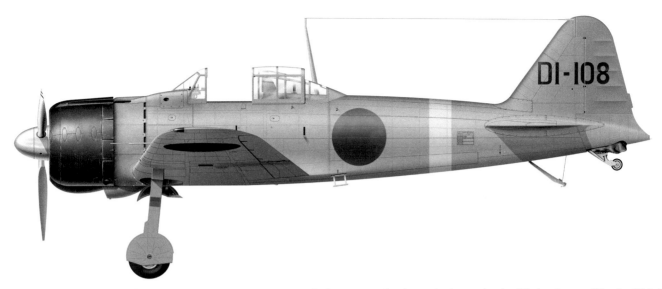

The Japanese Type 0 carrier dive bomber (manufacturer name: Mitsubishi A6M2 mod. 21) was also known by the Allied codename "Zero" or "Zeke" (in Japanese: *zero shiki kanjō sentōki – kansen* or *zerosen* in short). During Operation AL, "Zeros" from the 2nd *Kidō Butai* escorted dive and torpedo bombers and strafed the ground military facilities. *Ryūjō* Zeros' pilots were considered experienced airmen in 2nd *Kidō Butai*, and this example, DI-108, was flown by a wingman, PO1c Koga Tadayoshi. (Artwork by Jean-Marie Guillou)

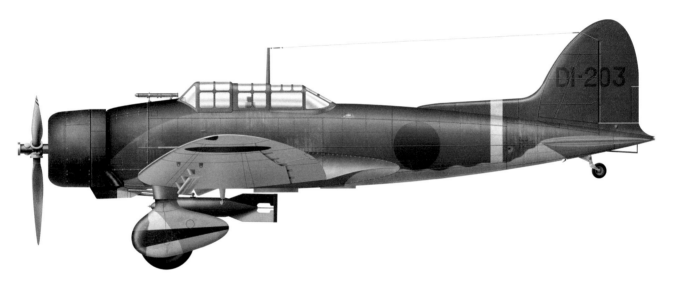

The Japanese Type 99 carrier dive bomber (manufacturer's name: Aichi D3A) was known by the Allied codename "Val" (in Japanese: *kanjō kyūkōka bakugekiki - kambaku* in short). As during the operation in the Indian Ocean, *Ryūjō*'s air group did not dispose of any dive bombers during the raid on Dutch Harbor. (Artwork by Jean-Marie Guillou)

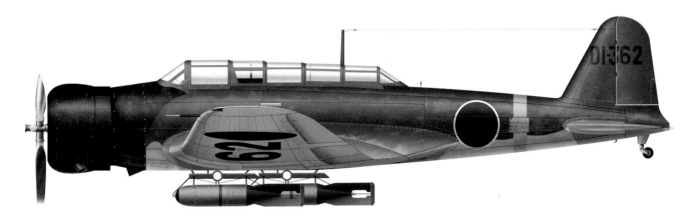

The Japanese Type 97 carrier torpedo bomber (manufacturer name: Nakajima B5N) was known by the Allied codename "Kate" in Allied (in Japanese: *kanjō kōgekiki* – literally "carrier attack bomber"; *kankō* in short). During Operation AL, "Kates" from *Ryūjō* attacked the most important military targets in Dutch Harbor and provided air reconnaissance. Torpedo bombers from the 2nd *Kidō Butai* had a good reputation among other pilots, as they participated in successful operations in the Philippines and the Indian Ocean. DI-362 was flown by an unknown wingman. (Artwork by Jean-Marie Guillou)

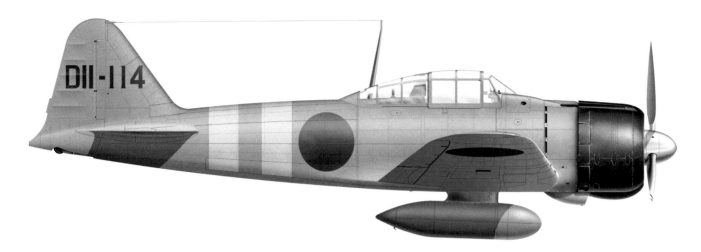

During Operation AL, "Zeros" from the 2nd *Kidō Butai* escorted dive and torpedo bombers and strafed the ground military facilities. DII-114 was flown by an unknown wingman from *Jun'yō,* whose pilots were considered much less experienced airmen than their colleagues from *Ryūjō.* (Artwork by Jean-Marie Guillou)

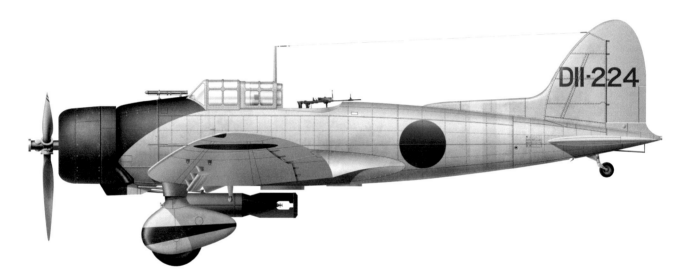

During Operation AL, "Vals" from *Jun'yō* bombed primarily targeted ground facilities. Their crews were considered the least experienced in the entire 2nd *Kidō Butai.* DII-224 was flown by an unknown wingman. (Artwork by Jean-Marie Guillou)

The Japanese Type 97 large flying boat (manufacturer name: Kawanishi H3K) was known by the Allied codename "Mavis" (in Japanese: *kyū nana shiki ōgata hikōtei - kyū nana daitei* in short). During the initial phase of the Aleutian Islands campaign, Mavises from *Tōkō Kaigun Kōkūtai* provided crucial reconnaissance in the chain and attacked encountered American vessels. The Japanese lost their most valuable air patrol aircraft after withdrawing from the area. (Artwork by Jean-Marie Guillou)

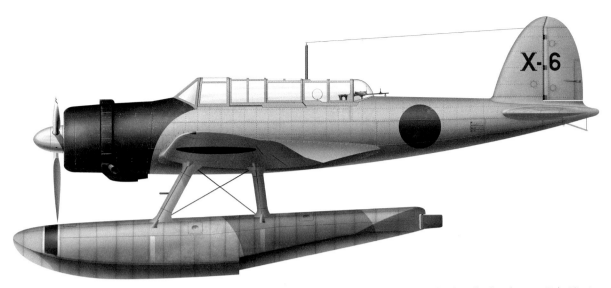

The Japanese Type 0 long-range reconnaissance seaplane (manufacturer name: Aichi E13A) was known by the Allied codename "Jake" (in Japanese: *zero shiki suijō teisatsuki - reisui* in short). Jake was a very widely used seaplane during the entire Pacific War and thus also appeared in the Aleutian Islands. During the initial phase of the campaign, the seaplane tender *Kamikawa Maru* brought some Jakes to provide air cover over the conquered Attu and Kiska, yet soon, she was ordered to withdraw due to bold American air attacks. (Artwork by Jean-Marie Guillou)

The Japanese Type 0 reconnaissance floatplane (manufacturer name: Mitsubishi F1M2) was known by the Allied codename "Pete" (in Japanese: *zero shiki suijō kansokuki - reikan* in short). Like the Jake, the Pete was widely used during the entire Pacific War and thus also appeared in the Aleutian Islands. During the initial phase of the campaign, the seaplane tender *Kamikawa Maru* brought some Petes to provide air cover over the conquered Attu and Kiska, yet soon, she was ordered to withdraw due to bold American air attacks. (Artwork by Jean-Marie Guillou)

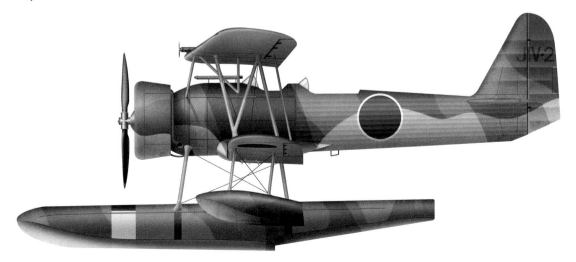

The Japanese Type 95 ship-borne reconnaissance floatplane (manufacturer name: Nakajima E8NM2) was known by the Allied codename "Dave" (in Japanese: *zero shiki suijō kansokuki – kyū go suitei* in short). This plane entered service in 1935 and was carried aboard all the capital ships – 16 cruisers and five seaplane tenders. However, Dave was already an outdated aircraft in late 1941, but some aircraft remained in service. They appeared in the initial stage of the Aleutian Islands campaign. They were soon replaced by more modern aircraft, such as the Jake. (Artwork by Jean-Marie Guillou)

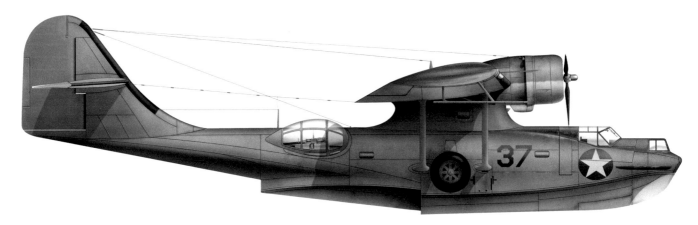

The American PBY-5A Catalina was a flying boat and amphibious aircraft introduced to the service in late 1936. With over 3,300 aircraft produced in total, Catalinas played a major role in all branches of American armed forces during the Second World War. In the Aleutian Islands campaign, flying boats from the 4th Patrol Wing carried out not only reconnaissance patrols in the area but also attacked Japanese ground targets and encountered ships. In the thick mists and unstable weather conditions, Catalinas were the only reliable aircraft able to spy on the enemy. (Artwork by Jean-Marie Guillou)

The American Curtiss SOC Seagull was a scout observation seaplane, which was introduced to the service in late 1935. At the beginning of the Pacific War, some cruisers still were equipped with Seagulls. Rear Admiral Smith used the seaplane during the bombardment of Kiska in August 1942. Later, the obsolete SOCs were replaced by the OS2U Kingfishers. (Artwork by Jean-Marie Guillou)

The Curtiss P-40 Warhawk was probably the most famous American fighter of the early Second World War. It was introduced into service in 1939 and quickly saw combat action in many campaigns all around the globe. The P-40E shown here belonged to the 11th Fighter Squadron, "Aleutian Tigers", based at Otter Point. The American fighter pilots engaged the withdrawing Japanese carrier-borne striking group and claimed several victories. Due to the vast distances between the American bases and the closest Japanese positions in Kiska, the P-40E was overshadowed by the newly introduced P-38 Lightning, which had far more operational range. (Artwork by Jean-Marie Guillou)

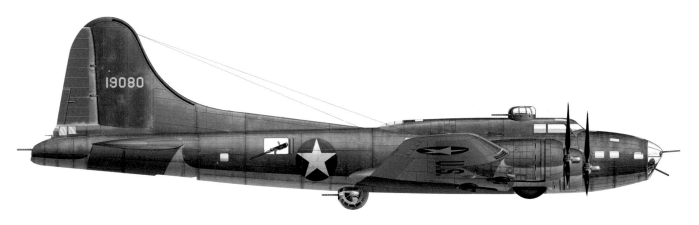

The Boeing B-17 Flying Fortress was the most famous American bomber of the Second World War. Introduced into service in 1938, it quickly became the primary USAAF bomber and was used primarily in Europe, where it dropped more bombs than any other aircraft during the war. The B-17E was developed in September 1941, this example belonged to the 11th Air Force and provided reconnaissance patrols during Operation AL. In the later period, B-17s also regularly appeared over Kiska and Attu, harassing the Japanese positions on both islands. (Artwork by Jean-Marie Guillou)

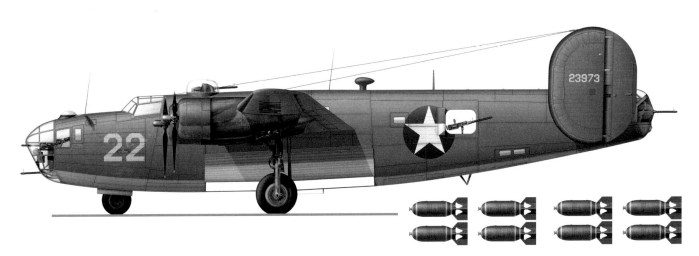

The Consolidated B-24 Liberator was introduced into service in 1941 and became a good alternative to the Flying Fortress in the heavy bomber role. The example shown, a B-24D, belonged to the 11th Air Force and after Operation AL regularly appeared over Kiska and Attu, harassing the Japanese positions on both islands. (Artwork by Jean-Marie Guillou)

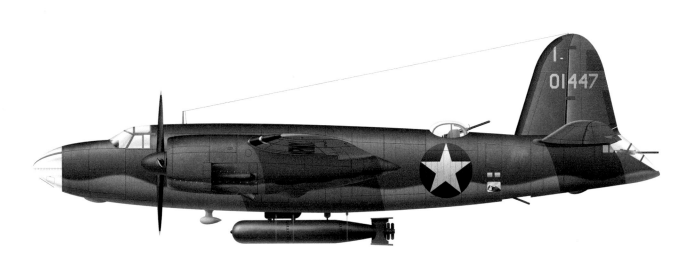

The Martin B-26 Marauder was an American medium bomber. It was introduced into service in 1941 and quickly received the reputation of being a "widow maker" due to the early models' high accident rate during take-offs and landings. The model B-26A shown here belonged to the 11th Air Force. During Operation AL, the B-26s tried to counterattack the 2nd *Kidō Kutai*, and the group led by Captain George W. Thornbrough caught the *Ryūjō* off guard, but the bombing run was unsuccessful. (Artwork by Jean-Marie Guillou)

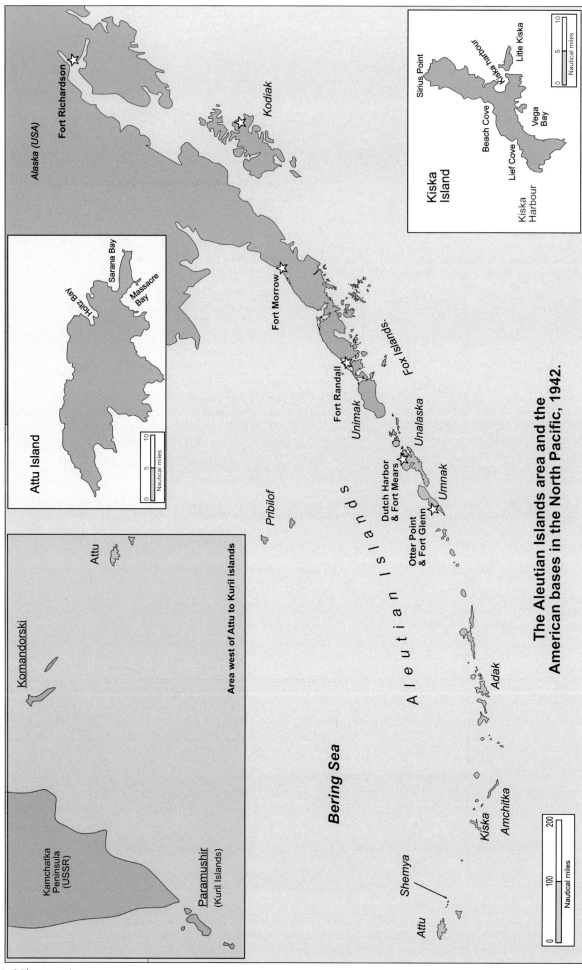

Kiska Island

Sirius Point
Little Kiska
Kiska Harbour
Beach Cove
Vega Bay
Lief Cove
Kiska Harbour
0 5 10
Nautical miles

Attu Island

Holtz Bay
Sarana Bay
Massacre Bay

0 5 10
Nautical miles

Alaska (USA)
Fort Richardson
Kodiak
Fort Morrow
Fort Randall
Unimak
Fox Islands
Unalaska
Dutch Harbor & Fort Mears
Otter Point & Fort Glenn
Umnak
Pribilof
Aleutian Islands
Adak
Amchitka
Kiska
Shemya
Attu

Bering Sea

Komandorski
Attu
Kamchatka Peninsula (USSR)
Paramushir (Kuril Islands)
Area west of Attu to Kuril islands

0 100 200
Nautical miles

The Aleutian Islands area and the American bases in the North Pacific, 1942.

(Map by Mark Thompson)

it was driven away by Japanese fighters. Bowers managed to escape and maintained radio silence according to the rules. Instead, he sent the ETA report, intentionally letting the base know that he had escaped the pursuit. However, the communication personnel read his message according to the procedures and understood that The Catalina would land in the next 30 minutes when she was more than an hour and a half from the base. This misunderstanding misled Americans regarding the actual position of the enemy task force, notably since at 0647 hours and 0720 hours, the other two flying boats also reported radar contacts at Seguam Island. Only at 1400 hours, Patrol Wing 4 realised that Bowers had come across Japanese carriers in the morning. The afternoon reconnaissance plans were hastily sent out to all nearby bases, indicating sectors where the 2nd *Kidō Butai* might be located. That day, however, any American aircraft did not find the enemy carrier task force, which according to various guesses, could have hidden in the fog near Seguam Island or west of Atka. One of the PBYs returning from patrol contacted a submarine by radar and later visually. On her bombing run, a bomb was accidentally released and exploded close to the submarine but severely damaged the plane, putting one engine out of commission. The Catalina landed safely at the base and did not report any casualties.[15]

Although *Ryūjō* and *Jun'yō* air groups' action reports for 6 June do not mention the pursuit of flying boats, the 2nd *Kidō Butai* maintained CAP comprised one Zero or two Vals for most of the day.

Table 20: Reconnaissance missions from *Ryūjō*, morning 6 June 1942.[16]

Unit	No.	Pilot	Observer	Radio operator	Notes
1st *shōtai* Kates/*Ryūjō* 150 degrees	1	PO1c Nishimura	Lt Yamagami (S)	PO2c Endō	take-off: 0737 landing: 1050
	2	Lt Samejima	PO1c Yoshihara	PO2c Itō	
2nd *shōtai* Kates/*Ryūjō* 170 degrees	1	Sea1c Futakuchi	SLt Satō (S)	PO2c Anzai	take-off: 0737 landing: 1052
	2	Sea1c Yamaguchi	PO2c Kobayashi	PO3c Izumi	
3rd *shōtai* Kates/*Ryūjō* 126 degrees	1	PO2c Horiuchi	WO Uchimura (S)	PO3c Yamauchi	take-off: 0737 landing: 1100
	2	PO2c Okuyama	PO1c Ōhashi	PO2c Ikehara	
4th *shōtai* Kates/*Ryūjō* 195 degrees	1	Sea1c Takahashi	PO1c Nemoto	PO2c Watanabe	take-off: 0737 landing: 1110
	2	Sea1c Tanishiki	PO2c Satō	PO2c Hoshino	

Table 21: Reconnaissance missions from *Ryūjō*, afternoon-evening 6 June 1942.[17]

Unit	No.	Pilot	Observer	Radio operator	Notes
1st *shōtai* Kates/*Ryūjō* 110 degrees	1	Lt Samejima (S)	PO1c Yoshihara	PO2c Itō	take-off: 1605 landing: 1920
	2	Sea1c Ōki	PO2c Kameda	PO3c Noda	
2nd *shōtai* Kates/*Ryūjō* 130 degrees	1	Ens Morita (S)	PO1c Itō	PO2c Urada	take-off: 1605 landing: 1920
	2	Sea1c Shitayoshi	PO2c Akiyama	Sea1c Takahashi I.	
3rd *shōtai* Kates/*Ryūjō* 150 degrees	1	PO1c Oda (S)	PO1c Miura	PO2c Kurahashi	take-off: 1605 landing: 1920
	2	Sea1c Tamai	PO1c Motohashi	PO2c Fujiki	
4th *shōtai* Kates/*Ryūjō* 174 degrees	1	PO2c Kawahara	PO1c Yamaguchi (S)	PO3c Ōbata	take-off: 1605 landing: 1925
	2	Sea1c Mizoguchi	PO3c Shimada	Sea2c Nakajima	

Table 22: Anti-submarine and CAP missions from *Ryūjō* and *Jun'yō*, 6 June 1942.[18]

Unit	No.	Pilot	Observer/navigator	Notes
Val/*Jun'yō* Anti-Sub	1	Unknown	Unknown	take-off: 1404 landing: ?
Val/*Jun'yō* Anti-Sub	2	Unknown	Unknown	take-off: 1610 landing: ?
Val/*Jun'yō* Anti-Sub	3	Unknown	Unknown	take-off: 1906 landing: ?
Unit	No.	Pilot		Notes
? *shōtai* Zeros/*Jun'yō* CAP	1	Unknown		take-off: 1934 landing: ?
	2	Unknown		
? *shōtai* Zeros/*Jun'yō* CAP	1	Unknown		take-off: 2140 landing: ?
	2	Unknown		
? *shōtai* Zeros/*Ryūjō* CAP	1	WO Uemura		take-off: 1000 landing: 1200
	2	PO2c Kitashino		

Additionally, at 0737 hours, Kakuta sent four pairs of Kates on reconnaissance patrols in 126-, 150-, 170-, and 195-degree sectors for over 180 miles distance. All the torpedo bombers returned to the carrier by 1110 hours and did not report any contact with the enemy. Since Kakuta was still unsure about the American moves, at 1605 hours, he sent another four pairs of Kates on reconnaissance patrols in 110-, 130-, 150-, and 174-degree sectors for over 200 miles distance. Again, the missions ended with no sighting reports, and all planes landed on *Ryūjō*'s deck by 1925 hours.

The Americans were unaware that the Japanese had begun preparations for landing on Attu and Kiska. According to the new instructions, the 2nd *Kidō Butai* was on a west-northwest course, which was changed to the northwest by midnight on 6 June, directly towards Agattu and Attu. Despite the raid on the American positions on Adak being abandoned, Kakuta's carriers were now responsible for providing air cover for invasion forces during their last leg of the route.[19]

After more than a week of waiting for orders to prepare for the landing operation, on the morning of 6 June, the Attu Invasion Force set a northerly course to bypass the island from the east. At 2000 hours, a direct approach to Attu from the northeast began. The Japanese entered Holtz Bay on 7 June at 0230 hours and dropped their anchors half an hour later.[20] The sea was calm, yet thick fog and darkness prevented a quick landing. Captain Tsuya Jirō and an independent construction company commander ordered the forming of a small scouting party and loaded its men on one Daihatsu landing craft. At the same time, around 0300 hours, the remaining soldiers were instructed to go down to the landing crafts and wait for further orders. The preparations lasted less than half an hour, after which the group carefully set off towards the shore.

Watching Holtz Bay closely, the commander of the landing party did not notice any threat and, at 0420 hours, ordered a faster approach. However, fog, described as "thick as milk", made it impossible to find the landing site indicated in the plans by binoculars. For the next 50 minutes, the Japanese looked for another appropriate site. Avoiding further postponement, they eventually chose a sandy beach in the western part of the bay. The first troops set foot on Attu at 0510 hours, and five minutes later, the commander informed the rest of the invasion forces about the successful landing.[21] The 1st Torpedo Squadron commander soon forwarded the report to the Fifth Fleet,

the Combined Fleet, and Naval Staff.[22] The rays of the morning sun, which chased away the mist, gradually revealed the picturesque landscape of the island.[23]

Without firing a single shot, Attu was seized by about 1,200 soldiers of the 301st Independent Infantry Battalion, commanded Major Matsutoshi Hozumi and supported by the 301st Independent Construction Company. The only buildings on the island were located in the Chichagof Bay area, inhabited by over 40 Aleuts and an American couple – Charles and Etta Jones.[24] Charles ran a civilian communications post and provided weather reports to Dutch Harbor, while Etta was a nurse and teacher to the residents. The married couple positively assessed their work so far:

> Aleuts look good to us. There are only 45 in the village [actually 43], and they live and work as a community. There are 9 or 10 houses, all well-painted, large and furnished. There is a lovely Russian Orthodox Church, and the chief tells us they have several thousand dollars in the treasury. They all speak a little English which is surprising because they are so far removed from other communities. They rarely see other people, except men on the occasional Coast Guard Cutters that put in there.[25]

Sunday morning of 7 June was to completely change the peaceful life of the local population and the American couple. Just before noon, Japanese soldiers began coming out of the hillside north of the village, one by one, firing in the air from time to time. Seeing the enemy, Charles hastily sent the warning, "Japs coming!" and then destroyed the radio station to prevent it from falling into the

The set of Japanese photographs from the invasion of Attu published by the *Weekly Photographic* (*Shashin Shūhō* No 228) magazine. (JACAR. Ref. A06031082300)

enemy's hands. This message was also received by warships of the Attu Invasion Force.[26] The Japanese quickly realised that there were no military facilities on the island and ordered Charles to repair the radio station. He refused to collaborate with the invaders, and the uncompromising attitude cost him his life. He was the only casualty of the invasion of Attu.[27] After a week, Etta was taken to Yokohama, where she lived in captivity until the war's end in various POW camps.

Neither was the local population protected from being forced to leave the island. Due to the construction plans of the Japanese Army, on 17 September 1942, 42 Aleuts (in the meantime, the 76-year-old chief John Artumonoff had died of natural causes) were moved to a camp near Otaru in

The 3rd Maizuru Special Naval Landing Force on Kiska. (NDL)

Hokkaido. Sixteen did not survive internment and never returned to the Aleutians.[28]

In the summary of the Attu capture operation, the Japanese reported that Chichagof Bay had been cleared of mines and that engineers had inspected the local seaplane base, which was estimated to hold up to eight large flying boats and several smaller seaplanes. On 9 June, the light cruiser *Abukuma* and the destroyers *Nenohi* and *Hatsushimo* departed to inspect the Semichi Islands to the southeast. At the same time, the destroyers *Wakaba* and *Hatsuharu* provided cover for the transport ship *Kinugasa Maru*, unloading supplies and equipment for the Army troops. At 1400 hours, the vessel reported about completing her task and was replaced by *Nissan Maru*, which was attached to the Attu Invasion Force by the Fifth Fleet on 6 June.[29]

Just before midnight on 10 June, *Abukuma*, *Nenohi*, and *Wakaba* left the anchorage in Chichagof Bay. A small infantry reconnaissance party was embarked on board the latter ship and investigated Amchitka the next day. It did not find any enemy forces and reported that a 1,000-metre-long airstrip could be built there in the future, providing seizing the island and establishing the local garrison.[30]

The Kiska Invasion Force began its approach to the island in the late hours of 6 June. Like the Attu Invasion Force, entering the anchorage passed without surprises. The light cruiser *Kiso*'s report sent on 7 June at 2100 hours informed that the Maizuru 3rd Special Naval Landing Force of Lieutenant Commander Mukai Hifumi landed at 0427 hours in Reynard Bay while two companies of Army infantry secured Little Kiska.[31] All of these were done with no casualties.[32] The communications outpost was captured, and a small group of naval personnel were taken prisoner. The Japanese also claimed that two soldiers fled inland during a chaotic chase after the escaping Americans. In contrast to Attu, no indigenous peoples were found.[33]

The only residents on Kiska, the westernmost American military outpost in the Aleutians, were a 12-person US Navy weather

outpost. They were accompanied by a Labrador female dog named Explosion. The outpost was established on 18 May, just two weeks before Operation AL commenced. It was a coincidence, but two men, including the commander, Lieutenant Mulls, were absent in the first days of June.[34] The rest of the team closely followed the news from Dutch Harbor, hoping the Japanese would withdraw to the west after the raid. However, they were afraid deep down inside that Kiska might be one of the objectives of their advance into the North Pacific, so they decided to conceal the storeroom.

On the night of 7 June, the Americans were awakened by the sound of breaking glass and machine guns. They quickly jumped out of the station and responded with their rifles. In a chaotic firefight, Mate Second Class Walter Winfrey was wounded in the leg, and Radioman Third Class M.L. Courtenay was shot in his hand. Mate Second Class J.L. Turner hastily burned the codebooks in the oven stove. Although the group managed to escape from an ambush, the Japanese captured two men at the back of the station. The other eight, including the wounded Winfrey, fled unarmed to a nearby hill, where they intended to hide in low clouds. They had to run and bend down since the machine gun mounted on the Daihatsu landing craft fired at them. According to the Americans, the 12.7mm bullets coming at high speed looked like "spinning baseballs" from above. To lose the Japanese soldiers, the escapees dispersed just before reaching the plateau. Further casualties were avoided, but the group failed to reunite at the top. The invaders gave up the pursuit and secured the captured buildings, quickly finding the hidden storeroom.

The following day, a reconnaissance patrol captured two Americans. Five other escapees gave up after a few days when it turned out that Winfrey's wound had become infected. It was so severe that the Japanese surgeon decided to perform the operation to extract the bullet in a hospital tent that had previously been set up on a nearby beach. From the entire weather station team, the Japanese failed to find only Mate First Class William C. House.

He hid in various locations on the island, freezing at night and eating only insects and roots. After 50 days of surviving in extreme conditions, House voluntarily surrendered. His physical appearance terrified the Japanese as he weighed only 36kg, which made a shocking impression even for his diminutive height.[35]

For most of 7 June, Japanese destroyers and minesweepers cleared the entrance to Kiska Harbor of sea mines. After securing the approach to the anchorage, the transport ships *Asaka Maru*, *Kumagawa Maru* and *Hakusan Maru* began unloading equipment and supplies for the new garrison of the island. The work continued for two days continuously, during which air cover was provided by seaplanes from *Kimikawa Maru* and *Kamikawa Maru*. The latter vessel arrived in the North Pacific on 6 June and supported the invasion of Kiska to relieve the 2nd *Kidō Butai* partly.

Speaking of the 2nd *Kidō Butai*, one hour before noon of 8 June, Kakuta set the course straight on Agattu. Until 18 June, both Japanese carriers provided reconnaissance missions east of Attu and Kiska to ensure the enemy did not plan any counterattack.[36] Eventually, on 20 June, they were recalled by the Combined Fleet and returned to Ōminato to await further orders.[37]

Coming back to Kiska – parallel to unloading supplies, the Japanese used equipment from *Awata Maru* and *Asaka Maru* to establish a seaplane base. On 13 June, both ships reported the completion of off-loading and, with part of the Kiska Invasion Force, set course for Ōminato.[38] The return trip was hazardous since the day before, the 11 AF carried out the airstrike on the island and sank the destroyer *Hibiki*.[39]

For the first week of Kiska's occupation, the Japanese garrison focused on consolidating their newly established positions. On 16 June, the anti-aircraft guns were deployed, and a day later, the Fifth Fleet commander ordered the merging of the remaining units of the Kiska Invasion Force and the Attu Invasion Force. On 18 June, the group of ships led by the light cruisers *Abukuma* and *Kiso*, set course for Japan. Operation AL was announced as a great success, but many *Nippon Kaigun* officers felt it was poor solace for the disastrous defeat in the Central Pacific. Without Midway, the Combined Fleet could not establish a defensive perimeter in the North Pacific. Even worse, yet unknown to the Japanese, they would have to drop their offensive mindset and quickly adapt to a stubborn defence.

6

SUMMER CAMPAIGN OF 1942

１９４２年夏の作戦
1942-nen Natsu no Sakusen

Just before 2400 hours on 7 June, as the Japanese invasion forces approached Attu and Kiska, Patrol Wing 4's commander ordered additional morning reconnaissance flights in search of enemy carriers. During four days of intensive operations, the unit lost six flying boats, and the crews did not have time to rest. Despite all odds, on the morning of 7 June, three PBYs from Otter Point checked the sectors north and west of Umnak and did not encounter any vessels. Due to the breakdown of the ECM machine on the *Casco*, Cold Bay did not receive Captain Gehres' order. PBYs were meant to explore the area north of their base but eventually went on the rectangular search southwards.

The Americans considered no contact with the Japanese throughout 6 and 7 June as a likely end of Operation AL. Although one of the civilian pilots reported stumbling upon a Katori-class light cruiser near Port Heiden, this was not confirmed by Cold Bay, which stated that the entire area was covered in heavy fog and radars

had not picked up any contacts. On that day, a trace of a group of Japanese transport ships, supposed to be in the Bering Sea, was not found either. Based on various data from radio transmissions, the 2nd *Kidō Butai* was believed to be on its way back to Japan. Additionally, the Catalinas sent on patrols on the night of 8/9 June,

The *San Francisco Chronicle* newspaper's cover. (Open source)

confirmed that the Japanese task force, at least its main part, had withdrawn from the chain area.

In the first days after the end of Operation AL, the American reinforcements started to arrive in the North Pacific as a replacement for the lost aircraft. On 8 June, four Catalinas of VP-43 landed at Kodiak, followed by eight PBYs the next day and VP-51's nine more flying boats on 11 June, bringing to four the number of Catalina squadrons in the Alaskan area. Along with VP-43 aircraft and personnel, the seaplane tender *Hulbert* also arrived on the stage, providing crucial support for Patrol Wing 4 from Nazan Bay off Atka.[1]

One of the troubling matters relating to the Japanese offensive in the Aleutian area was the loss of radio contact with the outposts at Attu and Kiska. From 7 June, both stations gave no sign of life, and the dense fog for the next two days made it impossible to carry out thorough air reconnaissance.[2] However, on the morning of 8 June, the LB-30 piloted by Captain Robert E. "Pappy" Speer headed down the islands from Otter Point and arrived over Kiska at 1300 hours. Speer decided to drop down to 200 feet and circle the harbour to check if his colleagues from the weather station were safe. Suddenly he saw some ships which he believed were US Navy vessels. Speer flashed a recognition signal and was greeted in return by a burst of gunfire. He pulled back into the clouds and ordered the encoding of the message while returning to Cape Field.[3] The Americans had some guesses about the Japanese moves, but it was not until 10 June that Catalinas piloted by Lieutenant (jg.) Bowers of VP-41 and Lieutenant (jg.) Dahl of VP-43 discovered enemy vessels and hastily erected military facilities on both islands.[4] On 11 June, after confirming these reports, the Americans had enough evidence that the Japanese had captured Attu and Kiska during Operation AL. TF-8's War Diary gave more specific data on Kiska, indicating one heavy cruiser, two light cruisers, one destroyer and six transport ships in the local harbour.[5] The invaders, being aware that the initial surprise must end someday, also noticed two enemy flying boats closely circling over their newly established bases.[6]

The American Response to the Occupation of Attu and Kiska
アッツ島・キスか島の占領に対するアメリカの反応
Attsu-tō, Kisuka-tō no Senryō ni tai suru Amerika no Han'nō

As B. Garfield noted, upon discovering Japanese vessels and troops at Attu and Kiska, the Americans needed to make appropriate decisions immediately. The easternmost Kiska posed a significant and direct threat to bases on Umnak and Unalaska. Still, in the strategic situation at the time, the US Navy and Army could patiently wait for further developments since, on 10 June, Rear Admiral Spruance's TF-16 was halfway to the Aleutians from Pearl Harbor. In the wake of the Battle of Midway, the American carriers were to follow up the victorious streak, this time in the Alaskan area. Besides involving the US Navy's high-calibre resources in the North Pacific, the second option included harassing Japanese positions on the chain, forcing them to withdraw to the Kuriles in the long-term.[7]

Despite the lack of imminent threat of another Japanese offensive in the Aleutians, the Americans could not simply ignore the occupation of Attu and Kiska. Apart from their military importance, the events of early June in the North Pacific also had political and propaganda significance. For the first time since the memorable war with Great Britain in 1812–1815, the enemy controlled part of the territory of the United States. President Roosevelt's administration assumed, somewhat correctly, that this fact would be exploited in the

American press, where the subject of a potential Japanese invasion of the West Coast was prevalent. For example, on 23 February 1942, the Japanese submarine *I-17* shelled and severely damaged a refinery in Ellwood, California. Soon after, on the night of 24/25 February, anti-aircraft batteries in Los Angeles roared unexpectedly once their crews allegedly sighted unidentified objects over the city. As a result of these two minor but highly publicised incidents, the American public was flooded with articles predicting an ominous invasion to happen in the next few days. The capture of Attu and Kiska, in no way affecting the defence of the West Coast, became a pretext for constant attacks on the US Army and US Navy for overlooking vital national interests. Some historians also pointed out that the loss of Kiska was a great humiliation for the Secretary of War, especially personally to Henry L. Stimson. This was also one of the multiple reasons why he insisted on reconquering the Aleutians as soon as possible.[8]

The loss of Attu and Kiska was also debated in Congress, where Anthony Diamond informed the House of Representatives that 25,000 Japanese troops were stationed in the Aleutian Islands. No one knew the precise numbers, albeit John M. Coffee stated confidently during his speech that "mainland Alaska will be invaded before the summer is over." Both Diamond and Coffee were absolutely wrong, but they effectively reminded other congressmen about the presence of the enemy on American territory.[9]

Moving away from the press and political views, the US Army and the US Navy also saw the possible threats resulting from the capture of Attu and Kiska by the Japanese. Lieutenant Bob Brocklehurst of the 18th Fighter Squadron recalled some American fears in the Alaskan Defense Command, "The impression we were given — and this was voiced oral stuff — was that we had nothing to stop the Japanese. [Our commanding officers] figured that the Japanese, if they wanted to, could have come up the Aleutians, taken Anchorage, and come down past down Vancouver to Seattle, Washington."[10]

On 10 and 11 June, TF-8 received several reports indicating the Japanese warships, including a heavy cruiser and possibly carrier planes at Kiska and invasion forces off Attu.[11] However, the Fifth Fleet avoided engaging its most valuable and kept only the light cruisers *Tama* and *Kiso* in the Aleutians. Still, their presence was a good reason for the Americans to take offensive actions. On the same day, Admiral Ernest J. King agreed with Admiral Nimitz's suggestion to use submarines and air forces to harass the enemy positions at Kiska.[12]

Nimitz, aware of the Japanese carriers supporting the landing operations in the Aleutians, acted much earlier and on 8 June, ordered TF-16 to rush for the North Pacific. *Enterprise* and *Hornet*, reinforced by fighters and bombers from the *Saratoga* Air Group, were meant to be a crucial asset in US Navy hands on the northern flank. However, with the likely retreat of the enemy carriers, Nimitz reverted TF-16 to Hawaii on 11 June. King supported this decision since both carriers could provide valuable support in the other operation and there was no need to commit them in the North Pacific. Once TF-16 was off the stage, Nimitz planned to merge the part of TF-8 and TF-1 to carry out training on the Dutch Harbor–Pearl Harbor line to await further developments.[13]

In response to recommendations to harass enemy positions in the Aleutians, Captain Gehres ordered all flying boats to cease further reconnaissance missions over the chain. Beginning on 11 June, PBYs were to focus on bombing and torpedo attacks on Japanese forces at Kiska. Patrol Wing 4 could speak of temporary shortness of breath, especially after Operation AL, yet new reinforcements allowed for the bigger offensive operations.

The seaplane tender *Gillis* also took part in the action, taking up a position in Nazan Bay on the night of 10/11 June where she could refuel and rearm flying boats faster than off Umnak. From 11 to 13 June, the American PBYs carried out 20 raids on Japanese positions, often also by dive-bombing attacks at 250 knots, having no proper bombsight equipment for that kind of task. The operation was aborted when *Gillis* ran out of fuel and ordnance. The seaplane tender was also spotted by one of the Japanese reconnaissance seaplanes and was forced to withdraw from the area hastily. Leaving Atka, the Americans burned all the buildings and military facilities on the island, evacuating white residents and some indigenous people. In the afternoon, *Hulbert* relieved

A unique shot of the destruction of the B-24 piloted by Captain Jack Todd on 11 June 1942 by anti-aircraft fire. (Maru Special)

Gillis and took off 62 more natives. The last inhabitants of Atka left the island aboard two Catalinas the next day.[14]

The air offensive involved crews unaccustomed to the Aleutian climate, having arrived directly from San Diego just four days earlier. However, besides several Catalinas damaged by the anti-aircraft fire, Patrol Wing 4 lost only one flying boat with the entire crew. On 14 June, a PBY piloted by Machinist Leland L. Davis of VP-43 headed over Kiska, bristling with anti-aircraft guns. One of the shells directly hit the aircraft and tore her apart.[15] Burning metal pieces fluttered down on the hillside below. The explosion was captured by a Japanese cameraman looking to the sky for the American plane. Despite this fatal loss, Patrol Wing 4 casualties totalled seven killed and two wounded men. It was a small price to pay for an unprecedentedly bold and improvised action during which the Japanese were attacked almost every hour of the day. Even Captain Gehres admitted, "Every flight was a flight that the crew should not have returned from. Every man knew this, and yet none wavered." Some crews were in the air for 19.5 hours daily, thus making Kiska the infamous "PBY Elimination Center" nickname. Nevertheless, Patrol Wing 4's three-day air offensive went down in history as "the Kiska Blitz", for which six Navy Crosses were awarded.[16]

While Patrol Wing 4 was actively harassing enemy positions on Kiska, they were also attacked by 11 AF aircraft. On the morning of 11 June, five B-24s took off from Cold Bay and headed west for a bombing mission. During the approach, the leader of the formation, Captain Jack Todd, went down from 6,000 metres and was hit by an anti-aircraft round, which exploded against the right wing near the fuselage. The bomber disintegrated, and pieces fell on and hillside near Trout Lagoon. Two other nearby Liberators were hit by fragments of Todd's plane but remained intact. The formation of B-24s then dropped bombs and set off on a return course without reporting any hits.[17]

The take-off of five B-17Es of the 36th Bombardment Squadron, scheduled to leave Umnak an hour later, was postponed due to technical failures. Eventually, the formation led by Colonel

Eareckson managed to scramble and attack the Japanese cruisers and destroyers in Kiska Bay from about 1,000 metres. Although the crews of the Flying Fortresses claimed to have seen their bombs hitting two cruisers and a destroyer, they scored only near misses with no casualties.[18]

The bombers of 11 AF stationed at Umnak, led each time by Eareckson, continued to attack Japanese ships in Kiska Bay in the following days, giving its contribution to "The Kiska Blitz". Six B-17Es and one B-24 went on 12 June, five B-17Es and three B-24s (two returned soon) on 13 June, and finally, three B-17Es and four B-24s on 14 June. Constantly changing weather meant the Flying Fortresses and Liberators failed to achieve significant results, although direct hits on enemy cruisers and a destroyer were reported.[19] The only real success of the American air offensive between 11 and 14 June, confirmed by Japanese documents, was the severe damage to the destroyer *Hibiki* inflicted by a Catalina of Patrol Wing 4 on 12 June. The ship was directly hit by one bomb that penetrated the starboard bow and exploded at the anchor chain locker near the waterline. The other three bombs fell short and were reported as near misses. Due to this attack, compartments under her fore guns were flooded, and she started sinking, but eventually, after more than three hours of damage control repairs, *Hibiki* was saved.[20]

On 15 June, the Americans decided to undertake a major reorganisation of their air forces in the Aleutian area. Patrol Wing 4 was merged with the 11 AF into the Air Task Group, more commonly referred to in reports as Task Group 8.1 of General Brigadier Butler. In addition to forming a new unit, Patrol Wing 4 changed its name to the Air Search Unit, also known as Task Unit 8.1.2, formally remaining under Captain Gehres's command with his Kodiak headquarters.[21] The summary of American air attacks against Japanese positions at Kiska and Attu from 4 to 13 June is as shown in Table 23.

The destroyer *Hibiki*. (Kure Naval Museum)

Table 23: American air attacks on Kiska and Attu, 4–13 June 1942.[22]

Date	US Navy air attacks	USAAF air attacks
4 June	2	3
6 June	1	-
7 June	1	-
11 June	7	1
12 June	8	2
13 June	5	2
In total:	24	9

Japanese on Attu and Kiska
日本に占領されたアッツ島およびキスカ島
Nihon ni Senryō Sareta Attsu-tō oyobi Kisuka-tō

Once the Japanese captured Kiska and Attu, they began the first stage of consolidating their newly established positions in the North Pacific. Apart from military objectives, occupying part of the American territory also had a propaganda dimension. Both islands soon received official Japanese names; thus, Kiska and Attu were respectively renamed Narukamitō (鳴神島) and Atsutatō (熱田島).

For geographical and strategic reasons, Kiska was chosen as the main Japanese outpost in the western Aleutians. Beginning on 8 June, transport ships *Awata Maru* and *Asaka Maru* unloaded the equipment necessary to establish the seaplane base.[23] At the same time, transport ships *Hakusan Maru* and *Kumagawa Maru* tried to deliver supplies for the local garrison, but American air attacks caused unexpected difficulties and delays.[24] The increased activity of enemy air forces, resulting in damage to the destroyer *Hibiki*, forced Hosogaya to reorganise the Northern Forces. On 13 June, the 21st Destroyer Squadron was assigned to the Kiska Invasion Force and then, with the light cruiser *Tama* and the destroyers *Hibiki* and *Akatsuki*, set course for Ōminato.

By 16 June, soon after the American air offensive ended, the Japanese reported the establishment of the garrison on Kiska. The local artillery detachment comprised four 120mm coastal guns,

four 70mm field howitzers, four 13mm anti-aircraft guns and two searchlights. In addition, one quadruple torpedo tube (of unknown calibre) was mounted ashore to protect the entrance to the harbour from enemy vessels trying to approach the anchorage undetected.

The small surface force assigned to defend the entire area consisted of the light cruiser *Kiso*, two destroyers, five gunboats, three submarine chasers, and several auxiliary vessels. By 15 June, the seaplane tender *Kamikawa Maru* also arrived in the vicinity of Kiska and with *Kimikawa Maru*, escorted by the destroyers *Shiokaze* and *Hokaze*, supported the local air force during reconnaissance and attack missions. By 20 June, the seaplane tender *Chiyoda* also delivered four midget submarines for the newly established base, allowing the Fifth Fleet to penetrate the American positions on Umnak and Unimak.[25]

The Japanese patrol wing in the Aleutians initially comprised six Jake seaplanes of *Kimikawa Maru*'s air group and the detachments of six Mavis flying boats from *Tōkō Kaigun Kōkūtai* which arrived from Japan's mainland via Kuriles in the evening of 8 June. Led by Commander Itō Sukemitsu, Tōkō-ku planes went on a reconnaissance patrol in six designated sectors eastward on 9 June but did not encounter any American vessels.[26] Over the next five days, scouting missions were repeated, and their results were as shown in Table 24.

Once *Kamikawa Maru* arrived off Kiska with new aircraft in the afternoon of 14 June, the Aleutian seaplane detachment had increased to 14 Petes, six Jakes and four Daves. Including six flying boats of Tōkō-ku mentioned above, the Japanese had 30 fully operational planes in the initial phase of the North Pacific campaign. Prior to entering Kiska Harbor, *Kamikawa Maru* catapulted four seaplanes to search for enemy submarines. An hour and a half later, American bombers attacked the Japanese, and two seaplanes were forced to remain in the air despite the lousy weather. One of them was damaged but remained operational due to quick repairs.[28]

When the Operation MI fiasco was eventually overprocessed at Tokyo at the end of the second week of June, the Combined Fleet turned its attention to the Aleutians. American air raids on Kiska strengthened the Japanese notion that the enemy was preparing for a

Type 0 reconnaissance seaplane (of the *Kimikawa Maru* air group), better known as the Aichi E13A or under the Allied codename Jake. The photograph was taken in June 1942 near Kiska. (Maru Special)

larger offensive and might also send their carriers as a main striking force. To support the Fifth Fleet in a possible naval battle with a large task group, at 1500 hours on 13 June, Admiral Yamamoto detached part of the 5th Carrier Squadron (without *Shōkaku*) with two destroyers, the light carrier *Zuihō*,[29] and part of the 5th Cruiser Squadron (heavy cruisers *Myōkō* and *Haguro*) and assigned them to new objectives in the Aleutian Islands. The 5th Carrier Squadron, operating only with *Zuikaku* in practice, was to proceed north, link up with the 4th Carrier Squadron (*Jun'yō* and *Ryūjō*) and remain under Rear Admiral Kakuta's orders during the upcoming action against the US Navy.[30]

Waiting for the reinforcements to arrive in the North Pacific, at 1100 hours on 15 June, Hosogaya issued Operational Order No.

109, pointing out the further arrangements for defensive operations against enemy bombers. Furthermore, the organisation of Japanese forces in the Aleutians after Admiral Yamamoto's 13 June dispatch was as shown in Table 25.

The forecast predicting slightly better weather and the support of carriers promised by the Combined Fleet encouraged the Japanese to respond to American air strikes. At 0810 hours on 14 June, five Mavis of *Tōkō Kaigun Kōkūtai* scrambled from Kiska led by Commander Itō. The flying boats proceeded towards Nazan Bay off Atka and, between 1115 and 1140 hours, dropped a total of sixteen 250kg bombs on enemy positions which were additionally machine-gunned. Without explicitly confirming the results of the attack, all Mavises returned to base by 1510 hours. Only one flying boat was damaged by anti-aircraft gun shells that pierced its tail.[32]

On 17 June, based on the Fifth Commander's order, the forces stationed at Kiska were reorganised into several smaller sub-units: Kiska Defense Unit (13th Submarine Chaser Squadron, destroyer *Hokaze*, four transport ships), Support Unit (destroyers *Wakaba*, *Hatsuharu*, and *Hatsushimo*), Seaplane Tender Unit (seplane tenders *Kamikawa Maru* and *Kimikawa Maru*, and destroyer *Shiokaze*) and Base Air Unit (part of *Tōkō Kaigun Kōkūtai*, two transport ships).[33] The ground forces comprised the 550-man detachment of

Table 24: *Tōkō Kaigun Kōkūtai* reconnaissance missions in the Aleutian area from Kiska, 9–14 June 1942.[27]

Date	Number of flying boats	Take-off and return to Kiska	Results
9 June	6	take-off: 0937–1015 return: 1840–1943	None
10 June	3	take-off: 0838–0846 return: 1602–1900	None
11 June	2	take-off: 1342–1406 return: 2024–2120	exchanged machine gun fire with the enemy plane
12 June	2	take-off: 0900–0925 return: 1620–12020	spotted one enemy submarine
13 June	2	take-off: 0844–0850 return: 1358–1515	None
14 June	5	take-off: 0810 return: 1510	Exchanged machine gun fire with the enemy plane and bombed land targets through heavy clouds; dropped 16 x 250kg bombs

The seaplane tender *Kamikawa Maru*. (Open source)

"Maizuru" 3rd Special Naval Landing Force and the 750-men Navy construction unit.[34]

The potential presence of Japanese aircraft carriers less than 450 kilometres from Kiska did not deter the Americans from further attacks on enemy positions in the Aleutian Islands. On the morning of 18 June, Colonel Eareckson sent one LB-30 to provide precise data on the enemy positions in advance, and then took off with four B-24s of the 30th Bombardment Group and three B-17s of the 36th Bombardment Squadron.[35] The planes dropped their bombs from 5,000 metres on Japanese vessels in Kiska Harbor, scoring direct hits on the transport ship *Nissan Maru*, which was set on fire and soon sank.[36] Ripped-off fragments of metal also slightly damaged *Kumagawa Maru*.[37] The positions on Kiska were so threatened by American air strikes that the Japanese decided to temporarily send four Petes from *Kamikawa Maru*'s air group to MacDonald

Table 25: Organisation of the Japanese naval forces assigned by the Combined Fleet to the Aleutians in the third week of June 1942.[31]				
Unit		Commander	Forces	Tasks
Main Force		Fifth Fleet Commander	heavy cruiser *Nachi* 6th Destroyer Division	Support during the operations
Support Force	1st Support Unit	3rd Battleship Squadron Commander	battleship *Hiei* 10th Destroyer Division tanker *Kyokutō Maru*	Direct support for the 2nd *Kidō Butai*
	2nd Support Unit	5th Cruiser Squadron Commander	battleship *Kongō* part of 5th Cruiser Squadron (heavy cruisers *Myōkō* and *Haguro*) 1st Torpedo Squadron (light cruiser *Abukuma*, 21st Destroyer Division) 9th Destroyer Division 21st Cruiser Squadron (light cruisers *Tama* and *Kiso*) tanker *Gen'yō Maru*	Support to destroy the enemy fleet
2nd *Kidō Butai*	1st Air Unit	4th Carrier Squadron Commander	4th Carrier Squadron (carriers *Jun'yō* and *Ryūjō*) heavy cruiser *Takao* 7th Destroyer Division destroyer *Uranami* tanker *Tōhō Maru*	Support to destroy the enemy fleet
	2nd Air Unit		part of 5th Carrier Squadron (carrier *Zuikaku*) light carrier *Zuihō* heavy cruiser *Maya* 4th Destroyer Division tanker *Fujisan Maru*	

Bay off Agattu. On 18 June, in response to Eareckson's air attack, anchored off Kiska *Hakusan Maru* and *Kumagawa Maru* were ordered to stop unloading supplies and equipment and return to Ōminato.[38] Prince Nobuhito Takamatsunomiya, the younger brother of Emperor Hirohito, looking at the reports from the Aleutians, recalled in his diary that during the raid, the anti-aircraft defences were utterly helpless and did not fire a single salvo at the enemy bombers. In addition, he mentioned that the Japanese later found empty tin tanks on the water's surface. Initially, the defenders thought that the Americans had tried unsuccessfully to attack the

base with chemical weapons, but it turned out later that they were only attached fuel tanks that were jettisoned after use.[39]

Bomber crews of 11 AF presented their missions against enemy positions on Kiska, carried out regularly throughout June, in a completely different light. If the weather allowed the planes to take-off and, on the route, they were not forced to return to the base, off Kiska Harbor, they were greeted by the fierce anti-aircraft fire from batteries on land and ships in the anchorage. The Japanese skilfully focused on one target, picking individual bombers not hidden in clouds, trying to prevent the enemy from approaching the

Type 97 large flying boat, better known as the Kawanishi E6K or under the Allied codename Mavis. (Maru Special)

target close enough. As a consequence, the bombs dropped by the Americans were mainly inaccurate, and the results of the air attacks did not compensate for the 11 AF losses. It should also be noted that besides the Japanese anti-aircraft defence, some other factors equally influenced the limited successes of the American bombers. The route from Umnak to Kiska and back to the base consisted of nearly 2,000 kilometres, which required bombers to use additional fuel tanks, better known as "Tokyo tanks". However, the extra fuel in planes decreased their capacity to carry bombs, leaving Flying Fortresses at only 30 percent and Liberators at 50 percent of their original loadout. The bombing missions against the Japanese were undoubtedly not facilitated by the primitive conditions at Cape Field. The Marston mat-covered runway was only 50 metres wide, which forced the pilots to approach for landing in one particular method, notwithstanding the bad weather or limited visibility. Although Cape Field was a crucial asset in American hands in the Aleutians, pilots hated it for the lumpy and rocky ground surrounding the runway, which did not leave any room for any mistakes. Additionally, all bombers were parked tightly, without keeping a safe distance between them, which posed a massive danger in case of a Japanese counterattack.[40] Still, the situation on Umnak was constantly improving since Colonel Benjamin B. Talley's engineers moved in and began building additional runways, taxiways, and hardstands. They replaced the tents with Pacific huts and Quonset huts, finally giving a touch of comfort and warmer beds to aviators and air personnel. On 20 June, after moving fighter and bomber squadrons and their support units forward, General Butler also sent Colonel Everett S. Davis and the advance headquarters of the 11 AF to Cape Field.[41]

Despite promises to provide air support for the Kiska garrison and seaplanes, the Japanese carriers present in the North Pacific did not see action over the chain from 16 to 20 June and remained at safe positions less than 300 miles to the west. *Zuihō* and *Jun'yō* did not conduct any air operations during this period,[42] while *Ryūjō* (coordinates: 47°48'N 170°38'E) sent two pairs of torpedo bombers to search for American surface vessels in the 150- and 180-degrees sectors on 17 June. After fruitless reconnaissance missions, all planes landed on the carrier in the afternoon, reporting blustery weather in

the area. In the meantime, another two pairs of torpedo bombers provided anti-submarine patrols. *Ryūjō*'s air group operations in the following days are unknown since all documents covering the events from 18 June to 24 August were lost with the carrier during the battle of the Eastern Solomons.[43]

The idle watch for the unlikely action of American aircraft carriers in the North Pacific was the main reason the Combined Fleet decided to call off the Main Force, Support Force, and the 2nd *Kidō Butai* to Ōminato at 2400 hours on 21 June.[45] Ironically, two days before, US Navy intelligence intercepted a dispatch indicating that the enemy was preparing for landing operations in the Aleutians. Additionally, two radar-equipped flying boats patrolling the area between the Prybilof Islands and St. Lawrence Island spotted a group of enemy vessels. Based on their location and course, PBY crews assumed that the Japanese were preparing to invade mainland Alaska, most likely the strategically important port of Nome.[46] The base soon received a warning about the approaching task force composed of three aircraft carriers, two battleships, five heavy cruisers, three light cruisers, 23 destroyers, and seven to 11 submarines. Albeit the report grossly overestimated the size of the Japanese task force and completely misinterpreted its intentions, the Americans suddenly faced the vision of imminent invasion. Once the reports also reached the politicians, they expressed the view that "the presence of this formidable force in Alaskan waters is a matter of grave concern and indicates that the whole chain is in danger of Japanese occupation".[47] Also General Marshall in his correspondence to Admiral Stark recognised the danger for the Alaska and the Aleutians, expressing that they are both in "a critical situation".[48]

The political debate on the Aleutians coincided with the next indecent off the West Coast. On 20 June, the Japanese submarine *I-26* closed to Vancouver Island to only five miles and fired 17 salvos at the telegraph station but did not score hits due to bad weather and poor visibility. Most of the shells fell in the vicinity of the lighthouse on Esteban Point, causing no substantial damage to the facility. The next day, Canadian vessels and aircraft went to hunt for *I-26* but could not locate the intruder, which escaped westwards and soon ended its war patrol.[49]

Table 26: Reconnaissance and anti-submarine missions from *Ryūjō*, 18 June 1942.[44]					
Unit	No.	Pilot	Observer	Radio operator	Notes
1st *shōtai* Kates/*Ryūjō* 150 degrees	1	PO2c Horiuchi	WO Uchimura (S)	PO3c Yamauchi	take-off: 1258 landing: 1427 returned after 90 miles due to bad weather
	2	PO2c Okuyama	PO1c Ōhashi	PO2c Ikehara	
2nd *shōtai* Kates/*Ryūjō* 180 degrees	1	PO2c Kawahara	PO1c Yamaguchi (S)	PO3c Ōbata	take-off: 1258 landing: 1420 returned after 70 miles due to bad weather
	2	Sea1c Tamai	PO1c Motohashi	PO2c Fujiki	
1st direct *shōtai* Kates/*Ryūjō*	1	Sea1c Tanishiki	PO3c Nihei (S)	Sea1c Toriyama	take-off: ? landing: ?
	2	Sea1c Mizoguchi	PO3c Shimada	Sea2c Nakajima	
2nd direct *shōtai* Kates/*Ryūjō*	1	Sea1c Shimada	PO2c Satō (S)	PO2c Hoshino	take-off: ? landing: ?
	2	Sea1c Ono	Sea1c Yoshimoto	Sea2c Suzuki	

The events related to the next Japanese submarine off the West Coast were overshadowed by intelligence and scouting data on the powerful enemy task force approaching Nome. For the first time since the Day of Infamy, the memorable strike on Pearl Harbor, panic broke out in the American headquarters. Calls went off at every major Army and Navy facility in Washington, Hawaii, the West Coast, and Alaska. Fear of the enemy amphibious operation in Alaska resulted in taking immediate countermeasures. On the night of 20/21 June, 46 civilian aircraft (some of them were modern DC-3s and antiquated Ford "Tin Goose" Trimotors) belonging to commercial airlines, which operated from Edmonton throughout Alaska, were temporarily requisitioned and used to support 15 military transport planes. Buckner also issued orders to local army posts to confiscate any plane that had landed in Alaska, regardless of the owner or the purpose of the flight. On the morning of 21 June, he collected 55 planes of various types that participated in the colossal airlift effort. In 218 trips, they transported 2,035 troops and over 883,000 pounds of cargo and equipment into Nome within 18 days. Heavy equipment, 20 anti-aircraft guns, fuel and other bulk cargo were shipped by sea from Seward.[50] This hastily improvised troop redeployment went down in history as Operation Bingo and ended in mid-July. However, the most crucial reinforcements arrived in 36 hours, establishing a substantial garrison at the very tip of mainland Alaska.[51] Some American soldiers were evacuated from isolated outposts in the Aleutian Islands to Nome and found themselves in an entirely new situation. Captain William J. Wheeler of the 36th Bombardment Squadron described the living conditions at the new base:

At Nome the crews are settled in tents. A few of them tried to dig foxholes but were stopped at a depth of eighteen inches by rock-like [permafrost]... Wernick's crew went into the town of Nome to see the natives in action. They report steak dinners for a nominal $2.50 served in the quiet and restful atmosphere of the Polar Bar Grill. Good whisky is reasonable and the assortment could be considered a minor miracle considering the difficulty of shipping such items from the States. Nome is proud of its boast that a greater tonnage of liquor is shipped in each year than food."[52]

The immediate response to the PBY's findings did not solve the primary American issue, who had to confirm the composition and plans of the enemy task force that suddenly appeared out of nowhere in the Bering Sea. TF-8 report of 18 June stated that Japanese forces in the Aleutian area were estimated at three aircraft carriers (*Ryūjō*, *Zuihō*, *Jun'yō*), two battleships (*Haruna*, *Kirishima*), five heavy cruisers (*Nachi*, two Maya-class, two Tone-class), three light cruisers (*Abukuma*, *Kuma*, *Nagara*), one seaplane tender, 20–22 destroyers, seven to 11 submarines, two to three converted seaplane tenders, six to nine transports of two types, several patrol ships, four to eight seaplanes/flying boats, 27 bombers based in the Kuriles and a garrison on the seized islands of Attu and Kiska. Additionally, the aircraft carrier *Zuikaku* was expected to arrive south of the chain in the following days.[53]

Comparing the TF-8 report with the actual composition of the *Nippon Kaigun*'s task force detached to the defence of the Aleutian area, one cannot deny that American estimates were highly accurate. US Navy not only precisely assessed the number of carriers and other vessels but correctly identified the carrier's types. The only mistake made on the night of

A photograph of Main Street in Nome taken by a soldier stationed there at the end of the war. (Valeria Edwards private resources via Radio Heritage Foundation)

20/21 June was an overly hasty prediction of the enemy's intentions. Albeit the Japanese had considerable forces on paper, they were not ready to use them for offensive operations in the Aleutians. Moreover, due to the strategic situation in the Pacific after the Battle of Midway, their carrier task force could not be stationed idle in the North Pacific. Once confirming that the US Navy was not preparing for the reconquest of Attu and Kiska, they left the Bering Seas, leaving a small surface force in the seized islands. On the morning of 20 June, the Japanese were still looking for enemy ships in the northeast of Kiska, but in the afternoon, they decided to return to Ōminato. On 29 June, the 2nd *Kidō Butai* carried out a reconnaissance mission south of Kiska for the last time.[54] The attention of the Combined Fleet gradually turned to the Solomon Islands in the South Pacific, which resulted in the withdrawal of all carriers from the North Pacific area in the coming weeks.

While the Navy General Staff, Combined Fleet and Fifth Fleet had different visions of the plans for the Aleutians, they all agreed that the newly established positions on Attu and Kiska should be held until the end of winter at least. On 23 June, the Imperial General Headquarters issued Army Order No. 647 and Detailed Navy Order No. 106, assigning the Fifth Fleet to "*chōki kakuho*" – the long-term defence of Attu and Kiska. The critical element of the future strategy in the Aleutian area, clearly emphasised in the order, was the cooperation of the *Nippon Kaigun* and *Nippon Rikugun*:

Detailed Navy General Staff Order No. 106

1. Pursuant to Detailed Navy General Staff Order No. 94, in the second phase of operations in the Aleutian Islands, the Army and Navy will cooperate closely together; the plan to destroy [the enemy's position] on Adak is cancelled, and Attu and Kiska should be held.

The Combined Fleet will provide the necessary forces to support the Kiska garrison and will cooperate with the Attu Army garrison.

2. From 2400 hours on 25 June, the Army Northern Seas Detachment will no longer be under the operational control of the Fifth Fleet commander.[55]

In parallel, the order addressed to the Army was as follows:

Army General Staff Order No. 647

1. The control over the Army Northern Seas Detachment will be transferred from the Fifth Fleet to the Imperial Headquarters at 2400 hours on 25 June.

2. The Army Northern Seas Detachment commander will cooperate with the Navy to secure the key positions on Attu. The task to destroy the enemy positions on Adak is cancelled.[56]

Based on the above-quoted orders, the *Nippon Rikugun* and *Nippon Kaigun* confirmed their long-term defensive strategy in the Aleutian area. The initially authorised strike against the American positions on Adak was cancelled for good since the offensive actions were considered too risky compared to potential gains. Yet, the defensive tasks were subjected to close cooperation between the Army and the Navy. The Japanese lost the transport ship *Nissan Maru* and several seaplanes due to enemy air raids in the first days after seizing Attu and Kiska, which proved the need to provide a more efficient anti-aircraft defence. Besides bringing more long-range artillery to both islands, the Navy and Army staff officers believed that best way to deter American bombers was to establish

Table 27: Comparison of the number of Japanese reconnaissance planes in the Aleutians, 15–23 June 1942.[57]				
	Jakes	Petes	Daves	In total
15 June	7	4	2	13
23 June	6	3	2	11

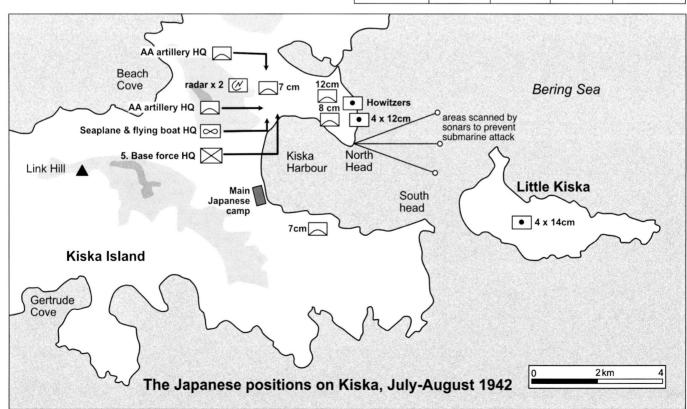

The Japanese positions on Kiska, summer 1942. (Map by Mark Thompson)

an independent air unit in the Aleutians. The Navy already had a small patrol wing in the area but expressed concern that any fully operational aircraft was worth its weight in gold should not be used

to wage the war of attrition in the North Pacific. On 23 June, the number of Japanese reconnaissance planes in the Aleutians (not assigned to the seaplane tenders) was as shown in Table 27.[10]

7
5 JULY 1942, ACTION OFF KISKA

7月5日の海戦
Shichigatsu itsuka No Kaisen

On June 21, two days before the Navy General Staff announced the long-term defence of the Aleutians, the Combined Fleet independently decided to reinforce the Attu and Kiska garrisons. Part of the 2nd Combined Special Naval Landing Force (968 men), the 11th and 12th Construction Units (324 men in total), six seaplane fighters and six midget submarines (initially part of the Midway Invasion Force) were soon sent to the North Pacific.[1] The Japanese Navy assigned this task to Captain Harada Kaku's team composed of seaplane tender *Chiyoda* (flagship), the 18th Destroyer Squadron (destroyers *Arare*, *Kasumi*, *Kagerō* and *Shiranui*) and transport ships *Argentina Maru*, *Kanō Maru* and *Kikukawa Maru*.[2]

It took the Japanese about a week to organise the first convoy. On 28 June, the 18th Destroyer Squadron (without *Kagerō*) departed Yokosuka, soon followed by *Chiyoda* and *Argentina Maru*, which headed for Kiska. The mission almost ended in a fiasco in its first hours due to the American submarine *Nautilus* (SS-168) being on war patrol in the vicinity of Tokyo Bay. Before dawn on 25 June, while passing off Ōshima Island, an undetected *Nautilus* fired two torpedoes when it encountered destroyer *Yamakaze* of the 24th Destroyer Division. Both missed the target, and in response, the Japanese ship attacked with depth charges. The American submarine avoided more severe damage and fired two torpedoes again after more than two hours following the victim. One of them proved to be a direct hit and was enough to sink *Yamakaze*.

The *Nautilus* then proceeded towards Yokosuka, where she spotted two ships and one cruiser in the early morning of 28 June. Her skipper, Lieutenant Commander William H. Brockman Jr., decided to try his chances and kick the hornet's nest. He did not know that the encountered vessel was not a cruiser but the seaplane tender *Chiyoda* that left for Kiska that same day. At about 1600 hours, Brockman ordered the firing of torpedoes at the largest Japanese ships. All of them missed their targets. The escort destroyers immediately spotted the intruder and sent a warning message to the Yokosuka Naval Base asking for help. The destroyer *Kagerō*, supported by minesweepers, escort ships, and minelayers, soon rushed to intercept the submarine. Several dozens of depth charges were dropped at a location where it was believed that the enemy vessel had hastily submerged just a quarter of an hour earlier. The American boat's report later emphasised that the entire crew was terrified to hear the number of explosions. Still, despite receiving some minor damage, *Nautilus* managed to get out of the death trap and return to Midway.[3]

After the end of the pursuit of the American submarine, *Kagerō* returned to Yokosuka, where she awaited *Kanō Maru* to be loaded with men and supplies. According to the original plan, the two ships were to set off on 3 July, yet due to logistical problems, the Japanese decided to detach *Kikukawa Maru*, which seemed to be a more suitable vessel for the mission. Finally, it was not until 9 July

that a small convoy of one transport ship and a destroyer departed Yokosuka and headed Kiska.[4]

The Combined Fleet was still not satisfied with the organisation of the Navy forces assigned to the defence of the Aleutian Islands. Therefore, on 1 July, it decided to create the AO Defense Force (*AO Bōbi Butai*; AO – Aleutians) commanded by Captain Satō Toshiharu. The new unit was still formally under the orders of the Fifth Fleet, but now it could independently react to enemy attacks and ask for its own reinforcements. This plan, at the first glance, was a rational solution to establish a separate command in the Aleutians area that would focus on the specific task of keeping Attu and Kiska. In fact, the AO Defense Force comprised only the 5th Garrison Unit (reorganised 3rd "Maizuru" Special Navy Landing Force), the 13th Submarine Chaser Squadron, one patrol boat, and the *Tōkō Kaigun Kōkūtai* flying boats detachment. Looking at those resources, even the most optimistic Japanese Navy officer spoke negatively about the combat potential of Satō's group, believing he was incapable of fighting with the Americans.[5]

By 30 June, US Navy cryptanalysts had confirmed that all Japanese carriers had likely withdrawn from the Aleutian area, leaving only a small surface force and an unspecified garrison on Attu and Kiska.[6] The ADC and TF-8 were relieved and decided to continue the air offensive operations against the newly established Japanese bases in the chain. Slightly better weather conditions in the last days of June allowed American bombers to appear over Kiska more often than before, but the effects of their bombing missions left much room for improvement. Evidence of the 11 AF's increased activity can be found in *Kamikawa Maru*'s war diary. In addition to information about the enemy reconnaissance missions, it also contains entries about the Flying Fortresses and Liberators' visits over Kiska on 24 and 26 June. According to the Japanese, four B-24s carried out a horizontal air attack from about 6,000 metres on 2 July, targeting *Kamikawa Maru*, *Kimikawa Maru* and *Fujisan Maru* stationing off Agattu at the time.[7] The American planes were greeted by fierce anti-aircraft fire, and apart from recording a few near misses, the Japanese vessels suffered no damage.[8] On the other side, American reports indicate that on 2 July, not four but seven B-24s took part in the strike, whose crews sighted three cruisers, three large transport ships and five destroyers. They reported several near misses (including two very close ones), which was a reasonably credible claim compared to the outcome of the attack described by the Japanese.[9]

In the early morning of 3 July, seven B-24s and two B-17s took off from Umnak to drop bombs on potential enemy positions in the nearby islands. After reaching the destination, it turned out that the dense clouds and thick fog prevented picking the targets, and the group decided to return to base. On the way back to Cold Bay, the Liberators dropped bombs on the Japanese base on Kiska and did not encounter any anti-aircraft resistance. Still, the crews could not confirm the effects of their improvised attack.[10]

The Type 2 seaplane fighter, better known as the Nakajima A6M2-N or under the Allied codename Rufe. From mid-June, it was the primary defensive weapon in the Kiska area against American bombers. (Kokuritsu Kokkai Toshokan)

The course of the Aleutian campaign made it clear to the Americans that their strategy of harassing the enemy bases with long-range air attacks was not yielding measurable results. Waging the efficient war of attrition relied on many resources that 11 AF lacked at that time in the North Pacific.[11] The number of bombers, the high risk of losing experienced aircrews and the ammunition consumption made it impossible to carry out frequent strikes against the Japanese bases. Considering the treacherous weather, which probably was the worst foe for both sides, Theobald decided to cancel the scheduled raids on Attu and Kiska and focus on reconnaissance patrols in the Bering Sea and photographic missions over the area controlled by the Japanese.[12]

On the afternoon of 4 July, after more than a week's journey to the North Pacific, a convoy composed of *Chiyoda*, *Argentina Maru*, *Arare*, *Kasumi* and *Shiranui* arrived at Kiska.[13] All ships temporarily dropped anchor except for the seaplane tender and the transport ship that entered the harbour to start unloading the supplies and equipment. Six Rufe seaplanes of *Tōkō Kaigun Kōkutai* were brought ashore as a matter of priority, which were in use by the Japanese the next day.[14] The morning of 5 July greeted the convoy with thick fog, significantly reducing visibility at the Kiska anchorage. Seeing the danger of the enemy attack, the Japanese destroyers raised their anchors and went into combat readiness to screen completely defenceless *Chiyoda* and *Argentina Maru*.

The Japanese had a good hunch, as the American submarine *Growler* was just three miles northeast of Kiska that day. *Growler* (SS-215) waited for the opportune moment to attack, but thick fog limited visibility to less than a mile. Unexpectedly, at about 0400 hours, the weather suddenly improved for the next 30 minutes. At 0413, observers on the submarine noticed the silhouettes of three vessels on course 90–110 degrees, bearing 244 degrees and at 7,000 metres distance. Accurate identification of the Japanese ships had not yet been possible, so the Americans initially assumed they had encountered cruisers that had just set off from Kiska. In the meantime, *Growler*'s skipper, Lieutenant Commander Howard Gilmore, passed the word to prepare for a surprise torpedo attack.

However, after several minutes, the enemy ships changed course and started to close to the island. Gilmore ordered to follow them, and when they stopped at 0539, he confirmed that they were the 1,700-ton Amagiri- or Fubuki-class destroyers. It took over 15 minutes to load No. 3 and No. 4 tubes again, and the submarine began slowly approaching the targets. If lookouts on the destroyers detected *Growler*, Gilmore was ready to fire torpedoes and escape into the dense fog.

Without hesitation, at 0555 hours, the submarine attacked three destroyers, firing one torpedo (heavy head) at each of the first two. Both proved to be a direct hit and struck amidship. She also fired two torpedoes (light head) at the last destroyer. The first "fish" missed the target and the second hit under the foremast. At 0600 hours, *Growler*'s crew noticed that the third destroyer fired her torpedoes from the tube nest between stacks.[15]

Again, Japanese accounts give a more credible outline of the events near Kiska on 5 July that the *Growler*'s attack can be described more accurately. The ship that suffered the most was *Arare*. Immediately after being hit by a torpedo (heavy head), the destroyer tried to shell the periscope seen on the water's surface with her main guns but soon due to severe damage to the keel, she broke in half. The ship sank in a few minutes, taking her 104 sailors to the bottom.[16] The second in line *Shiranui* was also hit by a heavy head torpedo. It exploded between frames No. 61 and No. 70, demolishing her engine room and killing three crew members. Her after compartments were flooded, and the ship became a sitting duck. In the meantime, *Kasumi* also fell victim to *Growler*'s salvo. One light head torpedo hit her in the hull under the main gun's turret No. 1, near frame No. 60, closer to the bow, tearing down the hull plating. A fire broke out on the vessel, quickly consuming the upper deck and control panels. At the same time, *Kasumi* began to take on water rapidly and lost steering control.[17] Crew casualties amounted to 10 men, most of whom were killed by the initial explosion.[18]

Soon after the *Growler*'s torpedo attack, the Fifth Fleet warned all ships: "one of our destroyers is sinking, another is on fire!". The Japanese knew the submarine had surprised them but did not expect

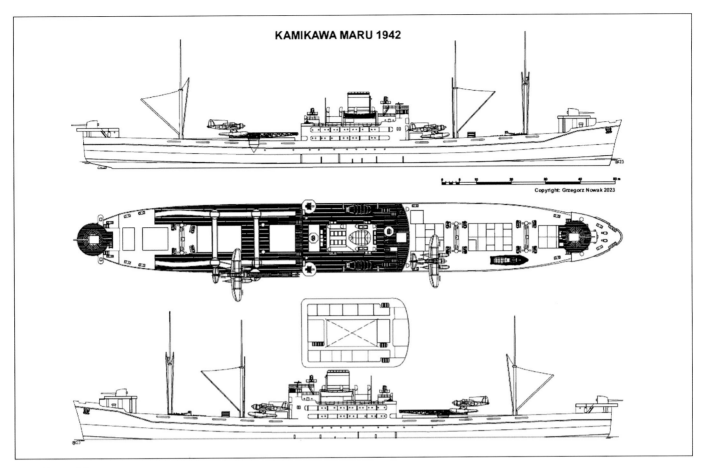

KAMIKAWA MARU 1942

Copyright: Grzegorz Nowak 2023

Kamikara Maru.

Kamikawa Maru (神川丸) was a seaplane tender initially built in December 1936 as a merchant vessel. She was requisitioned by *Nippon Kaigun* and refitted as a seaplane tender by October 1937. The vessel started her service by participating in the Second Sino-Japanese War. In May 1941, she was refitted in Sasebo and received the fully rotatable catapult on the starboard. In November 1941, *Kamikawa Maru* arrived at Sanya on Hainan Island to take part in the invasion of Malaya. Later, she supported the landing operations in British Borneo and clashed several times with Dutch fighters and bombers. After the conquest of the Dutch East Indies, she participated in the unsuccessful Operation MO and returned to Rabaul. The tender was assigned to the 11th Air Squadron as a part of Operation MI, but on 6 June, she was dispatched to the North Pacific to support landing operations on Attu and Kiska. At the beginning of the Aleutian Island campaign, she was a crucial ship for the Fifth Fleet, as she helped establish the seaplane base in Kiska. Her air group varied by the different period but mainly comprised 12 planes (nine operational and three spares) – four Jakes and eight Petes. (Drawing by Grzegorz Nowak)

the fatal blow to be dealt at escort destroyers. Instead of securing the seaplane tender and the transport ship, they prioritised saving *Kasumi* and *Shiranui* from sinking.[19] All the injured crew members were hastily transferred to *Chiyoda*, and the patrol boats rushed to intercept the intruder.[20]

The *Growler*'s crew initially observed the effects of their attack via the periscope but soon heard a distinctive whistling sound interpreted as a torpedo attack. Although Japanese records do not mention any torpedo counterattack that day, the American submarine was forced to submerge and withdraw. During the following hours, *Growler* avoided enemy patrol boats and reconnaissance planes that appeared in the sky. The submarine remained undetected and attempted to approach the Kiska anchorage again. Each time the Japanese were highly vigilant and left no illusions that another torpedo attack would mean exposing *Growler*'s position and certain death to the entire crew. Despite the risk, Gilmore wanted to try his luck one last time on 7 July. While approaching Kiska, however, the submarine was spotted and then attacked with depth charges by one of the Japanese escort destroyers. *Growler* luckily avoided hits, but Gilmore knew that further gambles would not bring any benefits, so he decided to return to Dutch Harbor.[21]

The balance of losses on 5 July was tragic for the *Nippon Kaigun*. Within five minutes of the ill-fated morning, *Arare* was lost, and *Shiranui* and *Kasumi* were severely damaged and unable to retreat

from the Aleutian area on their own. It was not until the following weeks that other destroyers towed them to the shipyards in the home islands. In late August, the Ministry of Navy decided that both vessels would be temporarily moved to "the special reserve" for the repairs period.[22] However, due to the extent of the damage, *Kasumi* remained at the shipyard until 30 June 1943 and *Shiranui* until 15 November 1943.[23]

To make matters worse, just the previous evening of 4 July,[24] the Japanese lost destroyer *Nenohi*, which was sunk off Cape Sabak (near Agattu) by the American submarine *Triton* (SS-201).[25] At the time, the ship was moving at nine knots in thick fog, covering *Kamikawa Maru* during a routine change of position to continue air operations in the Aleutians.[26]

The weather was so terrible that the *Kamikawa Maru*'s crew did not know what happened to the destroyer, which was literally lost on the route and had not given a sign of life for over 24 hours. Upon reaching Kiska, the skipper of the seaplane tender ordered the destroyer *Inazuma* to carry out a search mission for *Nenohi* off Agattu on 6 July. Unsurprisingly, this task was hampered by heavy fog in MacDonald Bay, but observers soon noticed men on the shore begging for help, a group of 36 survivors from *Nenohi* who left the sinking vessel at the last moment. They were soon transferred on *Inazuma* and properly provided with medical help. Their tales uncovered the mystery of *Nenohi* vanishing – she was unexpectedly

Japanese convoy heading to Kiska in the second half of June. In the background, the destroyer *Nenohi*, which will fall victim to the *Triton*. In the foreground, embarked float seaplanes Rufe for *Tōkō Kaigun Kōkūtai*. (Maru Special)

hit amidships by one torpedo. A colossal blast broke her hull in half, and she went down in minutes. The crew also testified to the steadfast attitude of her skipper, Lieutenant Commander Terauchi Saburō, who was last seen climbing onto the sinking part of the hull while chanting briskly *Nenohi banzai!* (Long live Nenohi!).[27] He and 188 men disappeared into the depths of the North Pacific. Many of those who escaped the death trap and bailed out the ship did not get to shore, freezing to death in the icy water.[28]

In a few hours of July's first week, the Fifth Fleet irretrievably lost two destroyers (*Arare* and *Nenohi*) and the other two (*Kasumi* and *Shiranui*) were put out of action for long months. Given that the AO Defense Force had almost begged to deploy more surface vessels to the North Pacific, the Navy General Staff could not reinforce the Kiska and Attu garrisons until the end of summer. The Japanese defeat at Kiska was also mentioned in the famous journal of Rear Admiral Ugaki Matome, Chief of Staff of the Combined Fleet, who presented the outcome of the American submarine attack in a laconic yet reliable manner.[29]

While the Japanese regarded the sinking of *Nenohi* as a typical operational loss, the mistakes made by the 18th Destroyer Division at the very end of the convoy's route, in a theoretically safe coastal zone, became the subject of various comments. Prince Takamatsunomiya mentioned in his diary that the Chief of Staff of the Fifth Fleet shared his opinion during a private conversation, emphasising the importance of the human factor, i.e. the fatigue of the crews after a long journey to the North Pacific. Nevertheless, both officers still did not know why the destroyers dropped their anchors, did not keep a considerable distance, and disregarded other

safety measures.[30] Captain Miyazawa Yoshito, the 18th Destroyer Squadron commander, later explained that the dense fog was seen by some officers as a positive factor – it could help protect the ships and discourage an enemy submarine from approaching the Kiska anchorage. Miyazawa also admitted that his men were not sufficiently familiar with the climatic conditions of the Aleutian area before leaving Japan, and it ultimately led to the tragedy.[31] Despite his accurate and fair assessment of mistakes that were made, Miyazawa himself, in a typical Japanese manner, felt responsible for losing three destroyers. Trying to save his unit's honour, he attempted to commit ritual *seppuku* on the day of the attack but was miraculously saved by medics on *Chiyoda*.[32]

Apart from the US Navy submarine operations in the Aleutian waters, the 11 AF continued, within the weather limitation, air strikes against the Japanese positions on Attu and Kiska. The TF-8 War Diary summarises the action taken from 14 June to 7 July as shown in Table 28.

Zero's Mystery Comes to an End
零戦の秘密が終わりになる
Zerosen no Himitsu ga Owari ni Naru

On 10 July, just over a month after the opening moves in the Aleutian campaign, the Americans unexpectedly discovered the secret of the famous Zero fighter, giving another crucial contribution to the final victory in the Pacific War.[34] At dusk on 9 July, the Catalina piloted by Lieutenant (jg.) William Thies took off on a routine reconnaissance patrol and navigated by dead reckoning, which could be considered unreliable and anachronistic, but in the weather conditions of the

The destroyer *Arare*, sunk by *Growler*. (Traces of War)

North Pacific often there was no other alternative. As expected, due to the strong crosswind, the crew of the flying boat lost its way and found itself about 240 miles east of the planned route. Thies first had to find the nearest landmark to establish his position and set the correct course. By a twist of fate, he found his PBY near Shumagin Island, and after confirming his position, decided to return to the base directly across Akutan Island. Catalina crews did not like to fly over the land because the sudden temperature jumps resulted in unpleasant turbulence, and thick fog often limited the visibility.

While flying over the corner of Akutan, one of the crew members suddenly shouted: "Hey! There's a plane down there. It has meatballs on its wings!". Thies decided to go down to get a better look at the spotted object. Although he did not know they had found the Zero fighter, he was convinced that the matter required further investigation. The wreck was circled for several minutes, its position marked on the map, and then PBY returned to Dutch Harbor. Once there, Thies tried to convince his commanding officer that he had to return to Akutan to examine the Japanese plane. Even though Patrol Wing 4 considered every crew in the Aleutians worth its

Table 28: Summary of the 11 AF air operations in the Aleutians, 14 June – 7 July 1942.[33]		
Date	**Forces**	**Target/Details**
14 June	2 x PBYs 4 x B-17s 3 x B-24s	flying boats and seaplanes stationing at Kiska
15–16 June	-	-
17 June	1 x PBY	submarine
18 June	4 x B-24s 3 x B-17s 1 x LB-30	Enemy ships reported in Kiska Harbor
19 June	-	-
20 June	3 x PBYs	Seven 500lb bombs dropped on Kiska shore base through a solid overcast
21 June	9 x B-24s (three returned)	Enemy ships reported in Kiska Harbor
22–24 June	-	-
25 June	1 x LB-30 11 x heavy bombers (only two dropped bombs)	A heavy cruiser and three destroyers in Kiska Harbor. Twenty hits observed in the town and supply area and a near miss on a destroyer
26 June	5 x B-24s	Bombed Kiska Harbor from an altitude of 2,700 to 3,300 metres
27 June – 1 July	-	-
2 July	7 x B-24s	Bombers sent off from Otten Point against Kiska; later reported several near misses and two very near misses on a transport ship and destroyer off Agattu Island.
3 July	7 x B-24s 2 x B-17s	Bombers sent off for an attack on the Near Islands but eventually B-24s dropped bombs on Kiska; no reports from B-17s
4–5 July	-	-
6 July	4 x B-24s 2 x B-17s 1 x LB-30	Planes took off to attack Kiska and Agattu Islands; the latter was obscured by clouds and planes were redirected to Kiska where B-24s dropped 40 and B-17s dropped 16 bombs through an overcast; no result nor enemy aircraft were reported
7 July	6 x B-24s	Ground targets at Kiska

weight in gold at the time, he obtained permission to conduct an independent investigation.

The following day, the first research team, accompanied by the photographer, Mate Arthur W. Bauman, set off in a small speedboat to the northeast. The plane was found without much difficulty. PO1c Koga's Zero from *Ryūjō* (Mitsubishi A6M2 mod. 21, serial number: 4593) crashed on 4 June while attempting an emergency landing on a grassy plain. As noted earlier in the book, according to *Nippon Kaigun* procedures, the accompanying wingmen should have destroyed the aircraft to prevent it from falling into enemy hands. However, not knowing whether Koga survived the accident, they left the battlefield, hoping he could be rescued by a submarine in the following days.[35]

Although the American research group was not sure whether or not it would fall into an enemy ambush, they could not find anyone on the island. Warrant Officer Robert Larson, the flying boat's co-pilot, described his impressions of first contact with the Zero in a little more detail:

Bauman took pictures and we made notes, then attempted to tip the plane right side up. It was more than we could handle, and about the best we could do was to prop the tail up so we could get the pilot and his gear out. We also removed the 20mm Oerlikon guns from the wings. Chief Petty Officer Duncan, a gunner's mate sent to evaluate the armament, had no trouble field stripping them. We accused him of getting his early training with the Japanese Navy.

We were rather surprised at the details of the airplane. It was well built, with simple, unique features. Inspection plates could be opened by pushing on a black dot with a finger. A latch would open and one could pull the plate out. The wing tips folded by unlatching them and pushing them up by hand. As it lay, we could see but one bullet hole in it, in the vicinity of the oil cooler. The pilot had a parachute and life raft, somewhat discrediting the then common theory that Japanese pilots weren't interested in survival. We could find no sword.

Thies knew from the beginning that they had found a Zero, which was additionally in excellent technical condition. The shortest member of the team, Albert Knack, crawled into the cabin of the plane, pulled out Koga's body, and then photographed for evidence before burying him near the plane. During the first inspection, the Americans were primarily interested in finding the information that might help in intelligence work. Still, the position of the Zero made it challenging to access all devices and the cabin. Soon, it became apparent that the plane needed to be turned over and taken out of the grassy water as soon as possible. Thies had neither the manpower nor the equipment, so he returned to the base with exciting news from his expedition.

A day later, a second team led by Lieutenant Robert C. Kirmse was sent to Akutan. The first attempt was made to lift the plane, but the Zero was firmly stuck in the mud. Kirmse could not also bring onto land the heavy equipment since the transport ship *Mary Anne* was damaged during the unloading, so he could not continue his mission. However, the Americans gave Koga a Christian burial this time, and he was inhumed on a nearby hill.

The third team arrived at Akutan on 15 July and managed to get the Zero out of the mud with a bulldozer, then carefully hauled it over wooden logs to the barge. The fighter was taken to Dutch Harbor, carefully turned right-side up by the harbour crane, and properly cleaned. The Navy's Chief Radioman, Bryan Franks, dismantled all the fighter's radio equipment and discovered to his surprise, that the New York-based Fairchild Aero Camera Company manufactured the radio direction finder. However, the Japanese were still relying on their equipment since the primary radio receiver was produced by Tōyō Electric Company (東洋電機製造株式会社, Tōyō Denki Seizō Kabushikigaisha).

On 25 July, the Akutan Zero left Dutch Harbor onboard the transport ship *St. Mihiel*, and a week later, it arrived in Seattle and was soon sent to San Diego for a detailed examination. After necessary repairs and modifications, the Japanese fighter scrambled again under the US Navy insignia on 20 September.[35] Analysing the Zero's technical strengths and weaknesses helped American pilots develop more effective methods of fighting with the famous enemy plane and designers to prepare better blueprints of new aircraft that had a decisive impact on the final victory in the Pacific War.

8
SUMMER EXCHANGE OF BLOWS

夏の打撃を行う
Natsu no Dageki o Okonau

Considering the envisaged offensive in the South Pacific in the third week of August, on the night of 7/8 July, the Combined Fleet decided to withdraw all four aircraft carriers from the Aleutians. After minor refits in the shipyards, the reorganised *Kidō Butai* was to proceed to Truk and actively participate in naval air operations against Allied positions in New Guinea, the Solomon Islands, northern Australia, and their advanced bases in New Caledonia and Fiji. As a direct result of this strategy for the second part of 1942, the Fifth Fleet was left alone in the North Pacific with limited resources and the task of defending the newly established positions in Attu and Kiska. Therefore, to better make use of the few ships at its disposal, the *Nippon Kaigun* created the Escort Unit commanded by Rear Admiral Ōmori Sentarō and composed of the light cruiser *Abukuma* and the 6th Destroyer Squadron (*Akatsuki*, *Inazuma*, *Ikazuchi* and *Hibiki*) and the 21st Destroyer Squadron (*Wakaba*, *Hatsuharu* and *Hatsushimo*). Two days later, the Combined Fleet issued Operational Order No. 181, establishing that the following units would be responsible for the defence of the Aleutian area from 14 July: Northern Forces, the Fifth Fleet, the 1st Torpedo Squadron, part of the *Tōkō Kaigun Kōkūtai*, part of the 3rd "Maizuru" Special Naval Landing Force, construction units and other patrol forces. Following the entry into force of this order, the heavy cruiser *Nachi* was also temporarily assigned to the 21st Cruiser Squadron.[1]

The task of the Escort Unit was to cover the convoy on the return route to Japan. Initially, the transport ship *Argentina Maru* was escorted by *Abukuma* and *Inazuma*, but only the latter

PO1c Koga's Zero from the light carrier *Ryūjō*, which crashed on Akutan on 4 June. (Naval History and Heritage Command)

The 'Akutan Zero'. This photograph was taken on 17 July at the Dutch Harbor marina, a week after the discovery of the slightly damaged plane. (Naval History and Heritage Command)

Rear Admiral Ōmori Sentarō. (NDL)

vessel accompanied it until 15 July, when they reached Yokosuka. On 12 July, *Chiyoda* accompanied by *Hatsuharu* set off from Kiska and entered the Inland Sea a week later.[2] On the evening of 18 July, a second convoy comprising the transport ship *Kikuchi Maru* and *Kagerō* arrived in Kiska.[3] As the 18th Destroyer Squadron had lost three of its four ships, *Kagerō* was assigned to the 15th Destroyer Squadron based on the Ministry of Navy order issued on 20 July.[4]

The most significant concern for the *Nippon Kaigun* in early July remained enemy submarine activity off Attu and Kiska. After *Growler's* successful torpedo attack, the Japanese expected that the Americans would continue to harass Japanese vessels off Kiska. Indeed, on 10 July, the submarine *Grunion* (SS-216) with Lieutenant Commander Mannert L. Abele in command, began her first war patrol north of Kiska. Five days later, *Grunion* encountered a Japanese destroyer of unspecified type and attacked her with four torpedoes. The enemy responded with depth charges, but they all missed the intruder. As it turned out later, Submarine Chasers No. 25 and No. 27 fell victim to the submarine's salvo.[5] This meant that the 13th Submarine Chaser Squadron, responsible for defending the entrance to Kiska's harbour, was left with only Submarine Chaser No. 26.[6] Additionally, *Grunion's* crew did not know that they had also killed the Japanese squadron commander, Lieutenant Commander Haruyama Aki. Less than two weeks after its establishment, the AO Defense Force command faced extreme difficulties keeping naval forces near Attu and Kiska. Furthermore, Captain Satō could not rely on reinforcements from the Combined Fleet since most of the ships were already during the preparation for being deployed to the South Pacific.[7]

However, *Nippon Kaigun* could also boast of the first measurable successes of their submarines in the Aleutians. In the late hours of 14 July, *I-7*, with Lieutenant Commander Koizumi Koi'ichi in command, spotted an American transport ship *Arcata* in the Unimak Isthmus, which was identified as a medium-sized freighter.[8] The vessel was en route from the Alaskan city of Bethel to Seattle. Koizumi felt confident enough that he even decided to reveal his position and shell the enemy ship to send her to the bottom despite scoring some torpedo hits earlier. Eight days later, 25 of 33 *Arcata*'s crew members, drifting on a rescue raft off Kodiak, were found by the destroyer *Kane* and the fishing boat *Yukon*.[9]

Just two days later, the Japanese submarine *I-2* encountered one large Army or Navy transport ship and a medium-sized freighter while patrolling the area south of Unimak. The *I-2* skipper ordered the enemy vessels destroyed with guns, but when his ship went to the surface, he was spotted by the flying boat. Since the presence of the American aircraft was a deadly threat to *I-2*, the Japanese submerged immediately, allowing both transport ships to escape.[10]

Besides submarines, the Japanese also tried to harass Americans with their seaplanes brought to the Aleutians area by convoys earlier this month. On 11 July, *Tōkō Kaigun Kōkūtai* sent aircraft over Umnak eight times, keeping the Americans busy for the whole day. Rufes first provided reconnaissance duties, then dropped 30kg bombs and machine-gunned enemy B-24 bombers stationed at Fort Glenn, trying to slow down their take-off. In the following days, *Tōkō Kaigun Kōkūtai* carried out scouting missions around Kiska, and on 16 July, two flying boats attacked one unidentified enemy vessel off Kanaga Island. One dropped one 250kg bomb but did not confirm scoring the hit, and the other strafed the target.[11] On 17 July, two flying boats carrying bombs repeated the attack on Kanaga Island and Seguam Island, again with no clear result. In response, B-24s and B-17s bombed Kiska and destroyed one seaplane fighter.[12]

On 20 July, three flying boats led by Lieutenant Matsumoto, armed with twelve 250kg bombs in total, raided a spotted destroyer off Atka Island and reported scoring several hits. In fact, the

Table 29: *Tōkō Kaigun Kōkūtai* activity in the Aleutians, 11–20 July 1942.[14]

Date	Pilot/Commander	Details
11 July (Rufe) take-off: 1050 (first *shōtai*) return: 2015 (last *shōtai*)	1. Lt Yamada 2. (unknown)	did not encounter the enemy
	1. PO2c Ōgawa 2. (unknown)	2 x 30kg dropped 220 x 20mm rounds expended 600 x 7.7mm rounds expended
	1. SLt Saitō 2. (unknown)	did not encounter the enemy
	1. Lt Yamada 2. (unknown)	2 x 30kg dropped
	1. Lt Yamada 2. (unknown)	did not encounter the enemy
	1. Ens Saitō 2. (unknown)	220 x 20mm rounds expended 400 x 7.7mm rounds expended
	1. PO2c Ōgawa 2. (unknown)	did not encounter the enemy
	1. PO2c Ōgawa 2. (unknown)	as above
11 July (Mavis) take-off: 1723 return: 1838	WO Iizuka	anti-sub mission around Kiska
14 July (Mavis) take-off: 1910 return: 2050 (first mission) take-off: 2115 return: 2235 (second mission)	PO1c Nakano	as above
15 July (Mavis) take-off: 0803 return: 1135 (anti-sub) take-off: 1623–1630 return: 1807–1820 (reconnaissance)	1. WO Iizuka	anti-sub mission around Kiska
	1. WO Iizuka 2. Ens Naitō	did not spot the enemy
16 July (Rufe) take-off: 0830 (first *shōtai*) return: 1620 (last *shōtai*)	1. Ens Saitō 2. (unknown)	did not encounter the enemy
	1. PO2c Ōgawa 2. (unknown)	
	1. Lt Yamada 2. (unknown)	
	1. Ens Saitō 2. (unknown)	
16 July (Mavis) take-off: 0910–0920 return: 1244–1517	1. SLt Obata	30 x 7.7mm rounds expended
	2. SLt Kijima	1 x 250kg bomb dropped
	3. Lt Matsumoto	did not encounter the enemy

Japanese attacked the seaplane tender *Gillis*, which did not record any damage that day.[13] Soon afterwards, until the end of July, *Tōkō Kaigun Kōkūtai* did not take offensive actions and focused on carrying out regular reconnaissance patrols around Kiska.

Table 29: *Tōkō Kaigun Kōkūtai* activity in the Aleutians, 11–20 July 1942. (*continued*)

17 July (Mavis) take-off: 0820–0825 return: 1148–1405 (first mission) take-off: 0820–0825 return: 1148–1405 (anti-sub mission)	1. WO Iizuka	spotted one enemy plane
	2. Ens Naitō	2 x 250kg bombs dropped on military facilities at Kanaga Island through an overcast
	1. Lt Yoneyama	2 x 250kg bombs dropped on Seguam Island through an overcast
17 July (Rufe) take-off: 0830 (first *shōtai*) return: 2000 (last *shōtai*)	1. PO2c Ōgawa 2. (unknown)	did not encounter the enemy
	1. Ens Saitō 2. (unknown)	as above
	1. Lt Yamada 2. (unknown)	as above
	1. Lt Yamada 2. (unknown)	as above
	1. Lt Yamada 2. (unknown)	240 x 20mm rounds expended 640 x 7.7mm rounds expended
	1. Ens Saitō 2. (unknown)	2 x 30kg bombs dropped 240 x 20mm rounds expended 750 x 7.7mm rounds expended (one seaplane damaged by two 7.7mm rounds)
	1. PO2c Ōgawa 2. (unknown)	200 x 20mm rounds expended 600 x 7.7mm rounds expended
	1. Lt Yamada 2. (unknown)	200 x 20mm rounds expended 300 x 7.7mm rounds expended
	1. Ens Saitō 2. (unknown)	200 x 20mm rounds expended 400 x 7.7mm rounds expended
	1. PO2c Ōgawa 2. (unknown)	180 x 20mm rounds expended 400 x 7.7mm rounds expended
	1. Ens Saitō 2. (unknown)	did not encounter the enemy
	1. PO2c Ōgawa 2. (unknown)	240 x 20mm rounds expended 800 x 7.7mm rounds expended
	1. Ens Saitō 2. (unknown)	2 x 30kg bombs dropped 240 x 20mm rounds expended 300 x 7.7mm rounds expended (one seaplane damaged)
	1. Lt Yamada 2. (unknown)	240 x 20mm rounds expended 550 x 7.7mm rounds expended (one seaplane damaged)
	1. Lt Yamada 2. (unknown)	did not encounter the enemy
18 July (Rufe) take-off: 1715 return: 1800	1. Lt Yamada 2. (unknown)	as above
18 July (Mavis) take-off: 1810 return: 2025	1. SLt Obata	did not spot the enemy

US Navy command ordered *Grunion* to return to the vicinity of the island to track the enemy's moves and harass his shipping lines. This time the Japanese had several vessels on the spot: Submarine Chaser No. 26, patrol ships *Ukishima* and *Ishizaki*, and the ocean escort ship *Ishigaki*, which had arrived from Attu just two days earlier. Nevertheless, on 30 July, *Grunion* attacked the transport ship *Kanō Maru* with four torpedoes. The first one went straight under her keel but failed to explode due to the magnetic pistol failure. The second torpedo was equally defective, and the warhead did not detonate on collision with the hull. The third torpedo exploded near the starboard engine room, causing minor damage to *Kanō Maru*.[15] The fourth and final fish missed the target and circled back, striking the periscope supports on the submerged *Grunion* without exploding. The Japanese did not see exactly what happened to the submarine, but after a while, they heard a dull explosion in the depths and noticed that large patches of oil began to appear on the surface gradually. This was considered sufficient evidence that the intruder had been destroyed.[16] Indeed, in American records, 30 July is the date of the last contact with *Grunion*, which was presumed lost with all crew.[17] In 2008, a group of US Navy researchers confirmed the discovery of its wreck about 10 miles northeast of Kiska. A detailed investigation showed that the unfortunate torpedo hit made the rear dive plane jam and triggered a sequence of events that caused the loss of depth control. *Grunion* went well below her maximum operational depth and imploded at about 300 metres.[18]

Patrol Wing 4 also suffered unexpected losses by the end of the month. On 20 July, a PBY piloted by Lieutenant Roy Green of VP-43 crashed on take-off, and the entire crew was lost. On 30 July, another Catalina flown

The second month of struggle in the Aleutian Islands ended with a surprise action in Kiska Harbor. After the first success, the

Table 29: Tōkō Kaigun Kōkūtai activity in the Aleutians, 11–20 July 1942. (continued)

19 July (Rufe) take-off: 0730 (first *shōtai*) return: 1745 (last *shōtai*)	1. PO2c Ōgawa 2. (unknown)	did not encounter the enemy
	1. Lt Yamada 2. (unknown) 3. (unknown)	as above
	1. Ens Saitō 2. (unknown)	as above
	1. PO2c Ōgawa 2. (unknown)	as above
19 July (Mavis) take-off: 1455 return: 2215	1. WO Iizuka	did not spot the enemy
20 July (Rufe) take-off: 0750 (first *shōtai*) return: 1930 (last *shōtai*)	1. SLt Saitō 2. (unknown)	did not encounter the enemy
	1. PO2c Ōgawa 2. (unknown)	dogfight with two B-17s 240 x 20mm rounds expended 300 x 7.7mm rounds expended (one seaplane seriously damaged)
	1. Lt Yamada 2. (unknown) 3. (unknown)	did not encounter the enemy
	1. SLt Saitō 2. (unknown)	did not encounter the enemy
	1. PO2c Ōgawa 2. (unknown)	as above
	1. Lt Yamada 2. (unknown)	as above
	1. PO2c Ōgawa 2. (unknown)	as above
	1. PO2c Ōgawa 2. (unknown)	as above
20 July (Mavis) take-off: 0810 (all scrambled) return: 1705 (last plane)	1. Lt Matsumoto 2. SLt Kijima 3. Ens Naitō	12 x 250kg bombs dropped on a transport ship in Kuluk Bay (Atka), then separately carried out a reconnaissance mission over Kanaga, Amchitka and Unimak
20 July (Mavis) take-off: 0513 return: 0722	1. Cdr Itō	did not spot the enemy

by Lieutenant (jg.) D.A. Brough crashed on landing outside Nazan Bay. Although three crew members were rescued, operational losses resulting from random accidents were always distressing for any flight personnel.[19] 11 AF air operations against the Japanese between 8 and 31 July were as shown in Table 30.

Bombardment of Kiska
キスカ島に対する砲撃
Kisuka-tō Shima ni tai suru Hōgeki

Like other Japanese strategic initiatives in 1942, the Combined Fleet plans in the South Pacific for August were intercepted by US Navy intelligence. The American command decided to accelerate preparations for the first counter-offensive in the Pacific War. It was clear from the beginning that the landing of the 1st Marine Division on Guadalcanal required decent surface and air cover. Admiral Nimitz had no choice but to commit most of the available carriers, one battleship and several cruisers and destroyers to support the amphibious operation. Theobald turned out to be the biggest victim of the envisaged offensive operation in the Solomon Islands since he could not count on any reinforcements in the nearest future. Similarly to Hosogaya, Theobald was now expected to continue the struggle for the Aleutians with limited resources. In early August, the Aleutians Defense Command had the following forces:

Task Force 8 "Tare", Rear Admiral Robert A. Theobald
(1) <u>Air Group</u>, Brigadier General William O. Butler
1.1. <u>Air Striking Unit</u>:
• Bombardment: 28th Composite Group, 30th Bombardment Group (11 heavy bombers and 23 medium bombers)
• Reconnaissance: 406th Bombardment Squadron, 8th Bomber-Reconnaissance Squadron of the RCAF (21 medium bombers)
• Fighters: 11th, 18th, 42nd, 54th, 57th Fighter Squadrons; 111th Fighter Squadron of the RCAF (98 fighters)
1.2. <u>Air Search Unit</u>, Captain Leslie E. Gehres:
• Patrol Squadrons 41, 43, 51, 62 (11 PBY flying boats, 20 PBY-5A amphibious flying boats).

• seaplane tenders *Avocet*, *Casco*, *Gillis*, *Hulbert* and *Teal*
• destroyer *Kane*

(2) <u>Escort and Patrol Group</u>, Rear Admiral John W. Reeves Jr.
• gunboat *Charleston*
• minesweeper *Oriole*
• old destroyers *Dent*, *Gilmer*, *Humphreys*, *Sands* and *Talbot*
• coast guard and patrol vessels

(3) <u>Submarine Group</u>, Lieutenant Commander Oswald S. Colclough
• submarines: *Finback*, *Grunion* † (30.07), *Trigger*, *Triton* and *Tuna*

The submarine USS *Grunion* in March 1942. (Open source)

Table 30: Summary of the 11 AF operations against the Japanese in the Aleutian Islands, 8–31 July 1942.[20]

Date	Forces	Target/Details
11 July	3 x B-24s	Dropped bombs one cruiser stationing in Kiska Harbor through an overcast
12–16 July	-	-
17 July	1 x PBY 3 x B-24s 3 x B-17s	Attacked one enemy submarine and military facilities on Kiska
18 July	2 x B-17s	Dropped bombs on military facilities on Kiska
19–20 July	-	-
21 July	2 x B-17s	Dropped 40 bombs on camp area of Kiska Harbor
22 July	8 x heavy bombers	Dropped bombs on camp area of Kiska Harbor
23–27 July	-	-
28 July	2 x PBYs	Attacked the enemy destroyer south of Vega Point (Kiska)
29–31 July	-	-

and destroyers. Pursuant to TF-8 Operation Plan No. 8-42, which came into force on 19 July, the bombardment of Kiska was initially scheduled for 22 July, but it was postponed for five days due to poor weather.[22] On 27 July, the weather was still terrible,[23] and forecasts for the following days were equally pessimistic, so on 1 August, under Operation Plan No. 9-42, the bombardment of Kiska was suspended once again.[24] The new deadline was set up on 7 August, and the new weather forecasts indicated a highly probable improvement in visibility and sea conditions. Despite the initial setbacks, the US Navy had a generally positive attitude towards the mission, as outlined in the Operations Report: "THE JAPS SHOULD BE AFFECTED BY DIVERSIONARY RAIDS AND ATTACKS. THESE ARE WELL WORTHWHILE."[25]

The Americans expected that during the upcoming mission, TF-8 might encounter strong enemy resistance. Japanese surface and air forces in the Aleutian area on 1 August were estimated at: two heavy cruisers (Nachi-class), one light cruiser, eight destroyers (Shigure-class), eight submarines, one seaplane tender, two freighters, six submarine chasers (plus many other patrol boats), four reconnaissance aircraft, six scouting seaplanes and eight seaplane fighters. The possibility that the enemy had one or more aircraft carriers in the North Pacific that might later arrive on the stage was also considered. Additionally, TF-8 was warned of minefields and hidden 150mm coastal artillery batteries during the approach to Kiska. Speaking about the island, the Americans predicted that only one heavy cruiser was stationed there, and no other enemy forces were spotted by the reconnaissance planes within a 30 mile arc, suggesting that the Japanese did not expect the bombardment.[26]

(4) Main Body, Rear Admiral William W. Smith
- heavy cruisers: *Indianapolis* (F) and *Louisville*
- light cruiser: *Honolulu*, *Nashville* and *St. Louis*
- destroyer: *Case*, *Gridley*, *McCall* and *Reid*
- fast minesweeper *Elliot*

(5) Tanker Group
- oiler *Ramapo*
- old destroyers: *Brooks* and *King*[21]

Theobald was aware that sooner or later, the Japanese would learn that the US Navy had redeployed most of its forces to the South Pacific. In the meantime, he intended to use the available surface forces to prevent the enemy from building-up new positions in the Aleutian Islands. Since the air raids had minimal results, and the war of attrition could not be based on individual submarine successes, Theobald decided to carry out the traditional bombardment of Japanese shore installations by a task group comprising cruisers

Since Admiral Nimitz insisted on putting more pressure on the enemy, Theobald decided to assign the Main Force of Rear Admiral William W. Smith for the bombardment of Kiska. A team composed of heavy cruisers *Indianapolis* (F) and *Louisville*, light cruisers *Honolulu*, *Nashville* and *St. Louis*, the destroyers *Case*, *Gridley*, *McCall*, *Reid* and the fast minesweeper *Elliot*, departed Kodiak in two groups on the afternoon and evening of 3 August, heading for 51°13'N 177°10'E. The plan was to approach the enemy positions from the south on 7 August, then enter Vega Bay, where Smith intended to open fire at about 1700 hours. Approximately 160 American and Canadian bombers, fighters and reconnaissance aircraft of the Air Striking Unit were to provide continuous support for the Main Force. Particular emphasis was placed on the accurate reconnaissance of Japanese forces during approach and retreat and disorganising their air and ground forces a few hours before the planned bombardment.[27] TF-8 command believed this would allow the Main Force to get close enough to the Kiska camp without the risk of the enemy counterattack.[28] Preparations for the mission had already begun with the entry into force of Operation Plan No. 8-42 when *Gillis* and *Casco* had taken forward positions at Nazan Bay and Kuluk Bay.[29] These movements did not go unnoticed by the Japanese, who scrambled three flying boats and attacked American tenders the following day, an action described in the previous section of the monograph.

Regardless of TF-8 plans for the Air Search Unit, Smith could rely on reconnaissance planes on his cruisers at any moment. Each disposed of at least two Curtiss SOC Seagull seaplanes, which could carry out scouting tasks and direct artillery fire.

In the early morning of 7 August, the Main Force was less than 170 miles southeast of Kiska. In one of the first points of the daily report, Smith recorded favourable weather conditions and recommended proceeding with the mission.[30] By 0945 hours, the destroyers and the minelayer finished refuelling, and the group proceeded on 345 degrees course at a speed of 25 knots to the so-called Point Mike (coordinates 51°10'N 177°19'E) designated as a concentration point prior to the bombardment.

Around noon Smith received a detailed weather report indicating calm sea, moderate north-westerly wind and eight to 10 miles of visibility. Overcast at 160 metres was also positive news for the Americans, who did not have to worry about being detected by enemy scouting planes from a long distance, albeit they must carry on with unreliable dead reckoning. Despite this, Smith decided to proceed with the bombardment of Kiska and slightly postponed the mission to 1800 hours. Based on the latest meteorological data, he expected to go straight into large masses of cold air at low altitudes, causing dense fog and reducing visibility.

Initially, the Americans planned that the Main Forces would be divided into three smaller groups that would simultaneously shell Japanese positions from different angles to provide accurate gunfire by each class of vessels. Therefore, all four destroyers were placed 14,000 metres from Kiska Harbor, three light cruisers 16,000 metres, whereas the two heavy cruisers kept 18,000 metres distance.[31]

At 1430 hours, the Main Force slowed to 15 knots to permit *Elliot* to stream sweeping gear and resumed 25 knots speed after an hour. At 1630 hours, the Americans reached Point Mike, from where they continued the approach (heading for Cape Vega) at 20 knots. According to the expectations, the group suddenly ran into a heavy fog.[32] The weather temporarily improved at 1747 hours, and the visibility was reported as less than seven miles. Three minutes later, each cruiser catapulted two seaplanes. *Indianapolis* began plotting radar ranges and bearings of what was believed to be Kiska Mountain and Segula Peak. One of the seaplanes gave an

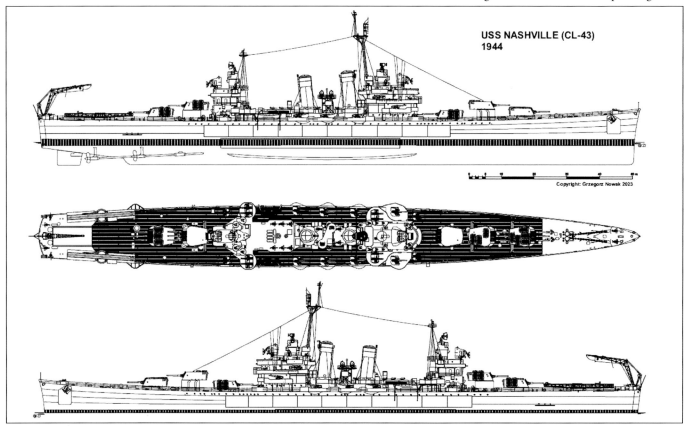

USS *Nashville* (CL-43) was one of nine completed *Brooklyn*-class cruisers, launched in October 1937 and commissioned in June 1938. During the outbreak of the Pacific War, she was stationed in the Central Atlantic and performed escort duties to Iceland. In March 1942, she was sent to the Pacific Ocean and participated in the Doolittle Raid. On 14 May, Nashville became the flagship of Task Force 8, and during the first month of the Aleutian Island campaign, she was one of the most important warships of Rear Admiral Theobald. (Drawing by Grzegorz Nowak)

The heavy cruiser USS *Indianapolis* in 1939. (Open source)

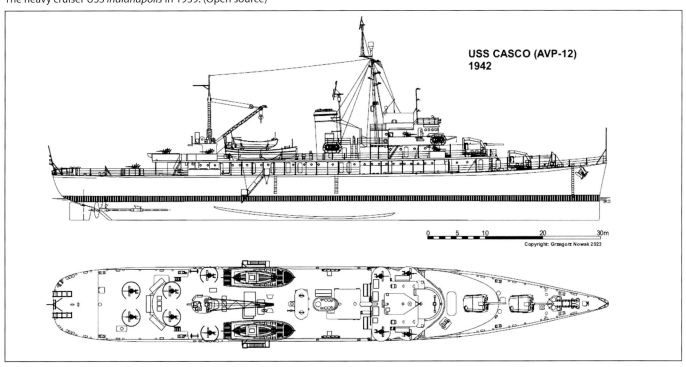

USS *Casco* (AVP-12) was one of 30 completed Barnegat-class small seaplane tenders, laid down at Puget Sound Navy Yard in May 1940 and launched in November 1941. She was equipped with one single 5-inch (127mm) 38-caliber dual-purpose gun mount, eight 40mm antiaircraft guns, eight 20mm antiaircraft guns and two depth charge tracks. At the beginning of her service, she carried out patrol duties and provided maintenance for seaplanes off the coast of the Pacific Northwest. On 5 May 1942, she arrived at Sitka and soon started establishing the seaplane base and providing the necessary equipment. *Casco* was mainly based at Cold Bay and sent her seaplanes on patrols over Dutch Harbor, Kodiak and Nazan Bay. (Drawing by Grzegorz Nowak)

estimated bearing of Vega Point, and Smith noticed to be slight to the westward of the predetermined line of approach. However, he had not yet received any news of the 11 AF air attack on Japanese positions, nor had he known anything about enemy forces in the harbour. At 1804 hours, the Main Force entered the thick fog again. Six minutes later, *Indianapolis* reached the hundred-fathom curve; this placed the heavy cruisers approximately five miles from Vega Point and the destroyers dangerously close to shore. The force

executed a simultaneous turn to the right by 50 degrees. At the time of execution, the destroyer *Case* estimated her position as two miles off Vega Point. Visibility was still bad, so after three minutes, another 40 degrees turn to the right was made, followed at 1816 hours by a change to course south. Smith considered the bombardment of Kiska blindly from a dead reckoning position as a great navigational risk to the ships and unwarranted by the existing situation. At 1815 hours, one of the scouting planes' crew confirmed that they could

Rear Admiral William Smith, executor of the Kiska bombardment operation on 7 August 1942. (USNI)

The Japanese spotted the two Seagulls circling over the Kiska base and tried to scare the intruders away with their anti-aircraft fire. After a while, they also sent six Rufes led by Lieutenant Yamada into the air to intercept enemy seaplanes and look around the island.[34] Based on the presence of floatplanes, the defenders guessed that an American surface vessel might be operating in the area. Smith had to make an immediate decision to begin the bombardment because the Japanese could withdraw their ships from the harbour and try to seek cover in the dense fog north of Kiska. At 1844 hours, the Main Force turned to an eastern course and received a report from the seaplanes about the clear visibility 10 to 15 miles east of Vega Point. Heading towards this area may have given the Americans a chance to get out of the fog, and by 1855 hours, visibility had improved to about 5 miles to the north and east. Five minutes later, Smith ordered a simultaneous turn to the left to course north and started the second approach to Kiska at 20 knots.[35]

At 1905 hours, *St. Louis'* seaplane confirmed excellent visibility over Vega Bay and proper bearing to Kiska Harbor. Accurate identification of enemy targets was still impossible due to low-altitude clouds. Fifteen minutes later, the Main Force ran into the heavy fog for the third time. Still, after several minutes, the leading destroyers reported a significant improvement in visibility to the island. They were also close to the positions from which they intended to open fire, so at 1942 hours, Smith ordered to change course to the east to create the formation for the most effective bombardment. *Indianapolis'* observers noticed the shoreline. Each of the three groups was instructed to fire independently. Soon after, all the ships got out of the fog, seeing the clear outline of Cape Vega. Even though the Main Force was slightly more to the southeast of the planned positions, heavy cruisers simultaneously came to course 350 degrees (T) to correct their position, and light cruisers closed the beach by simultaneous turns.

At 1950 hours, *Elliot* unexpectedly lost her port paravane, leaving the light cruisers unprotected from anchored mines. Despite that, the minesweeper maintained a proper relative position in the formation, so the rest of the team continued without further course corrections. At 1955 hours, the destroyers reported on range and bearing and opened fire, followed by the light cruisers two minutes later. The heavy cruisers were the last to begin the bombardment at 2000 hours. The original firing plan called for all groups to reach the firing positions simultaneously, but the bad weather made this impossible.

Looking at the first shells landing on the Japanese camp on Kiska, the Americans realised that enemy anti-aircraft batteries had opened fire, possibly thinking that 11 AF bombers had appeared over the base. At 1958 hours, *Case* spotted one Japanese destroyer at 10,000 metres escaping Kiska Harbor in an easterly direction. The

Curtiss SOC Seagull reconnaissance seaplane seen in 1939. (Open source)

see objects only a mile away. The two Seagulls were slowly running out of fuel and were forced to retreat east, where they intended to land in the base without taking additional risks.[33]

The Main Force stalemate was interrupted by a radiogram received at 1825 hours. Lieutenant R.A. O'Neill, leader of the *Indianapolis* spotting flight, reported getting an excellent view of Kiska Harbor through breaks in the overcast, flying at 500 metres. He spotted 10 transport or cargo ships, four submarines, and one destroyer or light cruiser. In addition, O'Neill mentioned that the entrance to the harbour was protected by one destroyer and one patrol vessel. He also confirmed that there were no signs of air attack in the last 24 hours, giving Smith clear evidence that the Army bombers did not provide the planned support four hours before the commencement of the bombardment.

The light cruiser USS *St. Louis*. (Open source)

American ship fired three salvos, but the enemy vessel disappeared behind Little Kiska.

At 2005 hours, it was already known that the Japanese figured out that they had been shelled by the enemy task force and made the first attempt to respond to this attack. The coastal gun batteries targeted *Elliot*, which reported several 127mm shells falling short. *Nashville* and *Honolulu* also reported near misses, and *Nashville* decided to provide the counter-battery fire with her port 5-inch guns, silencing the enemy shore positions. Almost at the same time, a large white chemical burst, looking like a "huge jellyfish", was noticed just over *Indianapolis'* starboard. The Americans were convinced that this burst was dropped through the overcast by an aircraft as a range marker for shore batteries or gunfire. At 2008 hours, an identical explosion of a chemical shell was recorded by the *Louisville* crew members, who also spotted an enemy seaplane fighter overhead but failed to open her anti-aircraft artillery. Weather conditions, particularly thick clouds, made it impossible for Seagulls to accurately identify the Japanese vessels stationed in Kiska Harbor. Therefore, the Main Force continued the bombardment of the previously marked targets. Although a number of columns of smoke were seen rising from South Head and the harbour vicinity, no direct hits on any enemy unit could be confirmed. *Case* reported the sighting of one transport that was making its way from Kiska towards Segula Island,[36] the

American ships decided to shell onshore targets that were identified as the anti-aircraft gun emplacements.

Catapulted Seagulls equally tried to contribute to the attack on the enemy positions, but they were chased away by the Japanese seaplane fighters. At about 2015 hours, *Elliot* unexpectedly detected a periscope. As the discovered enemy submarine was on a collision course with the light cruisers, they were forced to turn to starboard. The heavy cruisers also changed the course to starboard to avoid running into other ships, ceasing the artillery fire. By this point, the destroyers and light cruisers had already completed the bombardment mission, and at 2023 hours, all the ships were on course 230 degrees at 25 knots. *Indianapolis'* radar picked up another enemy seaplane following the group, but the intruder returned to base after a couple of minutes.

By 2036 hours, the Main Force recovered seven of the 10 catapulted seaplanes and slowed down to 20 knots. Due to low fuel, two Seagulls from *St. Louis* had returned to base earlier. The only aircraft missing was the second plane from *Indianapolis*, last seen by the wingman while escaping into thick clouds from a Japanese float fighter. At 2115 hours, the Smith changed the course to 140 degrees, but since his group was still tracked by one enemy aircraft, he quickly moved away from Kiska to the south. Twenty minutes later, a great splash was heard off *Louisville's* stern, assumed to be a missed bomb dropped by a Japanese seaplane. It was not until the night of 7/8 August, when the Americans were far enough from the island to change the course to 100 degrees towards Kodiak. The bombardment of Kiska was finally over.[38]

During the bombardment, the American ships fired 631 203mm, 3,534 150mm and 2,620 127mm rounds. Given the 30-minute one-sided artillery action against ground targets, one can deny that they expended a reasonably large amount of ammunition, which should wipe out or, at least, severely disorganise the Japanese garrison on the island. In reality, Smith initially did not know precisely what damage

Table 31: 5. *Kaigun Kōkūtai* activity during the bombardment of Kiska, 7 August 1942.[37]		
Hours	**Pilot/Commander**	**Details**
take-off: 1850 return: 1940	1. Lt Yamada (S) 2. PO2c Sasaki	fired 420 rounds and chased away two enemy seaplanes
take-off: 1850 return: 1950	1. SLt Saitō (S) 2. Sea2c Minazawa	spotted two enemy seaplanes at 1940 hours that escaped into clouds
	1. PO2c Suzuki (S) 2. PO3c Uchiyama	
take-off: 1950 return: 2050	1. Sea2c Narita	fired 400 rounds and chased away two enemy seaplanes
take-off: 1950 return: 2110	1. PO2c Ōgawa (S) 2. PO3c Uchiyama 3. Sea2c Minazawa	scrambled with 4 x 30kg bombs, fired 400 rounds in total at two enemy seaplanes and spotted the enemy *"Kidō Butai"* at 2050 hours
take-off: 2100–2215 return: 2235–2250	1. SLt Saitō (S) 2. PO2c Suzuki 3. PO2c Sasaki	did not encounter the enemy

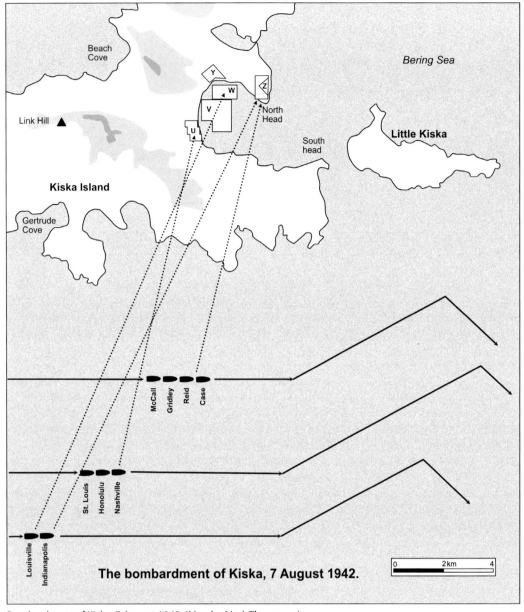

The bombardment of Kiska, 7 August 1942.

Bombardment of Kiska, 7 August 1942. (Map by Mark Thompson)

Prince Takamatsunomiya photographed in 1940. (NDL)

his team had inflicted on the enemy base.[39] Due to appalling weather, it took several days for 11 AF bombers to take pictures of military facilities on Kiska.[40] Still, it was not entirely clear which craters were caused by earlier air attacks and which by the August bombardment. Nevertheless, TF-8 summarised that the Main Force achieved the following score:

- 1 destroyer hit, possibly sunk,
- 1 transport hit and probably destroyed (beached and deck awash),
- 1 transport possibly sunk,
- various batteries silenced,
- moderate damage to shore installations, with unknown damage to stores and equipment.[41]

Despite the generally positive assessment of the Main Force's performance on 7 August, the bombardment of Kiska inflicted virtually no substantial damage on the Japanese shore camp. For many years, it was believed that the *Kanō Maru* had been set on fire, but the only actual losses were recorded by 5. *Kaigun Kōkūtai*, which mentioned three damaged flying boats and one destroyed seaplane fighter.[42] The Americans became convinced of the meagre effects of their sortie only on 10 October, when Army planes carried out more thorough reconnaissance missions. Based on photographs taken through overcast, they determined that most of the 1,600 artillery shell craters were located about 800 metres from the main Japanese camp. While some of the shells might have landed on targets, and in the meantime, the Japanese had managed to repair all the damage, most rounds were likely to have been fired in the wrong direction. Even before getting clear photographs of Kiska, the bombardment was aptly summarised by Smith:

(1) The bombardment of Kiska by a surface force of heavy ships would be of questionable value unless followed by the landing of troops. Results to be expected from indirect bombardment would not balance the risk to heavy ships under difficult conditions of approach in mineable waters, where enemy destroyers might be encountered in low visibility.

(2) Light cruisers were considered more adaptable to conditions in the area than heavy cruisers. With the prevalent low visibility, ships which could quickly produce a great volume of fire would have a decided advantage.

(3) The enemy could not be driven out of Kiska by surface bombardment alone. Visibility conditions permitting, more

damage to shore installations could probably be inflicted by a squadron of bombers.

(4) Attacks from the north by motor torpedo boats supported by destroyers could make Kiska Harbor untenable for the enemy.[43]

Besides the Japanese unit's records, Prince Takamatsunomiya's diary also contains interesting data on the losses recorded on Kiska due to the American bombardment. The 9 August entry listed two killed and one seriously and two slightly wounded men, and two Daihatsu landing craft destroyed.[44]

9

AMERICANS LAND ON ADAK; JAPANESE WITHDRAW FROM ATTU

アメリカはアダック島に上陸し、日本は
アッツ島から撤退する

Amerika wa Addaku-tō ni Jōriku shi, Nihon wa Attsu-tō kara Tettai suru

A few hours before the Main Force were about to begin the bombardment of Kiska, *Nippon Kaigun*'s attention was focused on the other half of the globe. On the same day, the 1st Marine Division, covered by three carriers, made a surprise landing on Guadalcanal, capturing an airfield built practically from scratch by the Japanese to launch the new offensive in the South Pacific. In response to the American counterattack, the Combined Fleet Staff, in consultation with the Naval General Staff, sent a warning to Fifth Fleet Command at 0600 hours on 8 August, advising extreme caution regarding a possible bombardment of Attu and Kiska by the US Navy.[1]

There is no evidence that the Japanese suspected that the US Navy intended to engage its surface forces to shell Kiska on the evening of 7 August. However, the concentration of American units in Nazan Bay did not escape the notice of *Tōkō Kaigun Kōkūtai*. On the morning of 3 August, four flying boats led by Lieutenant Commander Itō took off to attack the spotted destroyer off Atka. Each Mavis was armed with four 250kg bombs to maximise the potential outcome of the strike if any other vessels were encountered. After all, the Japanese crews attacked only two ships and reported three near misses, possibly without significant damage.[2] The Tōkō-kū targets were, in fact, seaplane tenders *Casco* and *Kane*, which recorded no losses.[3] The next day, the Japanese repeated the attack on Nazan Bay and sent two flying boats, each carrying two 250kg bombs. Again, no measurable success was achieved, mainly because P-38E fighters appeared off Atka. The new model of aircraft, unknown to the Japanese, had its baptism of fire in the skies of the Aleutian Islands and soon became one of the most famous fighters in the history.[4]

In response to Japanese offensive moves, Patrol Wing 4 raided enemy positions on Kiska on 8 April. Each of the six Catalinas was armed with one 454kg and two 227kg bombs and took off to strike vessels in the harbour or military facilities. During the attack, two Rufes of 5. *Kaigun Kōkūtai* were already in the air on routine patrol around the base rushed to intercept the PBYs. Flying boat crews reported scoring three hits on two transport ships and setting fire to ground installations. The Americans also claimed that both float fighters were shot down during the dogfight, although the Japanese report does not confirm this statement.[6] On the other side, two Catalinas were slightly damaged, and due to lack of fuel, Ensign Herrin of VP-41 made an emergency landing south of Umnak. The crew was soon rescued, albeit during the search mission, the flying boat commanded by Lieutenant (jg.) Raven of VP-41 failed to return, and the PBY was never found again.[7]

The limited air campaign over Kiska did not change the fact that the struggle for the Aleutians was fought in conditions unfavourable to both sides. Other negative factors included unstable weather, vast distances between islands, and insufficiently developed military infrastructure. While seaplane tenders tended to perform well in this theatre of operations, seaplanes themselves had very limited combat potential, especially when compared to carrier-borne fighters and bombers. The Japanese had experienced a series of large-scale air operations in the South Pacific, the hasty establishment of new forward bases, and efficient aircraft transit to distant fronts. In most cases, the attacking troops managed to seize airfields built by the Americans, British or Dutch, which were then used in later stages of the offensive. The situation was quite different in the case of the Aleutians, where the Japanese did not seize a fully operational airfield, even the single fighter strip. From the Attu and Kiska garrisons' perspective, the nearest allied air base was on the Kuriles, 1,200km to the southwest.

The AO Defense Force command was well aware that the successful implementation of strategic plans envisaging holding Attu and Kiska until the spring thaw of 1943 depended on allocating additional surface and air forces and building the first independent airfield in the Aleutians. After seizing both islands, the Japanese staff officers discussed the necessity to construct an air base in one of three potential locations: the Semichi Islands (near Attu), Amchitka (less than 120km east of Kiska), or Kiska as a last resort. Given the general capabilities of the Japanese in the North Pacific area, these were ambitious intentions that would certainly strengthen the position of the Fifth Fleet in the Aleutian Islands. However, on 19 June, the Combined Fleet and the Navy General Staff did not agree to deploy additional amphibious forces to capture the new islands adjecting to Attu or Kiska. Additionally, the Combined Fleet expressed its view that Kiska should be defended by the Army by building-up the strength of the local garrison and anti-aircraft artillery detachment. While no definitive dissent has been issued for building the new airport in the Aleutians, the Japanese believed that the construction works could not begin sooner than in early 1943.

The American air strikes on Kiska in June and July took an increasing toll on the Fifth Fleet, which persuaded the Combined Fleet to build a fully operational airfield in the Aleutian Islands. The negative stance of the Navy General Staff initially remained adamant, but after numerous talks and personal meetings, Tokyo headquarters gave formal approval on 15 July. Given the weather forecasts for the upcoming months, the construction of the airport was to begin in 1942. Additional equipment and forces to establish the local air units were to be allocated later, probably in late 1942 or early 1943. The Navy General Staff only agreed to build a fully operational

The seaplane tender USS *Casco*. (Open source)

Table 32: *Tōkō Kaigun Kōkūtai* activity on 3–4 August 1942.[5]

Date	Commander	Details
3 August (Mavis) take-off: 0820 return: 1730	1. Lt Cdr Itō (S) 2. SLt Obata 3. WO Iizuka 4. Lt Yoneyama	First proceeded to Kuluk Bay (Adak), then attacked enemy ships in Nazan Bay (Atak), scoring three near misses.
4 August (Mavis) take-off: 0820 return: 1415	1. Lt Yoneyama (S) 2. SLt Obata	Dropped 4 x 250kg bombs and expended 90 x 7.7mm rounds expended; encountered and shot down one enemy P-38.

Rufes at Attu. (Open source)

wide, presuming the need for expansion in the near future.[8]

Parallel to the Japanese debate on constructing the new airfield in the Aleutians, US Army made specific proposals to improve the infrastructure for bombers and fighters in the chain, preparing for the next stage of the war of attrition in the North Pacific. Based on Brigadier General Laurence S. Kuter's strategic analysis, on 14 July, Lieutenant General DeWitt suggested developing plans for the air offensive against enemy bases in the western Aleutians. The War Department, unable to allot reinforcements to the North Pacific, was rather pessimistic about this concept and advised continuing the campaign in its current shape. However, DeWitt was vehemently opposed to a passive strategy in the Aleutian Islands and believed that the Japanese should be inflicted with losses they would not be able to replace by regular Navy convoys from the Kuriles. Therefore, two days later, he proposed seizing Tanaga Island to build a new airfield from scratch and establishing a garrison with solid anti-aircraft defence.[9] The main advantage of his proposal was that the distance from the westernmost American base to Kiska would be reduced to less than 300km. In practice, this meant that the bombers could rely on the support of fighters during the air strikes on the Japanese base.

The Joint Chiefs of Staff discussed the suggestion of seizing Tanaga on 25 July but soon found that the US Navy preferred to capture the neighbouring Adak, excluding Theobald, who advocated Atka. Looking from a more

airfield on Kiska, rejecting the idea of parallel construction works on a fighter airstrip on another island. Nevertheless, the AO Defense Force command was satisfied with this decision and, by the end of July, prepared a detailed terrain analysis of all considered construction sites. After all, the Japanese selected Kiska as the most suitable place for their new air base in the Aleutians. The runway located in the central part of the island, in the so-called Katsuragawa area (桂川地区), was to be 950 metres long and 150 metres

neutral standpoint, Kuluk Bay was potentially a much better place for the warships, offering the same advantages as Tanaga and Atka. However, driven by the time needed to build the airfield, the US Army pushed for choosing Tanaga, believing that the entire project could be completed there in three to four weeks, while construction work at Adak required at least twice as long. Days passed, but Army and Navy officers found it hard to compromise. On 21 August, General Marshall finally resolved the stalemate and agreed on behalf

Brigadier General Laurence S. Kuter. (NARA)

of the US Army to seize Adak and carry out "cover" demonstrations at Tanaga and Atka, sending detailed explanations to DeWitt.[10] Following this decision, the next day, Theobald issued Operation Plan 10-42, setting the amphibious operation date on 30 August.[11]

Theobald warned Nimitz that the Japanese would likely launch a counterattack to push the Americans away from Adak, so the new garrison should comprise one division of 25,000 men. Buckner naturally supported this notion, but the US Army command refused to assign additional troops to the North Pacific, as Guadalcanal and North Africa remained the more critical theatres of operations. After all, despite Nimitz's pressure to send more infantry to the chain, the original plans for a 5,000-men garrison were retained.[12]

Considerations of the capture of Adak coincided with three important events on the American side: First, on 17 August, the Aleutian Defense Command received a cable that a dozen new B-24s and the 21st Bombardment Squadron personnel were en route to Alaska to reinforce the weakened 11 AF. As of 21 August, the bomber wing disposed of only 19 heavy and 24 medium bombers and 16 medium (reconnaissance) bombers. On the other hand, the fighter wing had 94 fighters, and Patrol Wing 4 had 50 flying boats (including amphibious PBYs).[13] Despite 11 AF's visible overwhelming numerical superiority over the Japanese, the effective use of air forces depended on reducing the operational distance to Kiska.

Secondly, on 20 August, the submarine *Gato* (SS-212) reported scoring four torpedo hits and sank one unidentified Japanese transport ship (probably *Kinka Maru*) escorted by one destroyer, an action that happened five days earlier.[14] Although the crew saw the silhouette of a vessel disappearing into the depths, the Japanese documents do not record any losses in the merchant fleet on that day.

On 19 August, during the Naval and Army staff meeting in Kodiak, the ACD commander read in front of several officers and secretaries a poem he had written, finding his inspiration in the Navy's attitude in the last months. In a rather peculiar way, Buckner wanted to present his point of view on the US Navy's actions in the North Pacific, which turned out to be extremely malicious and unprofessional personal criticism. Nevertheless, the so-called "Ode to Theobald" became so famous that it was repeatedly quoted behind the stages of the Army and Navy as a mocking piece having a specific humorous value. One can deny that the reception of Buckner's poem depended on the reader's attitude to the events in the Aleutians.

In far Alaska's icy spray, I stand beside my binnacle
And scan the waters through the fog for fear some rocky pinnacle
Projecting from unfathomed depths may break my hull asunder
And place my name upon the list of those who made a blunder
Volcanic peaks beneath the waves are likely any morning
To smash my ships to tiny bits without the slightest warning
I dread the toll from reef and shoal that rip off keel and rudder
And send our bones to Davey Jones – the prospect makes me shudder
The Bering Sea is not for me nor my fleet headquarters
In mortal dread I look ahead in wild Aleutian waters
Where hidden reefs and williwaws and terrifying critters
Unnerve me quite with woeful fright and give me fits and jitters

The conflict between Theobald and Buckner reached Washington and seriously alarmed Marshall, who approached the US Navy to probe King's view on changes in Alaskan command. In a letter to DeWitt from 3 September, he confirmed that King was willing to replace Theobald, and the US Army intended to remove Butler and Buckner but to do it in such a way as to avoid reflection on Buckner's behaviour.[15] Fortunately, personal animosities did not influence the decision to build a new airport and seize Adak. On the night of 27/28 August, submarines *Triton* and *Tuna* entered Kuluk Bay and went on the water's surface. Two small boats embarking three officers and 35 soldiers set off towards the shore.[16] The reconnaissance party of Colonel Lawrence Castner landed on the beach and started to

The submarine USS *Gato* seen in 1944. (Open source)

investigate whether the Japanese had occupied the island, even for a short period. After quickly inspecting critical positions, the party reported no evidence of an enemy present or past presence in the morning. Theobald waited for this message and passed the word to begin the amphibious operation. Seaplane tender *Teal* established a new base off Adak to cover the landing operation and *Case* act as an escort for tugs and barges of army engineers.[17] Soon after, the convoy comprising transport ships *J. Franklin Bell*, *St. Mihiel*, *Thomas Jefferson*, *North Coast*, cargos *Branch* and *Stanley Griffith*, and about 250 various types of landing craft and smaller boats, embarking 4,500 soldiers of Brigadier General Eugene Landrum set off from Unalaska.

The invasion forces were escorted by three US Navy groups formed from most of the available TF-8 vessels. The first group, commanded by Captain Francis S. Craven, consisted of the light cruisers *Nashville*, *St. Louis* and the destroyers *Brooks*, *Dent* and *Kane*. The second group, led by Read Admiral Smith, comprised the cruisers *Indianapolis*, *Louisville*, and *Honolulu*, and the destroyers *Gridley*, *McCall* and *Reid*. The last group of Captain Herbert J. Grassie, composed of destroyers *Lawrence*, *Humphreys*, *King*, *Lawrence* and *Sands*, two minesweepers and the submarine and supported by the Canadian vessels – auxiliary cruisers *Prince David*, *Prince Henry* and *Prince Robert* and corvettes *Dawson* and *Vancouver*, provided the direct cover for the convoy. All P-38 fighters and heavy bombers stationed on Umnak were in combat readiness and received the order to scramble immediately if any enemy counterattack was detected.[18]

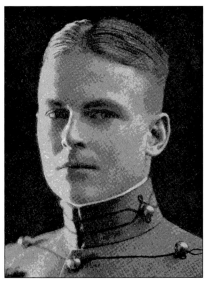

Colonel Lawrence Castner photographed in 1923. (Open source)

Anticipating the Japanese counterattack or other potentially dangerous moves, Patrol Wing 4 engaged its seaplane tenders to have eyes opened in every direction. At the end of August, the American vessels moved to positions from which they intended to carry out flights towards Adak and Kiska. However, on 26 August, one of *Williamson*'s flying boats under tow accidentally touched the guard rail, releasing two depth bombs into the water. The explosions severely shook the tender, flooding her after compartments and damaging the steering and starboard main engines. The towed PBY

The destroyer USS *Reid*. (Open source)

The seaplane tender USS *Williamson*. (Open source)

was lost, as well as four men reported missing, and 16 were wounded in this accident. After all, *Casco* assisted the damaged tender, and *Williamson* had to return to Dutch Harbor two days later.[19]

Before the Americans landed at Adak, the Japanese submarine *RO-61*, commanded by Lieutenant Commander Tokutomi Toshisada, sneakily approached Nazan Bay on 29 August. *RO-61*'s mission coincided with the recent arrival of *Casco* and *Gillis* and the destroyer *Reid* screening both tenders. Observing the activity of the enemy in recent days, the Japanese expected the Americans to be unaware of the threat. Additionally, the destroyer left the anchorage the following day due to a violent storm. In the evening, *RO-61* tried her chances and attacked *Casco* with torpedoes, scoring one direct hit in the engine room.[20] The explosion killed five and injured three men. The badly damaged vessel was beached to avoid sinking and personnel put ashore.[21] Tokutomi reported scoring two torpedo hits on the Northampton-class heavy cruiser and was attacked with depth charges, luckily escaping the area off Adak.[22] He was then tracked by one PBY but managed to run away from the enemy aircraft. When Tokutomi thought he could end the war patrol safely, *Reid* found him off Cape North. *RO-61* had to go on the water surface to avoid the destruction by the depth charges, and the American destroyer mercilessly sent it to the bottom with her guns.

Table 33: *Tōkō Kaigun Kōkūtai* activity in the Aleutian Islands prior to the withdrawal to Japan.[27]	
Number of operational days:	53
Number of days with action:	42
Number of days with dogfights:	9
Number of hours spent on patrol flights:	345
Number of clashes with the enemy aircraft:	160
Number of planes that participated in fight:	48
Number of enemy planes that participated in fight:	35
Damage dealt: 2 x B-17s, 1 x B-24, 1 x seaplane destroyed	
Losses: 3 x flying boats damaged, no crew casualties	

Of the 59 crew members, 17 men abandoned the ship, yet only five were captured. Tokutomi, like many of his companions and beloved *RO-61*, disappeared into the North Pacific depths.[23]

At this stage of the campaign in the Aleutian Islands, the Japanese had significantly lost the ability to respond to unexpected contacts with enemy warships. Given the past experience, *Reid* would soon be attacked by flying boats carrying 250kg bombs, a deadly weapon to any lone ship in the North Pacific. However, on

The Japanese seaplanes stationed at Attu. (NARA)

Table 34: Japanese convoys at Attu and Kiska from June to the end of August 1942.[28]

Date	Route	Ships	Supplies
15–19 June	Paramushiru – Kiska	*Magane Maru*	80 x 88mm AA guns shells and 1,030 x standard shells 10,000 x 13mm AA machine gun rounds
25–27 June	Ōminato – Kiska	*Inazuma*	ammunition, fuel
28 June–4 July	Yokosuka – Kiska	*Chiyoda Aruzenchin Maru*	6 x Rufe 6 x midget submarines 200 tons of concrete AA guns and machine guns ammunition and food supplies
4–10 July	Yokosuka – Kiska	*Akatsuki*	5th Base Unit command and workers (11 men) 120 x 40mm destroyer gun shells equipment for flying boats
5–15 July	Maizuru – Muroran – Kiska	*Hakusan Maru*	(unknown)
9–18 July	Maizuru – Muroran – Kiska	*Kikukawa Maru*	250 men from the construction unit equipment and spare parts for AA and coastal guns
10 July – X	Maizuru – Kiska	*Kumagawa Maru*	Transport ship ran aground and did not reach Kiska 32nd independent AA company 1,500 tons of supplies for seaplanes 611 tons of supplies for Attu garrison
19–21 July	Kapari Cape – Kiska	*Ikazuchi*	En route the destroyer was diverted to help *Kumagawa Maru*. 96 x camouflage mats 207 x telegraph poles
19–30 July	Maizuru – Ōminato –Katoka Bay – Attu –Kiska	*Kanō Maru*	1,300 m³ construction materials 1 x Rufe 4 x Daihatsu landing craft general supplies and coal
1st convoy: 12 August 2nd convoy: 30 August	Yokosuka – Paramushiru – Kiska	*Kimikawa Maru*	6 x Rufe (1st convoy) 5 x Rufe, winter equipment for soldiers (2nd convoy)
24–26 August	Paramushiru – Attu	*Kikukawa Maru*	transport ship took over *Kumagawa Maru* supplies
26–29 September	Paramushiru – Kiska	*Hinata Maru*	food supplies
2nd half of August	> Attu, Kiska	*Hiryō Maru* *Nagata Maru* *Imizu Maru*	Convoys divided into smaller groups, preparations for winter. 1,000 tons of general supply, 100t black coal, 400t charcoal (Attu) 2,300m³ rice, 150t charcoal (Kiska)

The monumental Japanese monograph on *Nippon Kaigun* operations in the North Pacific contains a summary of *Tōkō Kaigun Kōkūtai*'s flying boats and floatplanes activity in this area (excluding Paramushiru) as shown in Table 33.

In the first half of August, the Fifth Fleet made an important decision to supply the Attu and Kiska garrisons in advance, keeping in mind the upcoming cold season. In theory, the Japanese still had more than three months before the start of the calendar winter, but in practice, regular frosts in the Aleutian Islands were recorded as early as in the first week of October. Predicting difficulties in sending food rations, medications, coal, and winter equipment for soldiers in the last months of 1942, the first transport ships set off for the Aleutians already in August. The complete list of the Japanese convoys for Attu and Kiska from their capture to early September 1942 is shown in Table 34.

Between 14 and 24 August, the Combined Fleet organised military exercises of the Northern Forces in Mutsu Bay, which concluded with the Nippon Kaigun's command decision to withdraw several transport ships and destroyers from the Aleutian area. They were then assigned to the Eighth Fleet at Rabaul for the more important task – the Guadalcanal campaign. As a result of the 25 August order, the Japanese defence capacities in the North Pacific were significantly reduced, strongly influencing the views on keeping Attu and Kiska. On

14 August, Commander Itō received an order to withdraw the last three operational Mavises of *Tōkō Kaigun Kōkūtai* Command to Japan. Three days later, all aircraft first went to Paramushiru, where they proceeded directly to Yokohama, arriving in the afternoon. No enemy aircraft or ships were encountered along the way.[24] The burden of providing reconnaissance flights in the Aleutian area fell to the remaining 10 seaplanes of 5. *Kaigun Kōkūtai*,[25] which was formally detached from the *Tōkō Kaigun Kōkūtai* on 5 August and subordinated to the Fifth Fleet as part of the AO Defense Unit.[26]

the same day, the Imperial Headquarters issued Army Operational Order No. 675, calling a radical shift – the entire Attu garrison was to be transferred to Kiska. The Japanese not only hoped to solve the issue of the shortage of transport ships but also to keep the Americans away from the home islands unless they were ready for bloodshed during the reconquest of fortified Kiska. Additionally, the Japanese believed that moving the Army detachment to Kiska would help the Fifth Fleet to defend the island more effectively and, consequently, avoid dispersing the limited resources around the vast area North Pacific.[29]

Under Navy Operational Order No. 124, simultaneously published by the Imperial Headquarters, the Fifth Fleet was assigned to prepare the plan and execute the transfer of all troops and weapons from Attu to Kiska. Hosogaya assigned to this task four transport ships, screened by the 21st Cruiser Squadron, the 6th and 21st Destroyer Squadrons and other auxiliary ships. Once hastily embarking soldiers and supplies, the first echelon left Attu on 27 August and reached Kiska the following day. Northern Forces command was transferred by seaplane on 29 August. Following that, men and materials were transported step by step not to arouse American attention to the increased activity of vessels. On 16 September, the last Japanese departed from Attu, embarked on *Nagata Maru*, and arrived at Kiska in less than 24 hours.[30] The operation was then officially completed. One of the two seized islands in the western Aleutians has been abandoned.[31] The Imperial Headquarters did not know that this decision would soon become a severe mistake, and the Japanese Navy and Army would have to return to Attu soon and fight the bloodiest battle in the North Pacific in May 1943.

While the AO Defense Force was busy transferring troops from Attu to Kiska, the Americans landed on Adak on August 30, expecting the enemy resistance or at least a clash with the small detachment left on the island. Parallel to the preparations to begin the amphibious operation, *Hulbert* landed a Marine party on Seguam Island to investigate the island in daylight thoroughly. No Japanese or signs of their past habitation were found there, and the party returned to the ship.[32]

As a matter of urgency, the Americans first brought anti-aircraft and coastal guns to shore to protect the landing operation on Adak in the event of the enemy's counterattack. Subsequently, men and equipment of Colonel Benjamin Tally's 807th Aviation Engineering Battalion appeared on the beach and almost immediately began construction. Accurate terrain maps were not yet available then, but the experience gained from the Aleutian area was advantageous in managing the whole process of building the new airfield. As the Americans admitted later, improvisation played a prominent role in the entire process, allowing the engineers to find a convenient place for the runway independently. After all, they had to pick the only flat spot – a shallow tidal basin near Sweeper Cove. Within 10 days, after removing the sea water and installing a drainage system, a decent part of the tidal basin was secured and ready for further levelling and improvement work. On 10 September, the still provisional airstrip on Adak received the codename "Fireplace", and the first B-18 bomber of the 73rd Bombardment Squadron with the 11 AF commander on board landed without any obstacles. Conditions at the new airfield were described as "satisfactory", so three B-17s and six P-38s were deployed to Adak the following day.[33] Once the Marston mats were laid along the runway on 12/13 September, the Americans could add a fully operational airfield in the western Aleutians

Table 35: Summary of the 11 AF air attacks against the Japanese positions in the Aleutian Islands, 1 August –12 September 1942.[35]		
Date	Forces	Target/Details
3 August	3 x B-17s	Kiska Harbor (no hits observed)
4–7 August	-	-
8 August	1 x PBY 1 x B-24	Kiska Harbor (no hits observed)
9 August	-	-
10 August	6 x B-24s	Kiska camp (no hits observed)
11 August	5 x B-17s 4 x B-24s	Kiska camp (no hits observed)
12–27 August	-	-
28 August	3 x B-17s	Kiska Harbor
29 August – 3 September	-	-
4 September	1 x B-17 2 x P-38s	Kiska harbour and camp
5 September	-	-
6 September	1 x B-24 (recon)	one bomb hit scored on a small vessel between Attu and Kiska
7 September	3 x B-24s	Kiska Harbor
8–12 September	-	-

to the list of achievements, having the Japanese on Kiska at their fingertips.[34]

Overall, throughout August and the first two weeks of September, the 11 AF airstrikes against Japanese positions in the Aleutian Islands were as shown in Table 35.

The Japanese evacuation from Attu and the American capture of Adak, followed by the new airfield construction, concluded

Colonel Benjamin Tally (on right) being decorated. (NARA.)

the summer campaign in the North Pacific. The second half of September brought the autumn and the inevitable weather changes that influenced the further course of the struggle for the Aleutians, which interceded to a new phase with new opportunities and challenges for both sides. The Americans persistently continued their long-term strategy of closing the distance to the enemy bases; the Japanese stayed focused on supplying their garrisons until spring thaw and preparing for the imminent invasion in 1943. The Aleutian Islands campaign was fascinating from an operational and tactical point of view, forcing its belligerents to fight over a vast area considered crucial for their national interests with limited resources. Still, it was undoubtedly overshadowed by the events in the South Pacific, namely the Guadalcanal campaign, which led to a series of spectacular land and naval battles that changed the course of the Pacific War. It is vital to notice that once the *Nippon Kaigun* and *Nippon Rikugun* were broken on Hell Island until the end of 1942 and confronted the need for evacuating their troops in the following weeks, the Japanese positions in the Aleutians became stronger and stronger despite the Americans' efforts to soften up the local defence with the air war of attrition. More importantly, the relatively small Fifth Fleet still had an advantage against TF-8 and could actively support the defensive operations. To change this situation, the US Navy, in collaboration with US Army, had to learn the lesson and adopt a new strategy to neutralise the enemy naval forces and reconquer the Aleutians as soon as possible.

An example of using Marston mats. These were laid on the Navy's auxiliary field on Tanaga Island in the following months. (Open source)

The American camp on Adak in early September 1942, just after landing on the island. (NARA)

APPENDIX 1
RYŪJŌ'S AND *JUN'YŌ'S* AIR GROUP ROSTERS DURING OPERATION AL, JUNE 1942.

龍驤飛行機隊 *Ryūjō* hikōkitai *Ryūjō* Air Group			
No.	戦闘機隊 (Sentōkitai) (Fighter Group)	艦上攻撃機隊 (Kanjō kōgekitai) (Torpedo Bomber Group)		
-	Pilot	Pilot	Observer	Radio operator
1	Lt Kobayashi (B)	PO1c Nishimura	Lt Yamagami (B)	PO2c Endō
2	WO Uemura	Lt Samejima	PO1c Yoshihara	PO2c Itō
3	PO1c Kurihara	Sea1c Futakuchi	SLt Satō	PO2c Anzai
4	PO1c Tomoishi	SLt Shibata	PO1c Itō	PO2c Kikuta
5	PO1c Yoshizawa	PO2c Horiuchi	WO Uchimura	PO3c Yamauchi
6	PO1c Miyauchi	Sea1c Takahashi	PO1c Nemoto	PO2c Watanabe
7	PO1c Sugiyama	PO1c Oda	PO1c Miura	PO2c Kurahashi
8	PO1c Endō	PO1c Ōshima	PO1c Yamano	PO2c Morita
9	PO1c Koga	Sea1c Shitayoshi	PO2c Akiyama	Sea1c Takahashi I.
10	PO1c Shikada	Sea1c Shimada	PO2c Satō	PO2c Hoshino
11	PO2c Kitashino	Sea1c Tanishiki	PO3c Nihei	Sea1c Toriyama
12	PO3c Morita	PO2c Okuyama	PO1c Ōhashi	PO2c Ikehara
13	PO3c Yoshihara	PO2c Fujii	PO1c Morishita	PO2c Itasaka
14	Sea1c Ishihara	PO1c Yamaguchi	PO2c Kobayashi	PO3c Izumi
15	(no pilot)	PO2c Kawahara	PO1c Yamaguchi	PO3c Ōbata
16	(no pilot)	Sea1c Mizoguchi	PO3c Shimada	Sea2c Nakajima
17	(no pilot)	Sea1c Ōki	PO2c Kameda	PO3c Noda
18	(no pilot)	Sea1c Tamai	PO1c Motohashi	PO2c Fujiki
19	(no pilot)	SLt Morita*	PO1c Itō*	PO2c Urada*
20	(no pilot)	Sea1c Ono*	Sea1c Yoshimoto*	Sea2c Suzuki*

Crews marked with * participated only in reconnaissance or anti-submarine missions after 5 June 1942.

	隼鷹飛行機隊 *Jun'yō* hikōkitai *Jun'yō* Air Group				
No.	**戦闘機隊 (Sentōkitai)** **(Fighter Group)**	**No.** *chūtai*	**艦上爆撃機隊 (Kanjō bakugekikitai)** **(Dive Bomber Group)**	
-	Pilot	-	Pilot	Observer/navigator
1	Lt Shiga (B)		Lt Abe (B)	WO Ishii
2	Lt Miyano		PO3c Takei	PO1c Harada
3	WO Kitahata		PO3c Nakatsuka	PO2c Kimura
4	PO1c Okamoto		PO1c Ōishi	WO Yamamoto
5	PO1c Kamihira	1st	PO3c Okada	PO2c Sugie
6	PO1c Kubota		PO2c Ikeda	PO2c Miyawaki
7	PO1c Yamamoto		PO1c Numata	PO2c Takano
8	PO1c Ōzeki		Sea1c Nagashima	PO2c Nakao
9	PO1c Numata		(no details)*	(no details)*
10	PO2c Hasegawa		PO1c Kawabata	Lt Miura
11	PO2c Sasakibara		PO3c Yamakawa	PO2c Nishiyama
12	PO2c Yotsumoto		Sea2c Murakami	PO2c Kataoka
13	PO3c Tanaka		WO Harano	PO1c Nakajima
14	Sea1c Yoshida	2nd	PO3c Kosemoto	Sea1c Nakata
15	(no pilot)		PO2c Miyatake	WO Tajima
16	(no pilot)		PO2c Gotō	PO2c Yamano
17	(no pilot)		(no details)*	(no details)*
18	(no pilot)		(no details)*	(no details)*
* *Jun'yō* air group action report does not indicate the details of crews for some missions (especially before 3 June and after 4 June).				

Lieutenant Abe Zenji, *buntaichō* of dive bombers from *Jun'yō*, who was transferred on the carrier from Akagi in early May 1942, and PO3c Yamakawa Shinsaku gave a deeper insight into the preparations of the biggest carrier in the 2nd *Kidō Butai*. Half of the 36 dive bomber crew members were freshmen, and even after the month of intensive training at the navy base on Kyūshū, they could not master all the necessary skills to become a smoothly working team. Therefore, Abe submitted to superiors a plea, asking to give *Jun'yō* air groups more time for practice. However, due to the importance of *Nippon Kaigun*'s strategic plans, it was rejected, and pilots unready to serve on the carrier were to be left in air bases on land. This also might be a reason why 15 of 18 *Jun'yō*'s Val crews and 14 out of 18 Zero pilots actively participated in Operation AL.[1]

APPENDIX 2
LIST OF JAPANESE AIRCRAFT

Code name	Japanese operational /abbreviated name	Technical name
Claude	Type 96 carrier fighter (96 kansen)	Mitsubishi A5M
Dave	Type 95 reconnaissance seaplane (95 teisatsuki)	Nakajima E8N
Jake	Type 0 reconnaissance seaplane (reisui)	Aichi E13A
Kate	Type 97 carrier attack plane (97 kankō)	Nakajima B5N
Mavis	Type 97 flying boat (daitei)	Kawanishi H6K
Pete	Type 0 scouting seaplane (reikan)	Mitsubishi F1M
Rufe	Type 2 seaplane fighter (2-shiki suisen)	Nakajima A6M2-N
Val	Type 99 carrier dive bomber (99 kambaku)	Aichi D3A
Zero	Type 0 carrier fighter (zerosen)	Mitsubishi A6M

APPENDIX 3
JAPANESE TERMINOLOGY RELATING TO THE ALEUTIAN ISLANDS CAMPAIGN

English name	Japanese name	Transcript
Aleutians campaign	アリューシャン作戦	Aryūshan Sakusen
Aleutian Islands	アリューシャン列島	Aryūshan Rettō
Adak	アダック島	Adakku-tō
Agattu	アガッツ島	Agattsu-tō
Alaska	アラスカ	Arasuka
Attu	アッツ島 熱田島	Attsu-tō Atsutatō
Kiska	キスカ島 鳴神島	Kisuka-tō Narukamitō
Kodiak	コディアック島	Kodiakku-tō
Umnak	ウムナック島	Umunakku-tō
Unimak	ウニマク島	Unimaku-tō
Operation AL	AL作戦	AL Sakusen
raid on Dutch Harbor	ダッチハーバー空襲	Dacchi Hābā kūshū
action off Kiska on 5 July	7月5日の海戦	Shichigatsu Itsuka no Kaisen
battle of the Komandorski Islands	アッツ島沖海戦	Attsu-tō oki Kaisen
The 2nd Mobile Force (Carrier Striking Force)	第二機動部隊	Dai Ni Kidō Butai
Northern Force	北方部隊	Hoppō Butai

BIBLIOGRAPHY

Japan Center for Asian Historical Records
アジア歴史資料センター

Ajia Rekishi Shiryō Sentaa

JACAR: Ref. C14121194900, Greater East Asia War, Second Stage Operations: Japanese Navy Operational Plans, S17.04.05, 4th Chapter: Outline of Operations (in Japanese).

JACAR: Ref. C16120633100: S17.07.01–S17.07.15, Pacific War Course Outline (3) (in Japanese).

JACAR: Ref. C13071036200, About Operations related to the occupation of strategic positions (in Japanese).

JACAR: Ref. C13071066400, Report to the throne: Regarding the future operations in the Southern Direction and the Pacific Ocean, S17.04.16 (in Japanese).

JACAR: Ref. C12070396400: S16.07.28 (2nd part) Imperial Navy Official Announcement, No. 3857 (in Japanese).

JACAR: Ref. *C08030325100: Kure Navy Base War Diary (4) (in Japanese).*

JACAR: Ref. C12070164200: Orders vol. 3, Shōwa 17th year, July (3) (in Japanese).

JACAR: Ref. C08030019000: S16.12.01–S19.06.30, Fifth Fleet War Diary, Operation AL (1) (in Japanese).

JACAR: Ref. C08030019100: S16.12.01–S19.06.30, Fifth Fleet War Diary, Operation AL (2) (in Japanese).

JACAR: Ref. C08030081200: S17.05.29–S17.07.31, 1st Torpedo Squadron Detailed War Diary (1) (in Japanese).

JACAR: Ref. C08030081300: S17.05.29–S17.07.31, 1st Torpedo Squadron Detailed War Diary (2) (in Japanese).

JACAR: Ref. C08030081400: S17.05.29–S17.07.31, 1st Torpedo Squadron Detailed War Diary (3) (in Japanese).

JACAR: Ref. C08030081500: S17.05.29–S17.07.31, 1st Torpedo Squadron Detailed War Diary (4) (in Japanese).

JACAR: Ref. C08030081600: S17.05.29–S17.07.31, 1st Torpedo Squadron Detailed War Diary (5) (in Japanese).

JACAR: Ref. C08030095000, S17.05.01–S17.08.07, 2nd Torpedo Squadron War Diary (2) (in Japanese).

JACAR: Ref. C0803007030: S16.06.01–S17.11.30, 22nd Squadron War Diary (1) (in Japanese).

JACAR: Ref. C08051583400: S17.06–S18.01, Jun'yō Air Group Action Report (1) (in Japanese).

JACAR: Ref. C08051585900: S16.12–S17.08, Ryūjō Air Group Action Report (3) (in Japanese).

JACAR: Ref. C08051580400: S17.04–S17.12, Zuihō Air Group Action Report (1) (in Japanese).

JACAR: Ref. C08030641200: S17.04.28–S17.07.09, Kamikawa Maru action report Operation MO, MI/AL (2) (in Japanese).

JACAR Ref. C08030641300: S17.04.28–S17.07.09, Kamikawa Maru War Diary, Operations MO, MI/AL (3) (in Japanese).

JACAR: Ref. C08051600400: S17.05–S17.07, Tōkō-ku Action Report (2) (in Japanese).

JACAR: Ref. C08051600500: S17.05–S17.07, Tōkō-ku Action Report (3) (in Japanese).

JACAR: Ref. C08051628400, S17.08–S17.10, 5-ku Action Report (1) (in Japanese).

JACAR Ref. C08030747700: S16.12–S18.05, Warship Nachi War Diary with charts (1) (in Japanese).

JACAR: Ref. C14121139500: [Japanese] Navy Aleutian Operation: part 1, Organisation (in Japanese).

JACAR: Ref. C14121139600: [Japanese] Navy Aleutian Operation: part 2, Outline of the Most Important Forces in the Archipelago (in Japanese).

JACAR: Ref. C14121139700: [Japanese] Navy Aleutian Operation: part 3, Chronology of Main Operation (in Japanese).

JACAR: Ref. C14121139800: [Japanese] Navy Aleutian Operation: part 4, Imperial Headquarters Preparations (in Japanese).

JACAR: Ref. C14121139900: [Japanese] Navy Aleutian Operation: part 5, Combined Fleet Preparations (in Japanese).

JACAR: Ref. C14121140000: [Japanese] Navy Aleutian Operation: part 6, Northern Force Preparations (in Japanese).

JACAR: Ref. C14121140100: [Japanese] Navy Aleutian Operation: part 7, Summary of Progress (in Japanese).

JACAR: Ref. C14121151000: [Japanese] Navy Aleutian Operation: part 7, Outline of progress, 1st part: General Progress (in Japanese).

JACAR: Ref. C14121151100: [Japanese] Navy Aleutian Operation: part 7, Outline of progress, 2nd part: 2nd Kidō Butai (in Japanese).

JACAR: Ref. C14121151200: [Japanese] Navy Aleutian Operation: part 7, Outline of progress, 3rd part: Invasion of Attu (in Japanese).

JACAR: Ref. C14121151300: [Japanese] Navy Aleutian Operation: part 7, Outline of progress, 3rd part: Invasion of Kiska (in Japanese).

JACAR: Ref. C14121151400: [Japanese] Navy Aleutian Operation: part 8, Campaign after the seizure, 1st part: Enemy contraction (in Japanese).

JACAR: Ref. C14121151500: [Japanese] Navy Aleutian Operation: part 8, Campaign after the seizure, 2nd part: General Progress (in Japanese).

JACAR: Ref. C14121151600: [Japanese] Navy Aleutian Operation: part 8, Campaign after the seizure, 3rd part: Northern Force Main Core Operations (in Japanese).

JACAR: Ref. C14121151700: [Japanese] Navy Aleutian Operation: part 8, Campaign after the seizure, 4th part: Convoy Escort Operations (in Japanese).

JACAR: Ref. C14121151800: [Japanese] Navy Aleutian Operation: part 8, Campaign after the seizure, 5th part: Air Force Operations (in Japanese).

JACAR: Ref. C14121151900: [Japanese] Navy Aleutian Operation: part 8, Campaign after the seizure, 6th part: Submarine Force Operations (in Japanese).

JACAR: Ref. C14121137000: Aleutian Campaign Daily Calendar, S17.05 (in Japanese).

JACAR: Ref. C14121137100: Aleutian Campaign Daily Calendar, S17.06 (in Japanese).

JACAR: Ref. C14121137200: Aleutian Campaign Daily Calendar, S17.07 (in Japanese).

JACAR: Ref. C14121137300: Aleutian Campaign Daily Calendar, S17.08 (in Japanese).

JACAR: Ref. C14121137400: Aleutian Campaign Daily Calendar, S17.09 (in Japanese).

National Institute for Defense Studies
防衛研究所
Bōei Kenkyūsho
NIDS: Chūō, Meirei, 33: S16.11.5, Combined Fleet Secret Operational Order No 1, Chapter 4: Second Stage (in Japanese).

NIDS: Chūō Meirei 56: Northern Forces, Northern Forces Secret Order No 1 (S17.01.30) (in Japanese).

NIDS: Chūō-Meirei 56: Northern Force Secret Operational Order No. 7, S17.05.21, Table of a rough estimate of fuel consumption during Operation AL (in Japanese).

NIDS: Chūō Meirei 56: Northern Force Secret Operational Order No. 10, S17.05.25, Summary of the Northern Force Commander address (in Japanese).

NIDS: Hokutō Arūshan 17: Records of Aleutian Campaign, Shōwa 21.06, (in Japanese).

NIDS: Hokutō Arūshan 27: Records of Aleutian Campaign, Kiska and Attu (in Japanese).

NIDS: Hokutō Arūshan 27: Chapter 4, Operation of seizing the western part of the Aleutian Islands, Section 1: Preparations at Imperial General Headquarters (in Japanese).

NIDS: Hokutō Arūshan 32: Records of Operation AL, Shōwa 20.08 (in Japanese).

National Archives
国立公文書館
Kokuritsu Kōbunshokan
Decision to ratify the Neutrality Pact between the Empire of Japan and the Soviet Union (in Japanese) <http://www.archives.go.jp/ayumi/kobetsu/s16_1941_02.html> (accessed 12th Nov 2019).

KKS: Ceremonial submission of the official note on treaty related to exchange of the Kuriles and Sakhalin (in Japanese) <http://www.archives.go.jp/ayumi/kobetsu/m08_1875_03.html> (accessed 12th November 2019).

Peace Treaty between Empire of Japan and the Russian Empire (in Japanese)

National Records and Administration Records
NARA: From Commanding Officer, Naval Armed Guard Detachment to The Chief of Naval Operations, Air Raids on Dutch Harbor, 14 June 1942.

NARA: NA-50, From The Commanding Officer to The Commander, Alascan Sector, Bombing at Dutch Harbor – report on, 6 July 1942.

NARA: COMTASKFOR 8, Subject: Action Report (Bombardment of Kiska Is, 8/7/42) (Enc A-C).

NARA: Patwing 4, 8/11/41 to 11/1/42 and Fleet Air Wing, 11/1/42 to 9/2/45.

NARA: USS Avocet – War Diary, 6/1/42 to 8/18/42

NARA: USS Gato – Submarine War Patrol Report.

NARA: USS Gillis – War Diary, 7/1-7/42, 7/8-31/42, 7/20/1942 to 8/4/1942, 8/5/42 to 9/18/42.

NARA: USS Growler – Report of First War Patrol.

NARA: USS Hulbert – War Diary, 6/1-30/42, 7/1-31/42, 8/1-31/42, 9/1-30/42.

NARA: USS Nautilus – Report of First War Patrol.

NARA: USS Teal – War Diary, 8/1/42 to 9/4/42

NARA: USS Williamson, War Diary, 6/10 to 27/1942 (Enc A), 6/27 to 7/27/1942, 7/28/42 to 8/10/42.

NARA: COMTASKFOR 8, War Diary, 5/1-31/42, 6/1-30/42, 7/1-31/42, 8/1-31/42, 9/1-30/42.

NARA: COMWESTSEAFRON, War Diary, 5/1-31/42, 6/1-30/42, 7/1-31/42, 8/1-31/42, 9/1-30/42

The George C. Marshall Foundation Library
PoGCM: 3-066 Memorandum for the President, January 21, 1942.

PoGCM: 3-173 To Lieutenant General John L. De Witt, April 29, 1942.

PoGCM: 3-216: Memorandum for the Commander in Chief, United States Fleet [King], June 7, 1942.

PoGCM: 3-226 To Admiral Harold R. Stark, June 18, 1942.

PoGCM: 3-287, To Lieutenant General John L. De Witt, August 21, 1942.

PoGCM: 3-311, To Lieutenant General John L. De Witt, September 3, 1942.

PoGCM: 3-324, To Lieutenant General John L. De Witt, September 11, 1942.

Hoover Library Archive
Theobald Papers

USSBS Interrogations
Interrogation Nav No. 20, USSBS No. 97: Aleutian Campaign, Carrier Aircraft Attack on Dutch Harbor.

Interrogation Nav No. 23, USSBS No. 100, Aleutian Campaign: Japanese Flying Boat Operation in the Aleutians.

Interrogation Nav No. 73, USSBS No. 367, Aleutian Campaign: Operations of the Japanese First Destroyer Squadron.

Interrogation Nav No. 118, USSBS No. 606: Aleutian Campaign, Information on Japanese Second Mobile Force and the Kiska Garrison from U.S. Prisoners of War.

Unpublished Documents and Reports
Assistant Chief of Air Intelligence, Historical Division Army, Air Force Historical Studies: Alaskan Air Defense and Japanese Invasion on the Aleutians, April 1944.

C.B. Breslin, *World War II in the Aleutians: The Fundamentals of Joint Campaigns* (Newport: Naval War College, 1994).

Demobilisation Office Records Section, *Japanese Monograph No. 46a: Aleutian Islands Operation Records* (in Japanese) (Tokyo: Unpublished Monograph, 1949).

Historic American Buildings Survey (HABS) No. AK-34, *Naval Operating Base Dutch Harbor & Fort Mears, Unalaska, Aleutian Islands* (Department of the Interior: Washington, 1987).

JBE-R: Lieutenant W.S.M. Johnson, *History of the Eleventh Fighter Squadron, from 16 January 1941 to 1 January 1944* (unpublished work, 1945).

Second Demobilisation Office, *Japanese Monograph No. 88: Japanese Navy Aleutian Islands Operation* (in Japanese) (Tokyo: Unpublished Monograph, 1947).

J.M. Steele, *War Plans and Files of the Commander-in-Chief, Pacific Fleet, "Nimitz Gray Book", vol. 1, 7 December 1941 – 31 August 1942* (New York: American Naval Records Society, 2010).

US Department of the Inferior, *World War II in the Aleutians* (Anchorage: National Park Service, 1991).

Books, Articles and Memoires
Abe, Z., "Bombing Dutch Harbor", in: M. Nakamura, *Japanese Navy Dive Bomber Units: War Memories Collection of 99 Kambaku, Suisei, Ginga* (in Japanese) (Tokyo: Kyō no Wadaisha, 1986), pp. 73–96

Abe, Z. *War Lessons of Carrier Bombers Commander – Conditions to win through* (in Japanese) (Tokyo: Kōjinsha, 2013)

Bates, R.W., *The Battle of Midway Including the Aleutian Phase, June 3 to June 14, 1942: Strategical and Tactical Analysis* (Newport: Naval War College, 1948)

Battle Experience: Solomon Islands actions: August and September 1942 including bombardment of Kiska, 7 August 1942, Chapter 15

Bōei Kenshūsho Senshishitsu (ed.), *Senshi Sōsho vol. 21: Army Operations in the Northern Area (1) Honourable defeat on Attu* (in Japanese) (Tokyo: Asagumo Shimbusha, 1968)

Bōei Kenshūsho Senshishitsu (ed.), *Senshi Sōsho vol. 29: Navy Operations in the Northern Area* (in Japanese) (Tokyo: Asagumo Shimbusha, 1969)

Bōei Kenshūsho Senshishitsu (ed.), *Senshi Sōsho vol. 43: The Battle of Midway* (in Japanese) (Tokyo: Asagumo Shimbunsha, 1971)

Bōei Kenshūsho Senshishitsu (ed.), *Senshi Sōsho vol. 77: The Imperial Headquarters' Navy Section, Combined Fleet (3): To February of 18th year of the Shōwa era* (in Japanese) (Tokyo: Asagumo Shimbunsha, 1974)

Bōei Kenshūsho Senshishitsu (ed.), *Senshi Sōsho vol. 91: Imperial General Headquarters, Japanese Navy General Staff: Combined Fleet (1)* (in Japanese) (Tokyo: Asagumo Shimbunsha, 1975)

Breu, M., *Last Letters from Attu* (Portland: Alaska Northwest Books, 2009)

Cloe, J.H., *Attu: The Forgotten Battle* (Anchorage: National Park Service, 2017)

Cloe, J.H. *The Aleutian Warriors: A History of the 11th Air Force and Fleet Air Wing 4* (Missoula: Pictorial Histories Pub Co, 1999, 4th ed.)

Conn, S., Engelman, R.C., Fairchild, B., *Guarding the United States and Its Outposts* (Washington: Center of Military History, United States Army, 1961)

Craven,W.F., Cate, J.L., *The Army Air Forces in World War II, vol. 4, The Pacific: Guadalcanal to Saipan, August 1942 to July 1944* (Chicago: University of Chicago Press, 1948)

Cressman, R.J., *The Official Chronology of the US Navy in World War II* (Annapolis: Naval Institute Press, 1999)

Denfeld, D.C., *The Defense of Dutch Harbor, Alaska From Military Construction to Base Cleanup* (Anchorage: Alaska District, U.S. Army Corps of Engineers, 1987)

Dickrell, J., *Center of the Storm: The Bombing of Dutch Harbor and the Experience of Patrol Wing 4 in the Aleutians, Summer 1942* (Missoula: Pictorial Histories Publishing Co., 2002)

Dull, P., *A Battle History of the Imperial Japanese Navy, 1941-1945* (Annapolis: Naval Institute Press, 1978)

Frank, W., Cate, J.L., *The Army Air Forces in World War II. Vol. 1: Plans and Early Operations, January 1939 to August 1942* (Chicago: University of Chicago Press, 1948)

Fuchida, M., Okumiya, M., *Midway* (in Japanese) (Tokyo: ebook: 2011)

Fukuda, Y., *The last ship sunk during the battle of Leyte: The traces of destroyer Shiranui* (in Japanese) (Tokyo: Hokushindō Shuppan Kabukigaisha, 2016)

Garfield, B., *The Thousand-Mile War: World War II in Alaska and the Aleutians* (Chicago: University of Chicago Press, 2001, sup. ed.)

Hata, I., Izawa, Y., Shores, C., *Japanese Naval Air Force Fighter Units and Their Aces, 1932–1945* (London: Grub Street, 2011)

Hays O. Jr., *Alaska's Hidden War: Secret Campaigns on the North Pacific Rim* (Fairbanks: University of Alaska Press, 2004)

Herder, B.L., *The Aleutians 1942-43: Struggle for the North Pacific* (Oxford-New York: Osprey Publishing, 2019)

Ike, N., *Japan's Decision for War: Records of the 1941 Policy Conferences* (Stanford: Stanford University Press, 1963)

Ishibashi, T., 'Attsu Shima oki Kaisen', *Sekai no Kansen No 272* (1979), pp. 139–145

Japanese Monograph No. 88, Aleutian Naval Operation March 1942–February 1943

Johnson, R.L., *Aleutian Campaign, World War II: Historical Study and Current Perspective* (Fort Leavenworth: Unpublished Master's Thesis, 1992)

Katsume, J., *Japanese Navy's submarines: their development and complete war records* (in Japanese) (Tokyo: Dai Nippon Kaiga, 2010)

R. Katsura, R., *Life of carrier Zuihō: all our fight* (in Japanese) (Tokyo: Kasumi Shuppansha, 1999)

Lacroix, E., Wells, L., *Japanese Cruisers of the Pacific War* (Annapolis: Naval Institute Press, 1998)

Lorelli, J.A., *The Battle of the Komandorski Islands* (Annapolis: Naval Institute Press, 1984)

Maru Special: Japanese Naval Operations in W.W.II, No. 98 (in Japanese)

MacGarrigle, G.L., *Aleutian Islands: The U.S. Army Campaigns in WWII* (Washington: U.S. Army Center of Military History, 1992)

McDermott Faulkner, S., Spude, R.L.S., *Historic Naval Operating Base Dutch Harbor and Fort Mears Unalaska Island, Alaska* (Anchorage: National Park Service, 1987)

Miyakawa, M., *Crossing the sea of despair in full anger: War testimonies of Shōwa, Revival of war stories* (in Japanese) (Tokyo: Kōjinsha, 1990)

Mori, T., *Japanese cruisers: warships mechanisms* (in Japanese) (Tokyo: Kōjinsha, 1993)

Morison, S.E., *Coral Sea, Midway and Submarine Actions, May 1942–August 1942, vol. 4 of History of United States Naval Operations in World War II* (Annapolis: Naval Institute Press, 2010, sup. ed.)

Morison, S.E., *Aleutians, Gilberts and Marshalls, June 1942 – April 1944, vol. 7 of History of United States Naval Operations in World War II* (Annapolis: Naval Institute Press, 2011, sup. ed.)

Office of Naval Intelligence, *United States Navy Combat Narrative: The Aleutians Campaign, June 1942-August 1943* (Washington: Naval Historical Center Department of the Navy, 1993)

Nakazawa, T., *Vice Admiral Nakazawa memories* (in Japanese) (Tokyo, Kankōkai, 1978)

Navy Department, Office of the Chief of Naval Operations, History of USS Triton (SS-201)

Oka, N., 'I-26 going for American West Coast: Untold records of raid on Kwajalein, Operation K and destruction of shipping', Maru Separate Volume, *Pacific War Testimonies Series, vol. 8, Days of victory: Army and Navy Records of initial hostilities* (in Japanese) (Tokyo: Asashobō, 1988), pp. 42–67

Parker, F.D., *A Priceless Advantage: U.S. Navy Communications Intelligence and the Battles of Coral Sea, Midway, and the Aleutians* (Center for Cryptologic History National Security Agency, 2017)

Parshall, J., Tully, A., *Shattered Sword: The Untold Story of the Battle of Midway* (Annapolis: Naval Institute Press, 2005)

Perras, G.R., *Stepping Stones to Nowhere, The Aleutian Islands, Alaska, and American Military Strategy, 1867–1945* (Annapolis: Naval Institute Press, 2003)

Piegzik, M.A., *Aleutians 1942–1943* (in Polish) (Warszawa: Bellona, 2022)

Prange, G., Goldstein, D.M., Dillon, K.V., *Miracle at Midway* (New York: Open Road Media, 2018)

Rearden, J., *Forgotten Warriors of the Aleutian Campaign* (Missoula: Pictorial Histories Publishing Company, 2005)

Rearden, J., *Koga's Zero: The Fighter That Changed World War II* (Alaska Northwest Books, ebook, 2014)

Rottman, G.L., *World War II Pacific Island Guide* (Westport-London: Greenwood Publishing Group 2002)

Steller, G.W., *Journal of a Voyage with Bering, 1741–1742* (Stanford: Stanford University Press, 1988)

Stevens, P.F., *Fatal Dive: Solving the World War II Mystery of the USS Grunion* (Washington: Regnery History, 2012)

Takamatsunomiya, N., *Takamatsunomiya Diaries, vol. 4* (in Japanese) (Tokyo: Chūō Kōronshinsha, 1996)

Terauchi, M., (ed.), *Naval Groups of Destroyers: Composition of Destroyer's Combat Forces and True Battlefield Stories* (in Japanese) (Tokyo: Shioshobō Kōjinsha, 2015)

Ugaki, M., *War Diary, vol. 1* (in Japanese), (Tokyo: PHP Kenkyūsho, 2019)

Yamakawa, S., "A direct hit", in: M. Nakamura, *Japanese Navy Dive Bomber Units: War Memories Collection of 99 Kambaku, Suisei, Ginga* (in Japanese) (Tokyo: Kyō no Wadaisha, 1986), pp. 97–156

Online Sources

Japanese blog on the Aleutian Islands campaign, <https://korechi-aleutian.blogspot.com/2021/06/3-al.html>, [accessed on 10 Jan 2023]

Dr. Mark DePue WWII Midway Presentation at Abraham Lincoln Presidential Library and Museum on 23.04.2021, Video Record: < https://www.youtube.com/watch?v=iY56CJtwsvo> (accessed 12.12.2022)

L. Milton, C. Crawford, *Japanese Occupation Site at Kiska Island*, in: Clio: Your Guide to History, https://www.theclio.com/entry/16114 [last access: 29.04.2020]

'Lt. Colonel Bob Brocklehurst and Tara Bourdukofsky reflect on the Battle of Attu', interview available <https://alaskapublic.org/2018/05/14/lt-colonel-bob-brocklehurst-and-tara-bourdukofsky-reflect-on-the-battle-of-attu/>, accessed on 10 Jan 2023

On Eternal Patrol – U.S. Navy Press Release Regarding USS Grunion (SS-216), RELEASE #08-054, 1 Oct. 2008. <http://lastlettersfromattu.com/thestory.asp>, [accessed on 20 Nov 2022]

Website on airfields in the Aleutian Islands: <http://www.airfields-freeman.com/AK/Airfields_AK.htm#ftglenn>, [accessed on 20 Nov 2022]

NOTES

Introduction

1   R.W. Bates, *The Battle of Midway Including the Aleutian Phase, June 3 to June 14, 1942: Strategical and Tactical Analysis* (Newport: Naval War College, 1948).

2   S.E. Morison, *Coral Sea, Midway and Submarine Actions, May 1942–August 1942, vol. 4 of History of United States Naval Operations in World War II* (Annapolis: Naval Institute Press, 2010, sup. ed.); S.E. Morison, *Aleutians, Gilberts and Marshalls, June 1942 – April 1944, vol. 7 of History of United States Naval Operations in World War II* (Annapolis: Naval Institute Press, 2011, sup. ed.).

3   B. Garfield, *The Thousand-Mile War: World War II in Alaska and the Aleutians* (Chicago: University of Chicago Press, 2001, sup. ed.).

4   J.A. Lorelli, *The Battle of the Komandorski Islands* (Annapolis: Naval Institute Press, 1984).

5   J.H. Cloe, *The Aleutian Warriors: A History of the 11th Air Force and Fleet Air Wing 4* (Missoula: Pictorial Histories Pub Co, 1999, 4th ed.).

6   R.L. Johnson, *Aleutian Campaign, World War II: Historical Study and Current Perspective* (Fort Leavenworth: Unpublished Master's Thesis, 1992).

7   J. Dickrell, *Center of the Storm: The Bombing of Dutch Harbor and the Experience of Patrol Wing 4 in the Aleutians, Summer 1942* (Missoula: Pictorial Histories Publishing Co., 2002).

8   G.R. Perras, *Stepping Stones to Nowhere, The Aleutian Islands, Alaska, and American Military Strategy, 1867–1945* (Annapolis: Naval Institute Press, 2003).

9   B.L. Herder, *The Aleutians 1942-43: Struggle for the North Pacific* (Oxford-New York: Osprey Publishing, 2019).

10 Bōei Kenshūsho Senshishitsu (ed.), *Senshi Sōsho vol. 21: Army Operations in the Northern Area (1) Honourable defeat on Attu* (in Japanese) (Tokyo: Asagumo Shimbusha, 1968), Bōei Kenshūsho Senshishitsu (ed.), *Senshi Sōsho vol. 29: Navy Operations in the Northern Area* (in Japanese) (Tokyo: Asagumo Shimbusha, 1969).

11 M.A. Piegzik, *Aleutians 1942–1943* (in Polish) (Warszawa: Bellona, 2022).

Chapter 1

1   G.W. Steller, *Journal of a Voyage with Bering, 1741–1742* (Stanford: Stanford University Press, 1988).

2   KKS: Ceremonial submission of the official note on treaty related to the exchange of the Kuriles and Sakhalin (in Japanese) <http://www.archives.go.jp/ayumi/kobetsu/m08_1875_03.html> (accessed 12.11.2019).

3   KKS: *Peace Treaty between Empire of Japan and the Russian Empire* (in Japanese).

4   D.C. Denfeld, *The Defense of Dutch Harbor, Alaska From Military Construction to Base Cleanup* (Anchorage: Alaska District, U.S. Army Corps of Engineers, 1987), pp. 20–21.

5   S. McDermott Faulkner, R.L.S. Spude, *Historic Naval Operating Base Dutch Harbor and Fort Mears Unalaska Island, Alaska* (Anchorage: National Park Service, 1987), pp. 9–11.

6   Decision to ratify the Neutrality Pact between the Empire of Japan and the Soviet Union (in Japanese) <http://www.archives.go.jp/ayumi/kobetsu/s16_1941_02.html> (12.11.2019).

7   Morison, *Coral Sea*, p. 77. The "diversion theory" related to Operation AL strategic objectives was first mentioned by R. Bates in his NWC analysis of the Battle of Midway published in 1948. The source of this information is unknown, especially since Japanese officers during the November 1945 interrogations confirmed the defensive nature of the advance in the North Pacific. Bates, *The Battle of Midway*, p. 3, Interrogation Nav No. 73, USSBS No. 367, Aleutian Campaign: Operations of the Japanese First Destroyer Squadron.

8   J. Parshall, A. Tully, *Shattered Sword: The Untold Story of the Battle of Midway* (Annapolis: Naval Institute Press, 2005), pp. 52–53.

9   Dr. Mark DePue WWII Midway Presentation at Abraham Lincoln Presidential Library and Museum on 23.04.2021, Video Record: < https://www.youtube.com/watch?v=iY56CJtwsvo> (accessed 12.12.2022)

10 It is worthwhile adding that the author also had initially misinterpreted the Combined Fleet's views on Operation AL and discovered additional Japanese documents in the NIDS while translating the Polish version of the monograph. Newly researched sources allow for taking responsibility off either Combined Fleet or the Navy General Staff, which both equally supported the advance in the North Pacific. Therefore, Polish readers

might feel confused due to notably different statements (at least some) in the same book published in two languages.

11 NIDS: Chūō, Meirei, 33: S16.11.5, Combined Fleet Secret Operational Order No 1, Chapter 4: Second Stage (in Japanese), p. 2.

12 NIDS: Hokutō Arūshan 27: Records of Aleutian Campaign, Kiska and Attu (in Japanese).

13 Bōei Kenshūsho Senshishitsu (Ed.), *Senshi Sōsho vol. 43: The Battle of Midway* (in Japanese) (Tokyo: Asagumo Shimbunsha, 1971), p. 47.

14 SS vol. 43 (in Japanese), pp. 47–48.

15 Maru Special: *Japanese Naval Operations in W.W.II*, No. 98 (in Japanese), p. 18

16 All citations are based on SS vol. 43 (in Japanese), p. 48.

17 Source: SS vol. 43 (in Japanese), p. 48. The idea of the defensive perimeter is described and covered in JACAR: Ref. C14121139700: [Japanese] Navy Aleutian Operation: part 3, Planning Process of the Main Operation (in Japanese), p. 1.

18 During the Imperial Conference on 6 September 1941, the Japanese believed the German-Soviet war could be resolved in the coming months. Although the imminent collapse of Stalin's regime was not expected, close American-Soviet cooperation through the northern communication route was raised as an essential issue to discuss. These considerations were part of a more extensive debate about Japan's expansion policy. N. Ike, *Japan's Decision for War: Records of the 1941 Policy Conferences* (Stanford: Stanford University Press, 1963), pp. 158–160

19 SS vol 29 (in Japanese), p. 206.

20 SS vol 29 (in Japanese), pp. 206–207.

21 SS vol 29 (in Japanese), p. 208.

22 JACAR: Ref. C13071066400, Report to the throne: Regarding the future operations in the Southern Direction and the Pacific Ocean, S17.04.16 (in Japanese), pp. 2–3.

23 JACAR: Ref. C13071036200, Occupation of strategic positions (in Japanese), pp. 3–6.

24 JACAR: Ref. C14121194900, Greater East Asia War (…) Outline of Operations (in Japanese), pp. 7–8.

25 SS vol. 29 (in Japanese), pp. 208–209.

26 T. Ishibashi, 'Attsu Shima oki Kaisen', Sekai no Kansen No 272 (1979), pp. 139–145.

27 Imperial General Headquarters mentions the 301st Independent Infantry Battalion and the 301st Independent Engineer Company. NIDS: Hokutō Arūshan 27: Chapter 4, Operation of seizing the western part of the Aleutian Islands, Section 1: Preparations at Imperial General Headquarters (in Japanese), p. 4.

28 SS vol. 29 (in Japanese), pp. 196, 209.

29 *The Fifth Fleet previously existed in 1938–1939 as part of the Second China Area Expeditionary Fleet as an auxiliary force for the planned landings in China. It participated in the operations on Hainan Island, after which was assigned to the China Area Fleet.* Bōei Kenshūsho Senshishitsu (ed.), *Senshi Sōsho vol. 91: Imperial General Headquarters, Japanese Navy General Staff: Combined Fleet (1)* (in Japanese) (Tokyo: Asagumo Shimbunsha, 1975), *p. 516.*

30 T. Nakazawa, *Vice Admiral Nakazawa of Japanese: Memories of Chief of Naval Planning and Personal Affairs Bureau Director* (in Japanese) (Tokyo: Genshobō, 1979), pp. 64–65.

31 JACAR: Ref. C12070396400: Imperial Navy Official Announcement, No. 3857 (in Japanese), p. 19 .

32 Nakazawa, *Vice Admiral Nakazawa memories* (in Japanese) (Tokyo, Kankōkai, 1978), p. 66.

33 SS vol. 29 (in Japanese), p. 206.

34 Although Nakazawa did not remember any documents with the recommendation, the analysis of the necessity to protect the northern approach to Japan, drafted by the Fifth Fleet before Operation AL, can be found in the National Institute of Defense Studies. NIDS: Chūō Meirei 56: Northern Forces, Northern Forces Secret Order No 1 (S17.01.30) (in Japanese).

35 SS vol. 80 (in Japanese), pp. 419–420.

36 In Japanese archive documents, Operation MI and AL are referred to as AF and AO respectively. JACAR: Ref. C14121139800: IHQ Preparations (in Japanese), p. 1.

37 SS vol. 29 (in Japanese), pp. 209–210.

38 JACAR: Ref. C14121139800: IHQ Preparations (in Japanese).

39 SS vol. 29 (in Japanese), pp. 209–211.

40 JACAR: Ref. C14121139800: IHQ Preparations (in Japanese), p. 2; NIDS: Hokutō Arūshan 17: Records of Aleutian Campaign, Shōwa 21.06, (in Japanese); SS vol. 43 (in Japanese), pp. 93–94.

41 JACAR: Ref. C14121139500: part 1, Organisation (in Japanese), p. 2.

42 Based on JACAR: Ref. C14121139600: [Japanese] Navy Aleutian Operation: part 2, Outline of the Most Important Forces in the Archipelago (in Japanese), p. 1.

43 Due to severe damage to the flight deck Shōkaku was sent to Kure Naval Yards for repairs and Zuikaku's air group was decimated and unfit to participate in Operation MI.

44 SS vol. 29 (in Japanese), pp. 227–228.

45 The table shows the actual composition of the air group (jissū), which differs from the fixed number (teisū) established by the Japanese Navy on 1 June 1942. According to the initial plans, the Ryūjō air group was to consist of 16 Zeros and 20 Kates, plus additional spares.

46 Jun'yō's teisū: 12 Zeros (+3 spares), 18 Vals (+2 spares), and 18 Kates.

47 Ryūjō had small elevators and could not operate bulky dive bombers.

48 Source: SS vol. 29, pp. 229–233. The table is based on JACAR: Ref. C14121140000: [Japanese] Navy Aleutian Operation: part 6, Northern Force Preparations (in Japanese), pp. 1–4, JACAR: Ref. C08030019000: Fifth Fleet (1) (in Japanese), pp. 35–39. During operations in the North Pacific, the Fifth Fleet had three basic organisations that would change depending on the operation phase: the table shows the composition prior to the strike on Dutch Harbor. The tables in Senshi Sōsho also list the Ogasawara Islands (Bonin Islands) Patrol Force that did not participate in Operation AL. The vessels shown in brackets were temporarily attached to the unit.

49 Multiple testimonies say that Jun'yō's dive bomber group comprised 18 Vals. Abe, *Bombing Dutch Harbor*, p. 82, Yamakawa, *A direct hit*, p. 126.

50 Some Japanese sources also indicate that Jun'yō had 18 Zeros and 18 Vals and Ryūjō had 18 Zeros and 18 Kates. However, those figures do not reflect the actual composition of air groups which were primarily based on number of available crews and planes on the carrier. The full roster of Ryūjō and Jun'yō is included in Appendix 1. JACAR: Ref. C14121151100: part 7, 2nd Kidō Butai (in Japanese), p. 1.

51 NIDS: Chūō-Meirei 56: Northern Force Secret Operational Order No. 7, S17.05.21, Table of a rough fuel consumption estimate during Operation AL (in Japanese).

52 SS vol. 29 (in Japanese), p. 216.

53 NIDS: Chūō Meirei 56: Northern Force Secret Operational Order No. 10 (in Japanese).

54 JACAR: Ref. C08030019100: Fifth Fleet (2) (in Japanese), p. 20. JACAR: Ref. C14121151100: 2nd Kidō Butai (in Japanese), p. 2.

55 JACAR: Ref. C08030081200: 1st Torpedo Squadron (1) (in Japanese), p. 6.

56 JACAR Ref. C08030747700: Nachi (1) (in Japanese), p. 34, Nakazawa, *Vice Admiral Nakazawa memories* (in Japanese), p. 75.

57 SS vol. 29 (in Japanese), p. 245.

58 JACAR: Ref. C14121140100: part 7, Summary of Progress (in Japanese), pp. 1–2, JACAR: Ref. C14121137000: Aleutian Campaign Daily Calendar, S17.05 (in Japanese), pp. 1–5.

59 JACAR: Ref. C08051585900: Ryūjō (in Japanese), p. 10.

60 JACAR: Ref. C08051583400: Jun'yō (in Japanese), p. 1.

61 Abe, *Bombing Dutch Harbor* (in Japanese), p. 79.

62 Source: JACAR: Ref. C08051585900: Ryūjō (in Japanese), pp. 10–11, JACAR: Ref. C08051583400: Jun'yō (in Japanese), pp. 1–2. All hours are indicated in the local time zone (+11:00 hours) according to Ryūjō's coordinates.

63 M. Fuchida, M. Okumiya, *Midway* (in Japanese) (Tokyo: ebook: 2011), chapter 8.

64 Abe, *Bombing Dutch Harbor* (in Japanese), p. 75, Z. Abe, *War Lessons of Carrier Bombers Commander – Conditions to win through* (in Japanese) (Tokyo: Kōjinsha, 2013), p. 100.

65 All hours are indicated in the local time zone (+12:00 hours) according to Ryūjō's coordinates. Source: JACAR: Ref. C08051585900: Ryūjō (in Japanese), pp. 12–15, JACAR: Ref. C08051583400: Jun'yō (in Japanese), pp. 3–5.

66 SS vol. 29 (in Japanese), p. 244.

67 All hours are indicated in the local time zone (-11:00 hours) according to Ryūjō's coordinates. Source: JACAR: Ref. C08051585900: Ryūjō (in Japanese), p. 16.

Chapter 2

1 The first talks regarding the Japanese offensive in the Aleutians took place on 18 May as part of a larger debate on Operation MI. J.M. Steele, *War Plans and Files of the Commander-in-Chief, Pacific Fleet, "Nimitz Gray Book"*, vol. 1, 7 December 1941 – 31 August 1942 (New York: American Naval Records Society, 2010), p. 502, F.D. Parker, *A Priceless Advantage: U.S. Navy Communications Intelligence and the Battles of Coral Sea, Midway, and the Aleutians* (Center for Cryptologic History National Security Agency, 2017), pp. 38–50.

2 The Maru Special (in Japanese), p. 18.

3 Office of Naval Intelligence, *United States Navy Combat Narrative: The Aleutians Campaign, June 1942-August 1943* (Washington: Naval Historical Center Department of the Navy, 1993), pp. 4–5.

4 The Maru Special (in Japanese), p. 18.

5 PoGCM: 3-173 To Lieutenant General John L. De Witt, April 29, 1942.

6 Assistant Chief of Air Intelligence, Historical Division Army, Air Force Historical Studies: *Alaskan Air Defense and Japanese Invasion on the Aleutians, April 1944*, p. 49.

7 Garfield, *Thousand Mile War*, pp. 16–17.

8 In fact, the Americans managed to gather 13 destroyers and three seaplane tenders off Kodiak.

9 *Gray Book*, vol 1, pp. 511–513.

10 The Maru Special (in Japanese), p. 19.

11 Nimitz also could consider sending *Saratoga* to the North Pacific if Theobald were in severe danger of being overrun by the enemy carrier. *Sara* was to return to service in the early morning of 5 June with her hull repaired at the San Diego Repair Yard. Nimitz planned to send the carrier to Pearl Harbor, and after refuelling, she could proceed directly to Dutch Harbor.

12 First created as the Air Force, Alaskan Defense Command, it became an integral unit as the Alaskan Air Force on 15 January 1942, and eventually was redesignated the Eleventh Air Force on 5 February.

13 G.L. Rottman, *World War II Pacific Island Guide* (Westport-London: Greenwood Publishing Group 2002), p. 452.

14 Gray Book, vol. 1, p. 540.

15 Air Force Historical Studies: *Alaskan Air Defense*, p. 107, HLA: Theobald Papers, Summary of Original Forces, Gains and Losses, 11 AF, 26 May – 14 July 1942.

16 Buckner was promoted to Brigadier General in 1940 and to Major General in August 1941.

17 Cloe, *The Aleutian Warriors*, pp. 64–65.

18 G.L. MacGarrigle, *Aleutian Islands: The U.S. Army Campaigns in WWII* (Washington: U.S. Army Center of Military History, 1992), p. 6. Also, *Gray Book* (vol. 1, p. 515) says about over 23,000 men but does not include active US Navy and US Army civilian personnel.

19 Herder, *The Aleutians*, p. 8.

20 Cloe, *The Aleutian Warriors*, p. 5.

21 PoGCM: 3-066 Memorandum for the President, January 21, 1942.

22 Denfeld, *The Defense of Dutch Harbor*, pp. 36–37.

23 Cloe, *The Aleutian Warriors*, p. 104.

24 Herder, *The Aleutians*, p. 8.

25 There was a tendency to consider the Aleutians as primarily a Navy sphere of operations with ground troops and air units – in necessary, ground troops alone – in a supporting role only. Assistant Chief of Air Intelligence, *Alaskan Air Defense*, pp. 23–24.

26 *Gray Book*, vol. 1, p. 538.

27 Garfield, *Thousand Mile War*, p. 18.

28 Cloe, *The Aleutian Warriors*, p. 16.

29 *Air Force Historical Studies: Alaskan Air Defense*, p. 33.

30 G. Prange, D.M. Goldstein, K.V. Dillon, *Miracle at Midway* (New York: Open Road Media, 2018), pp. 163–164.

31 Cloe, *The Aleutian Warriors*, p. 53.

32 Herder, *The Aleutians*, p. 28.

33 *Air Force Historical Studies: Alaskan Air Defense*, p. 14.

34 NARA: Patwing 4, pp. 95–96.

35 Cloe, *The Aleutian Warriors*, p. 106.

36 Cloe, *The Aleutian Warriors*, p. 104.

37 NARA: COMTASKFOR 8, War Diary, 6/1-30/42, p. 11.

38 NARA: Patwing 4, p. 94, *Air Force Historical Studies: Alaskan Air Defense*, pp. 107–108, Dickrell, *Center of the Storm*, p. 23. Various American records and testimonies show contradictions in numbers and dislocation of the 11 AF aircraft. However, the situation at the most critical bases (Cold Bay and Otter Point) can be reconstructed.

39 ONI, *The Aleutians Campaign*, pp. 5–6.

40 NARA: Patwing 4, p. 96.

Chapter 3

1 Commander Okumiya Masatake claimed in the post-war interrogation that one torpedo bomber had a forced landing in the sea immediately after take-off, and the crew was rescued. Still, the original *Ryūjō* air group action report does not confirm this testimony. Additionally, Abe claimed in his memories that 18 Vals scrambled from *Jun'yō*. Interrogation Nav No. 20, USSBS No. 97: Aleutian Campaign, Carrier Aircraft Attack on Dutch Harbor, Abe, Bombing Dutch Harbor (in Japanese), p. 82.

2 JACAR: Ref. C08051585900: *Ryūjō* (in Japanese), pp. 17–22.

3 SS vol. 29 (in Japanese), p. 245.

4 JACAR: Ref. C08051585900: *Ryūjō* (in Japanese), pp. 17, 20.

5 JACAR: Ref. C08051583400: *Jun'yō* (in Japanese), pp. 6–10.

6 Abe, Bombing Dutch Harbor (in Japanese), p. 83.

7 JACAR: Ref. C08051585900: *Ryūjō* (in Japanese), pp. 17, 20, JACAR: Ref. C08051583400: *Jun'yō* (in Japanese), pp. 6–10. Aircraft damaged during the attack are marked #.

8 NARA: Patwing 4, p. 97.

9 Perras, Stepping Stones, p. 80.

10 Dickrell, Center of the Storm, p. 38.

11 NARA: Patwing 4, pp. 10, 97, JACAR: Ref. C08051585900: *Ryūjō* (in Japanese), p. 20, JACAR: Ref. C08051583400: *Jun'yō* (in Japanese), pp. 6–8 The American report also indicates one wounded (no name details) and one missing person (AP1c Merlyn B. Dawson). The Japanese report claimed that Endō's shōtai set the taxiing flying boat on fire.

12 Herder, The Aleutians, p. 32.

13 NARA: NA-50, From The Commanding Officer to The Commander, Alascan Sector, Bombing at Dutch Harbor – report on, 6 July 1942, pp. 2–3.

14 NARA: From Commanding Officer, Naval Armed Guard Detachment to The Chief of Naval Operations, Air Raids on Dutch Harbor, 14 June 1942, pp. 1–2.

15 JACAR: Ref. C08051585900: *Ryūjō* (in Japanese), p. 21.

16 NARA: Patwing 4, p. 97.

17 JACAR: Ref. C08051585900: *Ryūjō* (in Japanese), p. 21.

18 SS vol. 29 (in Japanese), p. 246.

19 JACAR: Ref. C08051583400: *Jun'yō* (in Japanese), pp. 7–9. JACAR: Ref. C08051585900: *Ryūjō* (in Japanese), pp. 18–22.

20 All hours are indicated in the local time zone (-11:00 hours) according to *Ryūjō* coordinates. Source: JACAR: Ref. C08051585900: *Ryūjō* (in Japanese), p. 23.

21 NARA: COMTASKFOR 8, War Diary, 6/1-30/42, p. 37.

22 Cloe, The Aleutian Warriors, p. 119.

23 JACAR: Ref. C08051585900: *Ryūjō* (in Japanese), pp. 24–30, JACAR: Ref. C08051583400: *Jun'yō* (in Japanese), pp. 11–14. * There is an error in *Ryūjō*'s air group action report regarding the take-off time of some torpedo bombers and fighters. The blurred handwritten notes make it impossible to read the number four or seven unambiguously, but neither makes sense. It is not possible that the first planes of the second striking group took off as early as 0950 hours, almost an hour before the dive bombers from *Jun'yō*. Similarly, they could not scramble at 1250 hours, after the decision to abandon the mission and return to the 2nd Kidō Butai. Looking at the order of entries in the report, it should be assumed that it was probably 0650 hours Tokyo time, therefore 1150 hours local time.

24 JACAR: Ref. C08051583400: *Jun'yō* (in Japanese), p. 11.

25 JACAR: Ref. C08051583400: *Jun'yō* (in Japanese), pp. 11–12.

26 JBE-R: Lieutenant W.S.M. Johnson, History of the Eleventh Fighter Squadron, from 16 January 1941 to 1 January 1944 (unpublished work, 1945), p. 37.

27 JACAR: Ref. C14121151100: 2nd Kidō Butai (in Japanese), p. 3.

28 SS vol. 29 (in Japanese), p. 246.

29 Garfield, Thousand Mile War, pp. 36–37.

30 NARA: Patwing 4, p. 97.

31 JACAR: Ref. C08051585900: *Ryūjō* (in Japanese), pp. 31–32.

32 NARA: Patwing 4, p. 98.

33 J. Rearden, Koga's Zero: The Fighter That Changed World War II (Alaska Northwest Books, ebook 2014), p. 48.

34 SS vol. 29 (in Japanese), pp. 246–247.

35 NARA: COMTASKFOR 8, War Diary, 6/1-30/42, pp. 13–16.

Chapter 4

1   NARA: Patwing 4, p. 98.
2   Interrogation Nav No. 118, USSBS No. 606: Aleutian Campaign, Information on Japanese Second Mobile Force and the Kiska Garrison from U.S. Prisoners of War.
3   Interrogation Nav No. 118, USSBS No. 606.
4   NARA: Patwing 4, p. 98.
5   Garfield, *Thousand Mile War*, pp. 42–43.
6   NARA: Patwing 4, p. 99.
7   Based on Theobald War Diary, it is known that Thornbrough suspected that the Japanese task force, comprised of two aircraft carriers, one assessed as the Kaga-class, was south of Seguam Pass, about 140 miles from Dutch Harbor. NARA: COMTASKFOR 8, War Diary, 6/1-30/42, p. 22.
8   Garfield, *Thousand Mile War*, pp. 45–46.
9   W. Frank, J.L. Cate, *The Army Air Forces in World War II. Vol. 1: Plans and Early Operations, January 1939 to August 1942* (Chicago: University of Chicago Press, 1948), p. 469.
10 SS vol. 29 (in Japanese), p. 249.
11 JACAR: Ref. C08051585900: Ryūjō (in Japanese), pp. 36–37.
12 JACAR: Ref. C08051585900: Ryūjō (in Japanese), pp. 36–37.
13 Abe, *Bombing Dutch Harbor* (in Japanese), p. 84.
14 JACAR: Ref. C08051583400: Jun'yō (in Japanese), pp. 15–17.
15 JACAR: Ref. C08051585900: Ryūjō (in Japanese), pp. 38–41, JACAR: Ref. C08051583400: Jun'yō (in Japanese), pp. 15–19. Crews lost during the attack are marked with a cross and damaged aircraft with #.
16 NIDS: Hokutō Arūshan 32: Records of Operation AL, Shōwa 20.08 (in Japanese).
17 SS vol. 29 (in Japanese), p. 249.
18 SS vol. 29 (in Japanese), p. 249.
19 JACAR: Ref. C08051585900: Ryūjō (in Japanese), p. 39.
20 NARA: Patwing 4, p. 99.
21 NARA: Air Raids on Dutch Harbor, p. 3.
22 ONI, The Aleutians Campaign, p. 7.
23 NARA: Bombing at Dutch Harbor, pp. 3–4.
24 Heisō means PO3c in this case.
25 Yamakawa, *A direct hit*, pp. 129–131.
26 NARA: Bombing at Dutch Harbor, p. 5.
27 NARA: Air Raids on Dutch Harbor, pp. 3–4.
28 Interrogation Nav No. 20, USSBS No. 97: Aleutian Campaign, Carrier Aircraft Attack on Dutch Harbor.
29 JACAR: Ref. C08030019100: Fifth Fleet (2) (in Japanese), p. 25.
30 Abe, *Bombing Dutch Harbor* (in Japanese), pp. 88–89.
31 Johnson, *History of the Eleventh Fighter Squadron*, pp. 38–39.
32 Abe, *Bombing Dutch Harbor* (in Japanese), p. 90.
33 JACAR: Ref. C08051583400: Jun'yō (in Japanese), pp. 15–19.
34 JACAR: Ref. C08051585900: Ryūjō (in Japanese), pp. 38–41.
35 JACAR: Ref. C08051583400: Jun'yō (in Japanese), pp. 15–19. JACAR: Ref. C08051585900: Ryūjō (in Japanese), pp. 38–41.
36 *Air Force Historical Studies: Alaskan Air Defense*, p. 110.
37 NARA: Bombing at Dutch Harbor, p. 6, ONI, The Aleutians Campaign, p. 13, Historic American Buildings Survey (HABS) No. AK-34, Naval Operating Base Dutch Harbor & Fort Mears, Unalaska, Aleutian Islands (Department of the Interior: Washington, 1987), p. 28.
38 Cloe, *The Aleutian Warriors*, p. 132.
39 JACAR: Ref. C08051585900: Ryūjō (in Japanese), pp. 33–35. JACAR: Ref. C08051583400: Jun'yō (in Japanese), pp. 20–21.

Chapter 5

1   JACAR: Ref. C08030081200: 1st Torpedo Squadron (1) (in Japanese), pp. 9–10, JACAR: Ref. C0803007030: 22nd Squadron (1), p. 11.
2   JACAR: Ref. C08030081200: 1st Torpedo Squadron (1) (in Japanese), p. 10, JACAR: Ref. C0803007030: 22nd Squadron (in Japanese), p. 13, SS vol. 29 (in Japanese), p. 250.
3   Nakazawa, *Vice Admiral Nakazawa memories* (in Japanese), pp. 80–81.
4   JACAR: Ref. C14121151000: part 7, Outline of progress, 1st part: General Progress (in Japanese), p. 5.
5   JACAR: Ref. C08030081200: 1st Torpedo Squadron (1) (in Japanese), p. 11.
6   SS vol. 29 (in Japanese), p. 251.
7   JACAR: Ref. C08051583400: Jun'yō (in Japanese), JACAR: Ref. C08051585900: Ryūjō (in Japanese).
8   Cloe, *The Aleutian Warriors*, p. 135.
9   ONI, The Aleutians Campaign, p 14.
10 NARA: COMTASKFOR 8 War Diary, 6/1-30/42, p. 41.
11 NARA: COMTASKFOR 8 War Diary, 6/1-30/42, p. 40.
12 NARA: COMTASKFOR 8 War Diary, 6/1-30/42, p. 41.
13 MacGarrigle, *Aleutian Islands*, p. 9.
14 NARA: COMTASKFOR 8 War Diary, 6/1-30/42, p. 41.
15 NARA: Patwing 4, pp. 100–101.
16 JACAR: Ref. C08051585900: Ryūjō (in Japanese), pp. 42–43.
17 JACAR: Ref. C08051585900: Ryūjō (in Japanese), pp. 44–45.
18 JACAR: Ref. C08051585900: Ryūjō (in Japanese), p. 46, JACAR: Ref. C08051583400: Jun'yō (in Japanese), pp. 22–23.
19 Some American publications try to convince that the abandonment of the raid on Adak was caused by discovering the airfield at Otter Point while returning from the second raid on Dutch Harbor on the evening of 5 June. Rear Admiral Kakuta feared that the strike planned for 5 June would be hindered by enemy fighters and bombers, yet the Japanese sources do not confirm this hypothesis.
20 JACAR: Ref. C14121151200: part 7, Outline of progress, 3rd part: Invasion of Attu (in Japanese), p. 1.
21 JACAR Ref. C14121137100: Aleutian Campaign Daily Calendar, S17.06 (in Japanese), p. 6, JACAR: Ref. C0803007030: 22nd Squadron (1), p. 16.
22 JACAR: Ref. C08030081300: 1st Torpedo Squadron (2) (in Japanese), p. 2.
23 SS vol. 21 (in Japanese), p. 116.
24 Japanese Monograph No. 88, Aleutian Naval Operation March 1942–February 1943, p. 51.
25 http://lastlettersfromattu.com/thestory.asp [last access: 20.11.2022].
26 JACAR: Ref. C08030081200: 1st Torpedo Squadron (1) (in Japanese), p. 12.
27 Dickrell claims that Jones committed suicide. Dickrell, *Center of the Storm*, p. 64.
28 J.H. Cloe, *Attu: The Forgotten Battle* (Anchorage: National Park Service, 2017), pp. 32–33.
29 JACAR: Ref. C08030081200: 1st Torpedo Squadron (1) (in Japanese), pp. 13–14.
30 SS vol. 29 (in Japanese), pp. 255–256.
31 JACAR: Ref. C08030081300: 1st Torpedo Squadron (2) (in Japanese), p. 2.
32 JACAR: Ref. C14121137100: Aleutian Calendar June (in Japanese), p. 5.
33 SS vol. 29 (in Japanese), p. 256.
34 Japanese sources confirm about 10 American soldiers on Kiska. JACAR: Ref. C14121151300: part 7, Outline of progress, 3rd part: Invasion of Kiska (in Japanese), p. 2.
35 L. Milton, C. Crawford, Japanese Occupation Site at Kiska Island, in: Clio: Your Guide to History, https://www.theclio.com/entry/16114 [last access: 29.04.2020].
36 JACAR: Ref. C08051585900: Ryūjō (in Japanese), pp. 47–65, JACAR: Ref. C08051583400: Jun'yō (in Japanese), pp. 24–27.
37 Nakazawa, *Vice Admiral Nakazawa memories* (in Japanese), p. 78.
38 The seaplane base was opened on 11 June. JACAR: Ref. C14121151200: Invasion of Attu (in Japanese), p. 2.
39 JACAR: Ref. C08030019100: Fifth Fleet (2) (in Japanese), p. 34.

Chapter 6

1   NARA: Patwing 4, pp. 102–103, NARA: USS Hulbert – War Diary, 6/1-30/42, pp. 2–4.
2   Garfield, *Thousand Mile War*, p. 103.
3   Cloe, *The Aleutians Warriors*, p. 152.
4   NARA: Patwing 4, p. 103.
5   NARA: COMTASKFOR 8 War Diary, 6/1-30/42, p. 98.
6   JACAR Ref. C14121137100: Aleutian Calendar June (in Japanese), p. 10.
7   Garfield, *Thousand Mile War*, p. 104.
8   Garfield, *Thousand Mile War*, p. 104.
9   Garfield, *Thousand Mile War*, p. 127.
10 'Lt. Colonel Bob Brocklehurst and Tara Bourdukofsky reflect on the Battle of Attu', interview available <https://alaskapublic.org/2018/05/14/lt-colonel-bob-brocklehurst-and-tara-bourdukofsky-reflect-on-the-battle-of-attu/>, accessed on 10 January 2023.
11 NARA: COMTASKFOR 8 War Diary, 6/1-30/42, p. 98.
12 *Gray Book*, vol 1, p. 575.
13 *Gray Book*, vol 1, p. 575.
14 NARA: Patwing 4, p. 105, NARA: USS Hulbert, War Diary, 6/1-30/42, p. 5.
15 NARA: Patwing 4, p. 104.
16 Herder, *The Aleutians*, p. 42.

17 Cloe, *The Aleutians Warriors*, p. 155.
18 JACAR Ref. C14121137100: Aleutian Calendar June (in Japanese), p. 10.
19 NARA: COMTASKFOR 8 War Diary, 6/1-30/42, pp. 110–129.
20 M. Miyakawa, *Crossing the sea of despair in full anger: War testimonies of Shōwa, Revival of war stories* (in Japanese) (Tokyo: Kōjinsha, 1990), p. 20.
21 NARA: Patwing 4, p. 107.
22 NARA: COMTASKFOR 8, War Diary, 6/1-30/42, pp. 183–184.
23 JACAR: Ref. C14121137100: Aleutian Calendar June (in Japanese), pp. 7–11.
24 JACAR: Ref. C14121151400: [Japanese] Navy Aleutian Operation: part 8, Campaign after the seizure, 1st part: Enemy contraction (in Japanese), pp. 1–2.
25 SS vol. 29 (in Japanese), p. 258.
26 JACAR: Ref. C08051600400: Tōkō-ku (2) (in Japanese), pp. 25, 27.
27 JACAR: Ref. C08051600400: Tōkō-ku (in Japanese), pp. 25, 27–29, 31–33.
28 JACAR: Ref. C08030641200: Kamikawa Maru (2) (in Japanese), p. 6.
29 R. Katsura, *Life of carrier Zuihō: all our fight* (in Japanese) (Tokyo: Kasumi Shuppansha, 1999), p. 73. The author claims that Zuihō received the order on 14 June.
30 SS vol. 29 (in Japanese), p. 260.
31 SS vol. 29 (in Japanese), pp. 260–261.
32 JACAR: Ref. C08051600400: Tōkō-ku (in Japanese), p. 33, Interrogation Nav No. 23, USSBS No. 100, Aleutian Campaign: Japanese Flying Boat Operation in the Aleutians.
33 SS vol. 29 (in Japanese), p. 269.
34 SS vol. 21 (in Japanese), p. 130.
35 Cloe, *The Aleutian Warriors*, p. 163.
36 JACAR: Ref. C14121137100: Aleutian Calendar June (in Japanese), p. 15.
37 N. Takamatsunomiya, *Takamatsunomiya Diaries, vol. 4* (in Japanese) (Tokyo: Chūō Kōronshinsha, 1996), p. 270.
38 SS vol. 29 (in Japanese), p. 270.
39 Takamatsunomiya, *Takamatsunomiya Diaries* (in Japanese), p. 271.
40 W.F. Craven, J.L. Cate, *The Army Air Forces in World War II, vol. 4, The Pacific: Guadalcanal to Saipan, August 1942 to July 1944* (Chicago: University of Chicago Press, 1948), p. 365.
41 Cloe, *The Aleutian Warriors*, p. 160.
42 JACAR: Ref. C08051583400: Jun'yō (in Japanese), JACAR: Ref. C08051580400: Zuihō (in Japanese).
43 JACAR: Ref. C08051585900: Ryūjō (in Japanese), p. 66.
44 All hours are indicated in the local time zone (+11:00 hours) according to Ryūjō coordinates. JACAR: Ref. C08051585900: Ryūjō (in Japanese), pp. 64–65.
45 SS vol. 29 (in Japanese), p. 262.
46 G.L. MacGarrigle, *Aleutian Islands*, p. 11.
47 ONI, *The Aleutians Campaign*, p. 15.
48 PoGCM: 3-226 To Admiral Harold R. Stark, June 18, 1942.
49 N. Oka, 'I-26 going for American West Coast: Untold records of raid on Kwajalein, Operation K and destruction of shipping', Maru Separate Volume, *Pacific War Testimonies Series, vol. 8, Days of victory: Army and Navy Records of initial hostilities* (in Japanese) (Tokyo: Asashobō, 1988), pp. 42–67.
50 Cloe, *The Aleutians Warriors*, p. 162.
51 Garfield, *Thousand Mile War*, pp. 128–129.
52 Garfield, *Thousand Mile War*, p. 131.
53 NARA: COMTASKFOR 8, War Diary, 6/1-30/42, p. 165.
54 JACAR: Ref. C08051580400: Zuihō (in Japanese), p. 22.
55 Bōei Kenshūsho Senshishitsu (ed.), *Senshi Sōsho vol. 77: The Imperial Headquarters' Navy Section, Combined Fleet (3): To February of 18th year of the Shōwa era* (in Japanese) (Tokyo: Asagumo Shimbunsha, 1974), p. 114.
56 SS vol. 29 (in Japanese), p. 277.
57 SS vol. 29 (in Japanese), p. 269.

Chapter 7

1   SS vol. 29 (in Japanese), p. 281.
2   SS vol. 29 (in Japanese), p. 271.
3   NARA: USS Nautilus – Report of First War Patrol, pp. 6–7.
4   JACAR: Ref. C08030095000, 2nd Torpedo Squadron (2) (in Japanese), p. 53.
5   SS vol. 77 (in Japanese), p. 110.
6   ONI, *The Aleutians Campaign*, p. 16.
7   Information on the position of seaplane tenders and transport: JACAR: Ref. C08030019100: Fifth Fleet (2) (in Japanese), p. 11.
8   JACAR Ref. C08030641300: Kamikawa Maru (3) (in Japanese), pp. 11–14.
9   NARA: COMTASKFOR 8 War Diary, 7/1-31/42, p. 31.
10 NARA: COMTASKFOR 8 War Diary, 7/1-31/42, p. 21.
11 NARA: COMTASKFOR 8 War Diary, 7/1-31/42, p. 15.
12 W.F. Craven, J.L. Cate, *The Pacific: Guadalcanal to Saipan*, p. 365.
13 JACAR: Ref. C14121137200: Aleutian Campaign Daily Calendar, S17.07 (in Japanese), p. 2.
14 SS vol. 29 (in Japanese), p. 272.
15 NARA: USS Growler – Report of First War Patrol, pp. 4–6.
16 Y. Fukuda, *The last ship sunk during the battle of Leyte: The traces of destroyer Shiranui (in Japanese) (Tokyo: Hokushindō Shuppan Kabukigaisha, 2016), pp. 75–76.
17 JACAR: Ref. C08030081600: 1st Torpedo Squadron (5) (in Japanese), pp. 2–5.
18 Japanese Monograph No. 88, p. 59.
19 JACAR: Ref. C08030081500: 1st Torpedo Squadron (4) (in Japanese), p. 17.
20 Fukuda, The last ship sunk*, pp. 75–76.
21 NARA: USS Growler – Report of First War Patrol, pp. 5–8.
22 JACAR: Ref. *C08030325100: Kure Navy Base War Diary (4) (in Japanese), p. 49.*
23 *Fukuda, The last ship sunk, p. 175.*
24 JACAR: Ref. C16120633100: S17.07.01–S17.07.15, Pacific War Course Outline (3) (in Japanese), p. 7.
25 Navy Department, Office of the Chief of Naval Operations, History of USS Triton (SS-201), p. 3.
26 JACAR: Ref. C08030019100: Fifth Fleet (2) (in Japanese), pp. 12–14.
27 JACAR: Ref. C08030081500: 1st Torpedo Squadron (4) (in Japanese), p. 18.
28 M. Terauchi (ed.), *Naval Groups of Destroyers: Composition of Destroyer's Combat Forces and True Battlefield Stories* (in Japanese) (Tokyo: Shioshobō Kōjinsha, 2015), p. 310.
29 M. Ugaki, *War Diary, vol. 1* (in Japanese), (Tokyo: PHP Kenkyūsho, 2019), p. 295.
30 Takamatsunomiya, *Takamatsunomiya Diary, vol. 4* (in Japanese), pp. 314–315.
31 SS vol. 29 (in Japanese), p. 272.
32 *Fukuda, The last ship sunk (in Japanese), p. 79.*
33 NARA: COMTASKFOR 8 War Diary, 6/1-30/42, 7/1-31/42.
34 NARA: COMTASKFOR 8 War Diary, 7/1-31/42, p. 66.
35 The Japanese tried to find Koga and destroy his Zero, but the submarine that was to approach the island was detected and shelled by Williamson, so abandoned the rescue mission and did not return to Akutan. J. Rearden, *Koga's Zero*, p. 58.

Chapter 8

1   Rearden, *Koga's Zero*, p. 136.
2   SS vol. 29 (in Japanese), p. 284.
3   JACAR: Ref. C08030019100: Fifth Fleet (2) (in Japanese), pp. 14–15.
4   JACAR: Ref. C08030095000: 2nd Torpedo Squadron (2) (in Japanese), p. 88.
5   JACAR: Ref. C12070164200: Orders vol. 3, Shōwa 17th year, July (3) (in Japanese), p. 28.
6   JACAR: Ref. C14121137200: Aleutian Calendar July (in Japanese), p. 13.
7   SS vol. 29 (in Japanese), p. 286.
8   Morison, *Aleutians*, p. 8.
9   SS vol. 29 (in Japanese), p. 322.
10 R.J. Cressman, *The Official Chronology of the US Navy in World War II* (Annapolis: Naval Institute Press, 1999).
11 SS vol. 29 (in Japanese), p. 322.
12 JACAR: Ref. C08051600500: Tōkō-ku (3) (in Japanese), pp. 13–19.
13 Takamatsunomiya, *Takamatsunomiya Diary, vol. 4* (in Japanese), p. 319.
14 NARA: Patwing 4, p. 110, NARA: COMTASKFOR 8, War Diary, 7/1-31/42, p. 113.
15 JACAR: Ref. C08051600500: Tōkō-ku (in Japanese), pp. 12–31.
16 JACAR: Ref. C14121137200: Aleutian Calendar July (in Japanese), p. 26. Two men were killed during the torpedo attack.
17 SS vol. 29 (in Japanese), p. 327.
18 On Eternal Patrol – U.S. Navy Press Release Regarding USS Grunion (SS-216), RELEASE #08-054, 1 Oct. 2008.
19 A detailed description of the discovery of the Grunion wreck and analysis of received damage on 30 July 1942 are included in: P.F. Stevens, *Fatal

Dive: Solving the World War II Mystery of the USS Grunion (Washington: Regnery History, 2012), pp. 147–165.

20 NARA: Patwing 4, p. 113.
21 NARA: COMTASKFOR 8, War Diary, 7/1-31/42.
22 ONI, *The Aleutians Campaign*, pp. 16–17.
23 NARA: Patwing 4, p. 109.
24 NARA: COMTASKFOR 8, War Diary, 7/1-31/42, p. 152.
25 NARA: COMTASKFOR 8, War Diary, 8/1-31/42, p. 12.
26 Battle Experience: Solomon Islands actions: August and September 1942 including bombardment of Kiska, 7 August 1942, Chapter 15, p. 33.
27 NARA: COMTASKFOR 8, War Diary, 8/1-31/42, p. 17.
28 The Americans planned to carry out the 500-mile reconnaissance flights from Atka three days prior to the bombardment of Kiska. NARA: Patwing 4, p. 109.
29 Battle Experience, p. 33.
30 NARA: Patwing 4, pp. 109–110.
31 NARA: COMTASKFOR 8, Bombardment of Kiska, p. 1.
32 NARA: COMTASKFOR 8 War Diary, 7/1-31/42, pp. 200–203.
33 NARA: Bombardment of Kiska, p. 1.
34 Battle Experience, pp. 34–35.
35 JACAR: Ref. C08051628400, 5-kū (1) (in Japanese), p. 5.
36 NARA: Bombardment of Kiska, p. 1.
37 NARA: Bombardment of Kiska, p. 2.
38 JACAR: Ref. C08051628400, 5-kū (in Japanese), pp. 5–9.
39 Battle Experience…, pp. 40–41.
40 NARA: COMTASKFOR 8, War Diary, 8/1-31/42, p. 47.
41 In the following days, the 11 AF made many attempts to take pictures of the island, but the bombers encountered overcast at low altitudes or had technical issues with their cameras.
42 ONI, *The Aleutians Campaign*, p. 20.
43 Some Japanese documents mention only one seaplane destroyed, but other accounts confirm damage to flying boats. JACAR: Ref. C14121137300: Aleutian Campaign Daily Calendar, S17.08 (in Japanese), p. 4.
44 ONI, *The Aleutians Campaign*, p. 20.
45 Takamatsunomiya, *Takamatsunomiya Diary, vol. 4* (in Japanese), p. 358.

Chapter 9

1 SS vol. 29 (in Japanese), p. 290.
2 JACAR: Ref. C08051600800: Tōkō-kū (1) (in Japanese), pp. 11–12.
3 NARA: Patwing 4, p. 111.
4 JACAR: Ref. C08051600800: Tōkō-kū (1) (in Japanese), p. 16. Some sources also state about the P-39 fighters. JACAR: Ref. C14121137300: Aleutian Calendar August (in Japanese), p. 3.
5 JACAR: Ref. C08051600800: S17.08–S17.10, Tōkō-kū Action Report (1) (in Japanese), pp. 11–12, 16.
6 JACAR: Ref. C08051628400, 5-kū (in Japanese), p. 11.
7 NARA: Patwing 4, p. 112.
8 SS vol. 29 (in Japanese), pp. 297–300.
9 NARA: Patwing 4, p. 114.
10 PoGCM: 3-287, To Lieutenant General John L. De Witt, August 21, 1942.
11 Craven, Cate, *The Pacific: Guadalcanal to Saipan*, p. 369.
12 Perras, *Stepping Stones*, p. 99.
13 NARA: COMTASKFOR 8, War Diary, 8/1-31/42, pp. 94, 168.
14 NARA: COMTASKFOR 8, War Diary, 8/1-31/42, p. 103, NARA: USS Gato – Submarine War Patrol Report, part 1, p. 42.
15 PoGCM: 3-311, To Lieutenant General John L. De Witt, September 3, 1942.
16 Garfield, *Thousand Mile War*, p. 170.
17 NARA: Patwing 4, p. 115, NARA: USS Teal, War Diary, 8/1/42 to 9/4/42, p. 7.
18 ONI, *The Aleutians Campaign*, p. 21.
19 NARA: COMTASKFOR 8, War Diary, 8/1-31/42, pp. 123, 133.
20 JACAR: Ref. C14121137300: Aleutian Calendar August (in Japanese), p. 10.
21 NARA: Patwing 4, p. 115. On 13 September, *Casco* was refloated.
22 SS vol. 29 (in Japanese), p. 324. Other Japanese sources claim that one torpedo hit the cruiser without specifying her class. JACAR: Ref. C14121151900: [Japanese] Navy Aleutian Operation: part 8, Campaign after the seizure, 6th part: Submarine Force Operations (in Japanese), p. 2.
23 J. Katsume, *Japanese Navy's submarines: their development and complete war records* (in Japanese) (Tokyo: Dai Nippon Kaiga, 2010), p. 148, NARA: COMTASKFOR 8, War Diary, 9/1-30/42, p. 29.
24 JACAR: Ref. C08051600900: Tōkō-kū (2) (in Japanese), pp. 13–14.

25 JACAR: Ref. C08051628400, 5-kū (in Japanese), p. 1.
26 SS vol. 29 (in Japanese), p. 308.
27 SS vol. 29 (in Japanese), p. 297.
28 SS vol. 29 (in Japanese), pp. 313–316.
29 SS vol. 29 (in Japanese), p. 305.
30 Detailed information on ships' movements and troops can be found in: SS vol. 29 (in Japanese), pp. 301–305 (Navy section) and SS vol. 21 (in Japanese), pp. 145–147 (Army section).
31 JACAR: Ref. C14121137400: Aleutian Campaign Daily Calendar, S17.09 (in Japanese), s. 6.
32 NARA: COMTASKFOR 8, War Diary, 8/1-31/42, p. 145.
33 NARA: COMTASKFOR 8, War Diary, 9/1-3042, p. 88.
34 Johnson, *Eleventh Fighter Squadron*, p. 47, Craven, Cate, *The Pacific: Guadalcanal to Saipan*, pp. 369–370.
35 NARA: COMTASKFOR 8, War Diary, 8/1-31/42, 9/1-30/42.

Appendix I

1 Z. Abe, "Bombing Dutch Harbor", in: M. Nakamura, *Japanese Navy Dive Bomber Units: War Memories Collection of 99 Kambaku, Suisei, Ginga* (in Japanese) (Tokyo: Kyō no Wadaisha, 1986), pp. 73–96, S. Yamakawa, "A direct hit", in: M. Nakamura, *Japanese Navy Dive Bomber Units: War Memories Collection of 99 Kambaku, Suisei, Ginga* (in Japanese) (Tokyo: Kyō no Wadaisha, 1986), pp. 97–156.

ABOUT THE AUTHOR

Michal A. Piegzik has a PhD in Japanese law, lecturing family law and children's rights at Edinburgh Napier University. He was awarded the Japanese Ministry of Education scholarship for exceptional research results. In 2016–2017 and 2020–2022, he researched Japanese civil law at the Tokyo Metropolitan University. The Pacific War is his life's passion which also, remarkably influenced his academic skills and career path. The author of six monographs and 20 articles related to law and history, *The Darkest Hour: The Japanese Naval Offensive in the Indian Ocean*, published by Helion and Company in 2022, was his debut in British historiography.